HARBOR & HAVEN

September 3, 1609. The Half Moon drops anchor and Henry Hudson discovers the site of New Amsterdam.

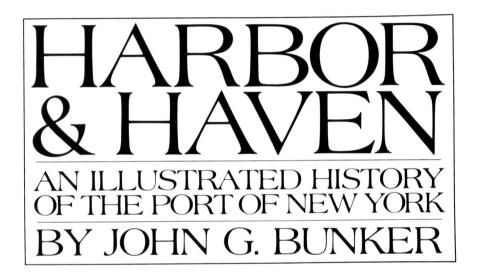

HARBOR & HAVEN

AN ILLUSTRATED HISTORY OF THE PORT OF NEW YORK

BY JOHN G. BUNKER

Sponsored by
THE MARITIME ASSOCIATION
OF THE PORT OF NEW YORK

Windsor Publications, Inc., Woodland Hills, California

International Standard Book Number: 0-89781-002-3
Library of Congress Catalog Card Number: 78-59898

Windsor Publications Inc., Woodland Hills 91364

"SHIP VIA THE
PORT OF
NEW
YORK"

TABLE OF CONTENTS

PREFACE

The author wishes to thank the Maritime Association of the Port of New York and its director, Nick Cretan, for sponsoring this history of a great port. Thanks are due to Mrs. JoAnn Levy for her capable and demanding editing. Special editorial assistance was provided by Debbie Durell, Paula Schoerner and Margaret Tropp. The cooperation of Mr. Charles Young, Librarian, Central Branch, Queens Borough Public Library, is appreciated for letting the author have access to the maritime files of the old New York *Herald Tribune*, a rich resource on port history since 1900. The very extensive collection of periodicals in the New York Public Library and the New York Historical Society were very helpful, as were the fine photographic collections of the New York Historical Society, the Museum of the City of New York and the Port Authority of New York and New Jersey. Photographs and drawings were also furnished by the Navy's Historical Section in Washington, the National Archives, the Library of Congress and the New York State Library in Albany. Thanks to Jeff Blinn and James Redding for photographs. Critiques of the manuscript by maritime historians Frank Brayand and Brad Mitchell are much appreciated, and special thanks are due to the Port Authority of New York for review.

Especially useful in the writing of this history have been the files of the old New York *Herald Tribune*, made available to the writer by the Queens Borough (N. Y.) Public Library. Helpful, too, have been microfilm copies of the New York Times and other newspapers in the New York Public Library and the New York Historical Society, which has an especially fine file of 19th century New York newspapers.

Annual reports of the Port Authority and other publications of the Authority have been of help, too. This material is available at the Authority's library in the New York World Trade Center.

CHAPTER 1

A VERY GOOD LAND TO FALL IN WITH

On the third of September in the year 1609 a tiny ship flying the blue, white, and orange flag of the Dutch East India Company came to anchor near the entrance to a spacious bay along the coast of North America. The air was warm and balmy. There were green, wooded hills to port and starboard, and crewmen were amazed to see a multitude of fish in the rippling waters overside. It was, according to the log of crewman Robert Juet, "a very good land to fall in with."

Early on the morning of the fourth, a large number of Indians darted out from shore in canoes, circling the ship and welcoming by friendly smiles and gestures these "winged strangers from the sea."

It was a momentous day in the history of America and the Western world, for the seaworn, crew-weary ship was named *Half Moon* and the captain who stood on her raised poop deck, absorbed by the excitement of discovery and the hope of what it might portend, was a navigator named Henry Hudson. In the often strange roles common to the great age of exploration, he was an Englishman commissioned by the Dutch to find a northern passage to the Orient.

Hudson and his *Half Moon*, a vessel that measured a scant eighty feet from bow to rudder, lay for some days in or near what is now known as the New York Narrows, the harbor entrance between Staten Island and Long Island, before hoisting anchor and venturing farther into the bay that opened up so awesomely before

them.

He and his crew were more than content, perhaps, to rest and make repairs after a long and storm-tossed voyage that originally had aimed at reaching the East Indies and the Orient eastward across the Arctic at seventy-seven degrees north latitude, a region beset by blustery gales, drifting icebergs, and other perils. Rebuffed by the elements in those northern reaches, Hudson had turned around and headed west, getting becalmed for several weeks on the foggy Grand Banks southeast of Newfoundland, and then making a landfall at Penobscot Bay on the Maine coast. Here the crew went ashore to cut down a tree and trim it into shape to replace a damaged foremast. They stopped briefly along the northern shores of Cape Cod and traded with the Indians, then rounded the Cape and coursed south till they reached the entrance to Chesapeake Bay. It may have been because of squally weather, or because he surmised that the English colony of Jamestown was in this area, or because he sensed this was too far south for a route to the Indies, but Hudson bypassed an exploration of the bay and headed north.

For several days the crew of the *Half Moon* traded with the Indians and took soundings of adjacent waters to be sure of safe navigation. A boat's crew went ashore on what is now Staten Island on the sixth. The men must have angered the natives in some way for John Colman was killed by an arrow and his companions were lucky to get back to their ship.

On the eleventh the *Half Moon* hoisted anchor and proceeded through the Narrows into a bay that second mate Robert Juet described as "a very good harbor for all winds." On the following day the cautious Hudson went farther up the bay, and *Half Moon* was inspected by more Indians in canoes. Word of the strange visitors must have spread by runners to every Indian village for a hundred miles around. The Dutch and English crewmen traded trinkets for oysters, a tasty and welcome relief to a long diet of stale biscuits and other unpalatable sea fare.

Hopeful that the wide, swift-flowing river he had found would lead to

On September 11, 1609, the Half Moon *passed through the gateway of the Narrows. Hudson then spent ten days exploring the river and frequently went ashore with some of his Dutch and English crew to trade with the Algonquins and also the Mohawks.*

the Orient, Hudson tacked his way back and forth up this broad and beautiful stream, the crew still fascinated by the multitude of fish and hooking many large salmon as the ship maneuvered slowly north against the current.

By the nineteenth of September Hudson had reached what is now Albany and stopped to trade knives, hatchets, and beads for skins and pumpkins.

Disappointed that this spacious stream did not lead to another open sea, and deciding he had reached the head of safe navigation for maneuvering under sail, Hudson heaved up the anchor on the twenty-third and headed south, reluctant to leave such a beautiful and bountiful land and, like many other navigators before and later, hating to report his failure to find a new route to the Indies. On October 4 *Half Moon* stood out into the Atlantic and squared away for home.

Hudson was not the first European to see the great harbor that was later to become New York. Some say that the Vikings preceded him by several

2

centuries. And it seems indisputable that Giovanni da Verrazano, a Florentine sailing for Francis I, King of France, discovered New York harbor in April of 1524 aboard a one-hundred-ton, tubby little three-masted vessel called the *Dauphine*, of which Antoine de Conflans was captain and sailing master. Verrazano reported being met by a fleet of some thirty Indian canoes. He took soundings of the bay and described "a very big river" that fed into it. After staying only a few days he up-anchored and continued his quest for a short route to the spice islands of the Indies.

In his report to the king, Verrazano described the land he found as "a very agreeable site located within two small prominent hills in the midst of which flowed to the sea a very big river...the people clothed with feathers of birds of various colors, came toward us joyously, uttering great exclamations of admiration." Verrazano also reported that the adjacent hills showed "indication of minerals," an observation that probably was thrown into his report as an added fillip to intrigue a gold-hungry sponsor. But his description did not excite the French king to plans for further exploration and colonization of this "very agreeable site."

It remained for Hudson and the Dutch to explore the spacious bay and the great river that led north from it, and to initiate plans for a settlement there.

Although Hudson had failed to find the fabled Indies, the trademinded Dutch, spurred on by the prospect of profits in furs, dispatched an expedition under Hendrik Christiaensen and Adrian Block to trade with the Indians. When they returned to Holland with a rich cargo of pelts the practical Dutch decided that even without gold, silks, and spices, this new land was worth attention.

A combine of merchants provided ships and cargo for a second voyage, and the same two mariners arrived in the fall of 1613 in the ships *Fortune* and *Tiger*. With an eye to establishing a trading post in this fur-rich land, Christiaensen worked his way upriver and built Fort Nassau at what is now Albany, the first Dutch commercial post in America.

Block and his men spent the winter of 1613-14 at Manhattan Island, trading with the Indians and filling their ship with the pelts of beaver, fox, squirrel, and other animals. During this winter the *Tiger* caught fire and was completely destroyed, but with the usual energy and inventiveness of the versatile mariner, the men, who spent the winter in Manhattan in four small huts, built a ship, which they named *Onrust*, meaning "restless." And restless they probably were after a long winter, eager to hoist sail and be off.

Traders returning to Holland with rich cargoes of pelts captured the interest of the practical Dutch, who decided that even without gold, silks, and spices, this new land was worth attention.

Far left, Giovanni da Verrazano, a Florentine sailing for Francis I, King of France, discovered New York harbor in April of 1524 aboard a one-hundred-ton, three-masted vessel called the Dauphine.

When the ship Tiger, belonging to Adriaen Block and his crew, was destroyed, the industrious sailors built the Onrust. It was not quite forty-four feet in length and less than twelve in width, but the Dutchmen sailed up the coast from Manhattan Island past Cape Cod and home to Holland. This reproduction of the Onrust is from an oil painting by Walter Bollendonk.

Capt. Adriaen Block and his crew built this ship to replace their burned vessel Tiger and named it Onrust, meaning "restless." It was the first vessel built in New York.

In 1621, the Dutch West India Company was awarded a monopoly on trade to North America, provided the company could establish its right by colonization. Hardship and inconvenience did not deter the sturdy pioneers.

Onrust was hardly worthy of the word *ship*, for it was barely forty-four feet in length and less than twelve in width, but in this little vessel the hardy Dutchmen set out to explore the coast. They sailed up the East River and through the narrow Hell Gate channel (which Block called Helle-gatt) into Long Island Sound, thence along the Connecticut shore to an island which they called Block Island. They visited Narragansett Bay, coursed past Martha's Vineyard and Nantucket, and sailed around Cape Cod—whose sands have claimed the timbers of many a sailing ship—into Cape Cod Bay. They crossed the bay to what is now Nahant, just north of Boston harbor, before heading back for the tip of Cape Cod.

The *Fortune*, meanwhile, had secured a full cargo of furs and had headed for home in the spring of 1614, leaving several men at Fort Nassau to continue business with the Indians. Amazingly, the *Fortune* fell in with the returning *Onrust* off Cape Cod. Block left crewman Cornelius Hendricksen in charge of *Onrust*, boarded the *Fortune*, and returned to Holland, arriving home in July of 1614.

It was on the basis of reports given by Block and Christiaensen that the Dutch government commissioned the short-lived United New Netherlands Company to establish trading posts in North America and explore its resources. And when it became known how rich this new land was in furs of all kinds, other traders soon followed in their wake.

Considering the detailed charts and the numerous navigational aids by which vessels today can leave one port and lay a direct course to another, it is amazing how these little ships took off boldly from Amsterdam, withstood the buffeting of the often stormy English Channel, and then found their way to New York without mishap, relying for their navigation on dead reckoning, the crude instruments of the day, and on what they could learn from those who had sailed the route before.

In 1621 the government gave the Dutch West India Company a monopoly on trade to North America. To establish this right, the company in 1624 outfitted a small vessel with the necessary people and stores for colonization, named her *Nieuw Nederlandt*, and dispatched her to the Hudson under Captain Cornelius Jacobsen. Aboard were thirty families of Protestant Walloons: 110 men, women, and children who somehow crowded into this vessel along with livestock, household goods, farming equipment, seeds, and trading goods. They were hardy people who were eager to wrest a better life from a far and unknown land. Hardship, crowding, and inconvenience were no deterrence to these sturdy pioneers.

They arrived in May, a time in New York State aglow in the beauty of trees and flowers and the promise of nature's bounty. A year later a second ship arrived with one hundred head of cattle and more farming equipment. The first colonists were soon harvesting a crop and doing well.

By the end of the second year they were able to build Fort Amsterdam, and Peter Minuit, leader of the colony, concluded history's greatest real-estate transaction, buying Manhattan Island for a boxful of trinkets worth about sixty guilders. There is reason to believe that a certain amount of subterfuge was involved in the deal.

The *Onrust* was the forerunner of what was to become a great shipbuilding industry in New York, for the forested hills of Manhattan and adjacent shores provided a rich resource in virgin ship timber. In the years to come this resource, plus clear-grained oak and pine from more

A seventeenth-century Dutch breech-loading swivel deck gun from Adriaen Block's ship Tiger, which burned off Manhattan in 1613. Timbers from the Tiger were found in 1916 during excavations for the subway at Dey and Greenwich streets.

4

Peter Minuit, leader of the colony, concluded history's greatest real estate transaction, buying Manhattan Island for a boxful of trinkets worth about sixty guilders.

By the end of the colonists' second year in the new land they had built Fort Amsterdam. This view is copied from an old engraving executed in Holland. The fort was erected in 1623, and finished upon the above model by Governor Twiller in 1635.

5

distant areas, provided the keels, hulls, and masts for hundreds, even thousands, of ships and boats built in New York yards.

A vessel called the *Wapen van Amsterdam* (flag of Amsterdam) was as historic as *Onrust*, for it was the first vessel to clear for Europe from New Amsterdam with an official manifest of cargo. For that reason this ship might be said to have opened regular trade between Europe and what was to become the largest and busiest port in the world. She set sail September 23, 1626, carrying 7,246 beaver skins, 853 otter skins, 48 mink, 36 wildcat, and 34 muskrat, plus "many logs of oak and nut wood," probably walnut, hickory, and chestnut, which the Dutch converted into fine furniture. The ship's cargo was valued at $25,000.

Furs were the silks and spices, the rich cargo that spurred the entrepreneurs of the port's early years; but furs were limited, and other exports, quite obviously, had to replace them. Flour became a very important export and, together with bagged grains, remained so for centuries.

Ships were an early export, too. In 1631 a new vessel called the *Nieuw Nederlandt* was launched on the East River. According to some writers she was a ship of eight hundred tons, but this is a figure hard to accept, considering that a commercial vessel of eight hundred tons would be large even a century later. Be that as it may, she must have been an impressive vessel, for she created much attention in Amsterdam for her size and the big timbers used in her. It is said that this vessel mounted thirty guns and was as large as most ships of the Dutch navy. In looking askance at such a sizable ship in these early days of the colony, it is pertinent to remember that wood was only one material required in building a ship; needed, too, were iron fastenings and hardware, a large amount of hemp, duck for the sails, anchors and anchor chain, and other appurtenances.

By the 1630s settlers had built homes on Long Island, and about 1638 a ferry service began hauling passengers and produce between the two islands, running (in present-day terms) from the foot of Fulton Street in Brooklyn to Peck Slip in Manhat-

tan. Rowboats were used at first; then large flat-bottom pulling boats that could carry hay, horses, and cattle, as well as people. Ferries later connected Manhattan with Staten Island and New Jersey. Sail and muscle power provided the propulsion.

The first facilities for ship docking and cargo handling came in 1647 when the town council of New Amsterdam authorized funds for a wharf, which received its first ship a year later. A second wharf was provided in 1659. Another important develop-

ment came in 1654 when a weigh house, with scales for weighing merchandise, was built on this pier. A collector of customs was appointed, and New Amsterdam was on its way to becoming a seaport.

In 1657 came another addition to the port's facilities. A pole was set up on a hill at the Narrows and on this a flag was hoisted when a ship was sighted coming in from the sea, alerting those who had business with ships and cargoes well ahead of the vessel's arrival at dock or at anchor. This was the port's first marine information

Peter Stuyvesant was appointed as director-general of New Amsterdam and arrived on May 11, 1647. He was honorable, active, and conscientious, but his autocratic disposition and his hostility to popular demands led to continual friction.

This map of New Netherland in 1656 was published in Holland by Adrian van der Donck, who headed the deputation that secured from the States-General the charter for the city. He founded Yonkers, which is twenty miles above New York.

6

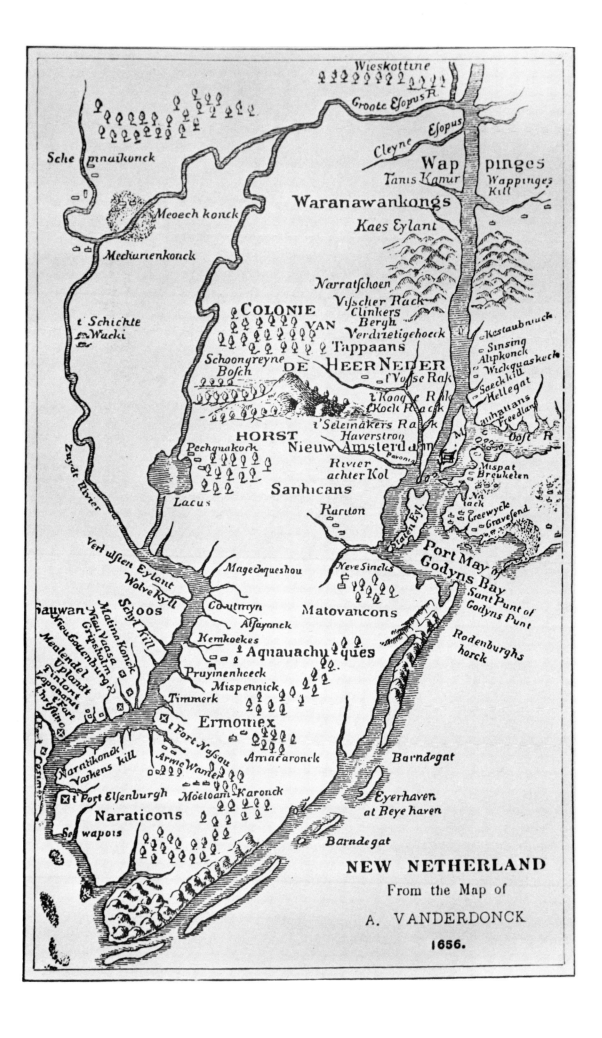

7

NEW NETHERLAND

From the Map of

A. VANDERDONCK

1656.

system, the beginnings of an elaborate reporting in future years for the maritime fraternity.

By the 1670s seaborne trade in the harbor of New York was varied and growing. Sloops, ketches, and other small craft freighted cargoes to and from towns along the sound, to river and bay points, and to the other colonies. These coasting vessels, tiny ships to our way of thinking today, also voyaged routinely to the Caribbean, returning with salt, molasses, sugar, and other products. Flour was an important export to the West Indies. Trade with Europe was increasing, too. Vessels arrived with tools, hemp, linens, hardware, paper, inks, and other merchandise needed in the colony, and sailed back with pelts, timber, flour, and grains. At this period a trade was also developing with faraway Brazil.

Although in 1635 furs were the primary export of the colony—more than 16,000 skins were sent to Amsterdam that year—by the 1670s furs were not as easily obtainable; agriculture had taken over many of the Indian lands, and the main industry of the colony had become the making of flour and meal.

Ships engaged in trade between New Amsterdam and the mother country had quaint and colorful names: *Sea Mew, White Horse, Orange Tree, Three Kings, Black Eagle, Pear Tree,* and *King Solomon.* A voyage took from six to eight weeks by way of the Canary Islands and the southern route.

The Dutch were not to long enjoy the fruits of the colony's growth. In 1664, during war between the Dutch and the English, an English fleet sailed into the harbor and demanded surrender of the fort and the city. The Dutch had no ability to resist, and the transfer was one of the easiest and most important acquisitions ever made in the days of empire building. King Charles II presented the colony to his brother, the Duke of York, and renamed New Netherland, in his brother's honor, New York. A Dutch fleet retook the city in 1673 during another Anglo-Dutch war, but at war's end it was given back to England under terms of the Treaty of Westminster.

Coastwise shipping and trade with the West Indies was the most important aspect of port commerce at this period. The coastwise trade had its beginnings in 1633 when Governor Winthrop of Massachusetts sent that colony's first home-built ship, the *Blessing of the Bay,* to New Amsterdam with an invitation for trade. Within a few years a lively commerce had developed between the two.

New York's first governor, Col. Richard Nicolls, was succeeded by Gov. Edmund Andros, who appreciated the port's geographical advantages and was determined to make it an important commercial center. He built a new city dock made of stone, extending from Whitehall Slip to Coenties Slip. The canal that ran along what is now Broad Street, and which served by this time more as a refuse sluice than a waterway, was filled in to make the area more presentable. Andros was the city's first environmentalist, for one of his first acts was to forbid the throwing of garbage and refuse into the harbor.

Port improvements were encouraged after the British occupation. From 1686 to 1730 there was a stipulation that everyone receiving a grant of waterfront land had to build a wharf on it.

By 1747 close to one hundred vessels were owned in New York, and eight hundred seamen found employment here. The tremendous growth of commerce in the next quarter-century is evident from statistics showing that the number of New York-owned vessels had increased to 709 by 1772. Privateers accounted for some of this increase in shipping.

A glowing portrayal of New York's booming maritime importance is attributed to the English statesman Edmund Burke, who penned these words in 1757:

"The city of New York contains upwards of 2,000 houses and above 12,000 inhabitants....It is well and commodiously built, extending a mile in length and half that in breadth, and has a very good aspect from the sea. The town has a flourishing trade and in which great profits are made. The merchants are wealthy and the people, in general, most comfortably provided for.

"From 1749 to 1750," he continued,

"232 vessels have been entered in this port and 286 cleared outwards. In these vessels were shipped 6,731 tons of provisions, chiefly flour, and a vast quantity of grain....In the year 1755 the export of flaxseed to Ireland amounted to 12,528 hogsheads."

The fortunes of the port of New York were greatly affected by various acts of Parliament aimed at shaping colonial trade to the benefit of English merchants and shipowners. The first of these restrictive measures were the Acts of Navigation and Trade, and one of their more onerous provisions was that the colonists could not sell to other countries any products needed in Great Britain, or buy and import certain goods except from Great Britain. Needless to say, this encouraged smuggling and subterfuge, and New York captains and merchants, along with those in the other colonies, became adept at evading the law.

Subsequent legislation, especially the Stamp Act of 1765, was aimed at making the colonies pay for costs of supporting British troops and the costs of royal government.

When the British ship *Edward* arrived in New York harbor in 1765 with the first stamps to be used to tax all legal documents and newspapers, it created such a furor among the populace that the stamps had to be rushed to Fort Orange to keep the *Edward* from being boarded and sacked. The Sons of Liberty demanded that Governor Colden repudiate the Stamp Act or suffer the consequences, namely hanging. In March of 1766 Parliament repealed the Stamp Act but most unwisely in 1767 levied even more stringent taxes on tea and other imports needed by the

In 1746, New York was a bustling center of activity and the port kept pace with its growth. Sloops, ketches, and other small vessels appeared as coastwise trade expanded to carry people and produce to other ports.

9

New Amsterdam (New York) about 1667.

colonies.

A boycott of the taxed goods followed immediately, and it was so effective that in 1768 imports from England through the port of New York dropped to almost nothing.

Ironically, the tax that incited rebellion would seem to have been a minor one—a levy of three pence a pound on tea. In December of 1773 Boston patriots dumped valuable cargoes of tea into the harbor, and in April of 1774 New Yorkers forced the British ship *Nancy*, which had discharged some of its cargo in Boston, to hoist sail and depart for England before selling the remainder in New York. The British ship *London* was not so fortunate. A party of citizens held Captain Chambers of the *London* prisoner in Fraunces Tavern while others boarded his ship and threw eighteen cases of tea onto the tide. It is not known whether the tea sank or floated away to be salvaged clandestinely by those not so patriotic.

By April of 1776 New York was in full-blown revolt. Citizens raided the armory and helped themselves to several hundred muskets; they also seized supplies that were being loaded aboard ship for British garrisons in Boston and Halifax. In May of 1776 the New York Provincial Congress became the ruling government of New York.

But the city's independence was short-lived. On June 29, 1776, General Howe arrived with nine thousand British troops, to be reinforced later by more British and Hessians. They were to control the port for the rest of the war except for the brief period in which Washington's Continentals held Manhattan.

The retreat of the American army to Manhattan from its precarious position on Long Island on the night of August 29-30, 1776, was one of the most momentous events that ever took place in the harbor of New York. If this evacuation had not been successful—if the Americans had been trapped and Washington captured—the Revolution would have died on the Brooklyn shore. It was a masterful operation and one that insured Washington's place in history as a military strategist of the first order.

To accomplish this withdrawal from an untenable situation, Washington

issued an order to "impress every kind of watercraft from Hell Gate on the Sound to Speyghten Duyvel Creek that can be kept afloat and that has either sails or oars and have them in the east harbor of the city by dark."

The retreat began immediately after dark and was carried out so quietly and swiftly that the British did not discover the movement until all but a few of the troops were safely across the river to Manhattan. The embarkation was made from the Fulton Ferry (where the Brooklyn

Bridge now is), the boats being manned by men who, in the words of an aide to Washington, "went to work with sailor-like cheer and dispatch." The troops were crammed into rowboats, flatboats, whale boats, and sloops, some so jammed with men that they had only a few inches of freeboard. Washington crossed in the last boat.

It is of interest to note that the ancient iron fence at the newly restored Bowling Green park, fronting the old U.S. Custom House at the foot of Broadway, is the same now as when

This Revolutionary War recruiting poster called all brave young men to join Washington's Continentals in the fight for freedom and independence.

Speaking at a Sons of Liberty meeting in New York City Hall on December 17, 1773, John Lamb asked, "Is it then your opinion, gentlemen, that the tea should be landed under this circumstance?" There was one prolonged and vociferous shout, which echoed far into the street, and was three times repeated, "No! No! No!"

The retreat of the American army to Manhattan from Long Island on August 29 began immediately after dark and was carried out so quickly and swiftly that the British did not discover the movement until all but a few of the troops were safely across the river. The embarkation was made from the Fulton Ferry, the boats being manned by men who, in the words of an aide to Washington, "went to work with sailor-like cheer and dispatch."

TO ALL BRAVE, HEALTHY, ABLE BODIED, AND WELL
DISPOSED YOUNG MEN,
IN THIS NEIGHBOURHOOD, WHO HAVE ANY INCLINATION TO JOIN THE TROOPS,
NOW RAISING UNDER
GENERAL WASHINGTON,
FOR THE DEFENCE OF THE
LIBERTIES AND INDEPENDENCE
OF THE UNITED STATES,
Against the hostile designs of foreign enemies,

TAKE NOTICE,

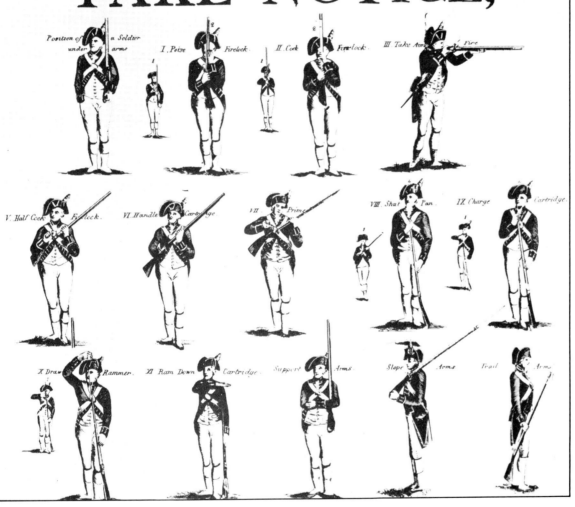

the British occupied this area, but with one exception. Prior to the Revolution, a royal crown topped the upright dividers along the fence. These symbols of royal majesty were sawed off by patriots on the night of July 4, 1776. It was in Bowling Green also that rebels pulled down the statue of King George the same night.

A little-known monument in Brooklyn's Fort Greene Park is a stark reminder of a tragic chapter in the history of the port of New York. This simple marker honors the thousands of American soldiers and seamen

and transports, one by using fire ships and another by blocking the channel between the Battery and Governor's Island by sinking boats loaded with stones. There were numerous other forays and engagements in the harbor and adjacent waters during the war.

In 1778 the French fleet, sent to help the United States and destroy the fleet of Lord Howe, operated for eleven days off Sandy Hook, failing to engage the British fleet but capturing many British merchantmen. In May of 1779 the American sloop *Providence*, ten guns, under Capt. Haysted

12

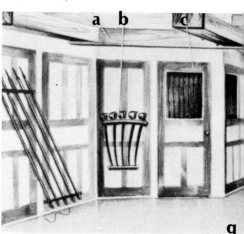

q

Cutaway Scene from the gun deck depicting equipment used during the Revolutionary War: a. Carlings; b. Cutlasses; c. Officer's Cabin; d. Hanging Knee; e. Drift Bolt; f. Spar Deck Beam; g. Gun Worm; h. Ceiling; i. Mizzenmast; j. Gunport; k. Lodging Knee; l. Breeching; m. Sponge Rammer; n. Intermediate Beam; o. Scuttlebutt; p. Removable Athwartships Bulkheads; q. Gun Secure Hook; r. Quoin; s. Train Tackle; t. Inhaul Tackle; u. Waterway Lock Strade; v. Twenty-four Pounder Shot; w. Hatch; x. Stanchion; y. Boarding Pikes.

who died in British prison hulks anchored in what was then Wallabout Bay, later the site of the Brooklyn Navy Yard. More than twelve thousand Americans died on board the British prison fleet from cold, disease, malnutrition, and neglect during the long, dark days of the Revolution. Many more were crippled for life as a result of their harsh imprisonment.

Conditions on board these foul-smelling, rotting hulks prompted a strong letter of protest from General Washington to General Howe in January of 1777:

"Those who have been lately sent out [from the hulks]," he said, "give the most shocking accounts of their barbarous usage, which their miserable emaciated countenances confirm."

Despite this protest little was done to change things, and many more men were fated to die needlessly in these infamous floating prisons along the Brooklyn shore.

In 1776 the patriots were active in harassing British shipping in the harbor. During August, several attempts were made to destroy British warships

Hacker, captured the British sloop *Diligent*, ten guns, in a fierce battle off Sandy Hook.

Captain Harradan, in the American privateer *Pickering*, sixteen guns, was attacked off Sandy Hook in 1779 by a British sloop of fourteen guns, a brig of ten, and a sloop of eight. In a two-hour battle he captured all three.

On June 12, 1780, Captain Kemp of the sloop *Comet* took eight of a fleet of fifteen convoyed British merchantmen just two miles off Sandy Hook; and on November 3, 1782, Captain Storer, commanding two small boats commissioned by the government of New Jersey, saw a British vessel anchored near Staten Island, and boarded and captured her in the first victorious engagement of the New Jersey "navy."

What was probably the smallest privateer under the American flag "sailed" boldly out of Amboy, New Jersey, on April 18, 1780. It was an open whaleboat with a Captain Marriner and nine dauntless companions. And dauntless they were. In two days they captured the British privateer brig *Black Snake* with its

f g h i j k l m n o p

r s t u v w x y

13

crew of twenty, and used her to take the British privateer schooner *Morning Star*, with a crew of thirty-three. He sailed both ships, with his whaleboat in tow, into Egg Harbor and delivered fifty prisoners to the American army.

The harbor was closed to commerce throughout the war, but there was considerable shipping activity, both coastwise and deep-sea, because the port was the center of British military activity. Movements of troops and supplies insured a considerable flow of shipping.

An accident to one of these British supply ships gave New York a romantic legend of treasure trove. The frigate *Hussar*, recently arrived from England in 1780 with gold and silver coins to pay British troops in America, was dispatched from New York to Newport, Rhode Island, up the narrow East River and through the dangerous Hell Gate passage into Long Island Sound. It was tacking to go through Hell Gate when it hit an unseen rock and went down in a matter of minutes, almost within a stone's throw of shore. More than two hundred British seamen and America prisoners locked below decks went down with the ship, along with a payroll said to have been in excess of $1 million.

Various salvagers over the years have brought up cannon, muskets, cannonballs, crockery, and even skeletons from the hulk of the *Hussar* but, so far, the strong room and its treasure hoard have eluded all attempts at recovery. The strong tides of Hell Gate and centuries of hard-packed mud are guarding well New York's most sought-for wreck.

The first use of a submarine against an enemy vessel in time of war took place in New York harbor during the Revolution. David Bushnell, a young Yale graduate, had conceived and built a tiny, self-propelled submersible with which he hoped to sink at least one of the British ships then at anchor in the port. The idea was to approach the vessel submerged, attach a torpedo to its hull by means of a screw device operated from within the submarine by its navigator, and then, it was hoped, to escape from the area before the torpedo and its 130 pounds of gunpowder were detonated by a clock timing arrangement.

A small boat towed the little submersible, which Bushnell named the *Turtle*, to within several hundred yards of the British frigate *Eagle*, after which the operator was on his own in this radical and as yet untried innovation in naval warfare.

Volunteering to risk his life in this historic experiment was Ezra Lee, a sergeant in Washington's army. Sitting in a cramped position inside the tiny turtlelike contraption, Lee oper-

A seaman in the days of the Revolutionary War.

14

The Turtle, one of the first working submarines, was designed during the Revolutionary War. The operator was to crank his way out to a British Man O' War and somehow attach a keg of gun powder to the copper-sheathed hull. Unfortunately, the inventor never devised a successful method of attaching it, and after repeated failures, dropped the keg and left. The keg exploded, and while it failed to do any damage to the ship, it caused her to move further out to sea.

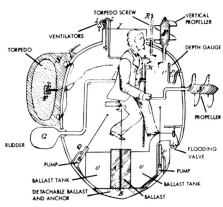

This plan of the city of New York was originally published in London in 1776 and republished in David T. Valentine's Manual of the Corporation of the City of New York in 1854.

ated the pumps and the ballast valve for rising and descending. He steered with a rudder and hand-cranked a mechanism that turned a wooden propeller. Glass plates in the top of his cubicle enabled him to get some idea of where he was going.

After some two hours of cranking and maneuvering against strong tidal currents, Lee finally positioned the *Turtle* beneath the *Eagle* and tried to attach the torpedo, which was carried on the back of the sub. But for some reason, perhaps because of the copper sheathing on the bottom of the frigate, the screw device on the torpedo would not work, and Lee had to retreat before his air supply was exhausted and the British discovered him. By that time he was probably near exhaustion as well. The British did spy the *Turtle* as it headed toward the Long Island shore and sent a boat to investigate. Lee released his torpedo and it blew up without doing any damage, other than causing the British to post extra lookouts on their ships at anchor and to accuse the Continentals of breaching the nice rules of war with an infernal machine. Had the attempt on the *Eagle* been successful it might have had some impact on the British occupation. At the very least it would have speeded the use of the submarine as a naval weapon.

16

George Washington marched back into New York at war's end in November of 1783 to find a city half in ruins from fire, neglect, and the ravages of occupation. Port facilities were in a state of decay and disrepair. Commerce and shipping were stagnant.

When the British fleet sailed away on December 5 the port of New York had to start from scratch; not only to rebuild its neglected facilities but, more importantly, to bring back trade lost through war and to open up new trade contacts all over the world. ♆

George Washington marched back into New York at war's end in November of 1783 to find a city half in ruins from fire, neglect, and the ravages of occupation.

The departing British, to prevent the hoisting of the American colors, greased the flagpole. David Van Arsdale, a sailor boy, attempted to climb the bare pole, but it was too slippery. Some of the bystanders ran to Goelet's Hardware Store, in Hanover Square, procured tools, and set to work to boring new cleats for the flagstaff. Nailing the cleats above him as he ascended, the sailor boy hoisted the American colors atop the mast as the echo from a salute of thirteen guns rang across the bay to the British ships.

The Frigate United States dressed with the colours of different Nations

CHAPTER 2
THE INTREPID
TRADERS

Merchants did not sit around after the Revolution waiting for better times to come or for trade to begin drifting back to their doorsteps. There was no federal largess in those days to help "disaster areas" and no government loans for distressed businesses.

No sooner had the British fleet left New York than traders and ship-owners began planning for business revival. Adventure was the keynote of the day and they planned boldly.

The port's postwar renaissance might well be dated from a cold day in February of 1784 when a little ship prepared to leave her East River slip for a voyage as historic for trade as Henry Hudson's was for discovery and exploration.

The name *Empress of China* was emblazoned in gold letters beneath the cabin windows of her squarish stern. As crewmen in tarred queues and canvas trousers loosed her jibs and topsails, onlookers waved and shouted good wishes, and the owners repeated their advice on the conduct of the voyage and the disposal of cargo. Capt. John Green judged the wind and the tide, and the mate, with his hands cupped to his mouth, shouted out the commands that would cut their ties with New York for many months to come: "Cast off forward! Cast off aft!"

Within a few minutes the swift current of the East River took the vessel in its grasp and, with sails sheeted home, the *Empress of China* began a voyage that would take her half the world around and open up fabulous new trade opportunities for the port of New York.

It was perhaps symbolic of the city's future as a commercial and shipping center that this vessel should have left from Manhattan. *Empress of China* was a kind of all-American enterprise. She had been built in Baltimore. The project was financed by Robert Morris and associates in Philadelphia, and the venture cargo, as it appears, had been accumulated by merchants in New York. It was there also that details of the voyage were worked out. The business of supervising the cargo, disposing of it at a profit, and obtaining goods for the return trip was assigned to a Maj. Samuel Shaw, a New Englander of exceptional shrewdness and enterprise.

Much was at stake as the ship squared away off Sandy Hook and coursed toward the southeast and the long haul to the Cape of Good Hope. Morris and friends had invested what for that time was the huge sum of $120,000 in the voyage. Under hatches were thirty tons of ginseng, an aromatic herb much favored by the Chinese for its medicinal value; pepper; woolen garments; and 2,600 fur pelts. In addition, Shaw had in his care a large amount of specie to be used to buy tea and other goods.

Captain Green and his crew of forty-five were off to find a port that none of them had ever seen, and to trade with a strange, mystical land that lay beyond uncharted seas. But the captain navigated his ship safely more than eighteen thousand miles to Canton via the Cape, across the vast and lonely reaches of the Indian Ocean, through the hazardous Straits of Sunda and up the South China Sea. There were guns, muskets, and cutlasses on board, and the ship carried a large crew that could be well used if any pirates tried to take her. Fortunately, none were encountered.

Once the vessel reached China it was up to Major Shaw to become friendly with the local merchants and to make the voyage worthwhile. This he accomplished with acumen and dispatch, and within a month the *Empress of China* was homeward bound with a cargo of tea and other goods. She arrived back in New York safely after a voyage of fifteen months, and netted a substantial

The United States was one of the frigates chiefly responsible for American success in the War of 1812. In this painting the ship is shown dressed with the flags of all nations.

profit.

Shaw was so impressed by the opportunities for trade in China that he sought and obtained the post of U.S. consul in Canton and lived there for many years.

Enterprise, adventure, and the willingness to take chances always have been a signal feature of New York's maritime community, from the days of Robert Morris to the time of Moore-McCormack, Farrell, Grace, Isbrandtsen, and others who have displayed the spirit of enterprise within the framework of more modern and more limiting trade and commerce on the seas. Latter-day merchants and shipowners lack none of the ambition and enterprise of their predecessors whose ships opened up trade for New York all over the world, but they do lack the free hand of laissez-faire common to the eighteenth century.

It was the boldness of her merchants and seamen, the willingness to risk lives and fortunes against the hazards of the sea, and the often-dangerous environment in far places that, more than anything else, laid the foundation for making New York the greatest port in the world.

Merchants and owners who saw ship, crew, and cargo sail away in these early days never knew when—or if—they would see them return. When a vessel slipped down the bay and eventually was lost to view beyond the Narrows, those left behind could do nothing but wait, wait and pray, for a safe return.

The second voyage from New York to China was made by the seventy-six-ton sloop *Experiment*, even smaller than *Empress of China*. Dauntless the bold argonauts who manned her! They faced a voyage to the faraway Orient with seemingly no more concern than a trip to the West Indies. Or so it would seem, considering the size of their ship and her crew of ten. *Experiment* carried a cargo of ginseng, wine, and specie. Tiny though she was, she made the round trip successfully and turned a profit on the venture.

The China trade soon attracted more ships, and, before long, New York merchants were receiving a steady flow of silks, tea, and chinaware.

Because China was a profitable market for furs, the fur seal and the sea otter became important to all ships in the China trade. In 1797 Capt. Edmund Fanning, then only twenty-eight years old, sailed from New York to the island of Juan Fernandez in the South Pacific, west of Chile, where his crew killed thousands of fur seals. When the hold was full, Fanning continued on to Canton, where he traded skins for tea and other cargo that sold for $120,000 in New York and netted Fanning and his associates $50,000 for the voyage. Such spectacular profits, of course, inspired others to follow suit. Within a gen-

eration the furbearing sea mammals were almost extinct through rapacious hunting, and the market in China was glutted with skins.

What was probably the city's first organization for trade promotion was formed in the 1790s by shipowners and merchants as a means of exchanging information and a convenient means of arranging joint ventures. Serving also as a place for dining and conviviality, it was called the Tontine Association, better known as the Tontine Coffee House, and was named for a Neapolitan who started a similar organization in France in 1653. The coffee house was

Maj. Samuel Shaw, a New Englander of exceptional shrewdness and enterprise, was assigned the business of supervising cargo aboard the Empress of China *on a voyage that would take her half the world around and open up fabulous new trade opportunities for the port of New York.*

The Tontine Coffee House, built in 1792 at Wall and Water streets, was probably the city's first organization for trade promotion. It was formed by shipowners and merchants as a convenient means of exchanging information and arranging joint ventures.

built at Wall and Water streets in 1792.

Cargo was arriving at New York docks from all over the world.

On August 7, 1807, this notice appeared in the New York *Daily Advertiser*:

Oliver Wolcott offers for sale the cargo of the ship Trident, from Hong Kong, consisting of Imperial Hyson, Sonchong, and Bohea teas in whole, half, and quarter chests, long and short pieces of white nankeens, lute strings, striped vest patterns, mock damask and five boxes of camphor of the best quality.

Not as exotic, but typical of New York's prosperous trade with the West Indies was an ad by W. and J. Robinson offering the cargo of the schooner *Ocean*, in from Demarara with twenty-two hogsheads of rum and three hogsheads of molasses. Other cargoes for sale that day included Havana sugar from the brig *Hetty* and earthenware from the ship *Magistrate*, just in from Liverpool.

American foreign trade grew rapidly after the turn of the century, increasing at the rate of about 700,000 tons a year from 1795 to 1805. But there were squalls on the horizon and prosperity was short-lived. The United States was caught in the feuding between the rampant Napoleon Bonaparte and the English. France and England enacted trade restrictions aimed at crippling one another, but seriously hurt American trade and shipping in the process. This running battle between the two great European powers, both of which were good customers for goods brought by American ships, made the latter subject to seizure and confiscation if caught trading with ports of these countries or their colonies. A more exasperating situation for young America, straining for trade expansio like a tiger on the leash, hardly can be imagined.

Equally aggravating as far as seamen and fiery patriots were concerned was the free and easy manner in which British men-of-war stopped American ships to see if there were any British navy deserters on board and, if so, to take them away. American captains claimed that all too frequently a strong, able Yankee would be admired by a British boarding party who suddenly discovered that he looked very much like a deserter from His Majesty's ship so-and-so. The protesting man would be taken off, and there was nothing the American captain could do about it except object to a government which had no power to protect American sovereignty on the seas.

Stopping American vessels to look for naval deserters was only one part of British highhandedness with American shipping for some years prior to the outbreak of war. It reached a high point of humiliation in September of 1807 when a boat's crew from the British frigate *Jason* boarded the New York pilot boat *Thorn* near the harbor entrance and tried to take over the ship. When the captain of the *Thorn* knocked a British seaman away from the helm and threatened to shoot if necessary, the *Jason*'s men departed, all the while heaping verbal abuse on the pilots.

In what it considered its only means of bringing England or France to terms on these various aggravations, the administration of Thomas Jefferson in 1807 enacted an embargo prohibiting American ships from leaving port in foreign trade.

The effect was disastrous, not to Great Britain or France, but to America's own shipping and commerce. By the end of a year there were said to be more than four hundred ships at anchor or tied up to piers in the port of New York alone, and thousands of seamen either unemployed or diverted from the sea to other occupations. There were so many sailors walking the streets in New York that the Navy Yard was able to employ three hundred of them for meals only, no pay.

Many businesses went bankrupt. With no foreign markets for New York's primary export—flour—the price soon fell from two dollars to seventy-five cents a barrel. Sugar, salt, tea, molasses, and rum became almost impossible to obtain.

Even before the embargo was lifted in 1809, another act of aggravation by Great Britain, which regarded America as an impotent nation and a handy punching bag, edged Americans closer to war. In June of 1807 the British frigate *Leopard* attacked the American frigate *Chesapeake* when the latter refused a request by the British commander to heave to and permit a boarding party to examine the crew for British deserters. Unprepared to fight, the *Chesapeake* suffered a destructive and bloody cannonade before she struck her colors and the *Leopard* took off some of her crew. The nation was stunned at this brazen effrontery to the American flag on the high seas. Stopping a homely little merchantman was one thing; to attack and humble an American warship was something else. But nothing could be done. The nation still was unprepared for war. The complete unpreparedness of the *Chesapeake* typified the state of the nation. Indecisiveness may have been a factor in the *Chesapeake* affair, too, just as the nation was still indecisive about what to do with Great Britain.

America's seagoing fraternity knew all too well what they would be up against in the event of war. At this time the British navy had on station in North American waters five ships of the line, nineteen frigates, forty-one brigs, and sixteen schooners, plus transports of various rigs. All told, the British navy could muster a thousand ships. America's naval force ready for sea could be counted off on the fingers of two hands.

It is impossible here to examine even briefly all the political and economic forces that brought on the War of 1812. Sufficient to say that after two years of negotiations over impressment of seamen, trade restrictions, and the *Chesapeake* affair, America was convinced that talk and diplomacy would achieve nothing and finally was ready to fight.

Like most wars, the War of 1812 could have been prevented by more willingness to understand each other's problems; in this case, America's need for unrestricted trade and Britain's need for all the help it could get in stopping Napoleon.

But when war finally came in 1812 there was a succession of brilliant American naval victories at sea, with New York sharing in the nation's exultation over tweaking the lion's tail.

On July 2, 1812, Capt. David Porter sailed from New York in the frigate

Robert Morris was the financier of the Empress of China voyage in February of 1784, which marked the beginning of trade with China and New York's future as the shipping center of the world.

The American frigate Chesapeake which was fired upon and boarded by the British in June, 1807. The Chesapeake Affair was but one of the inflammatory incidents leading to the War of 1812.

23

Essex flying a banner with the motto "Free Trade and Sailors Rights," words that proclaimed the basic reasons for the War of 1812. President Madison had called the habit of British cruisers stopping American ships on various pretexts "a crying enormity."

In September of 1812 there were no ticker-tape parades in Manhattan, but New Yorkers turned out to cheer Capt. Isaac Hull and his officers after the *Constitution*'s victory over the British frigate *Guerriere*. They were presented with swords and were given "the freedom of the city."

Soon after this, New Yorkers celebrated another victory when the U.S.S. *Wasp*, a sloop of war, scored a decisive victory over the British sloop of war *Frolic*. Again, public celebrations, speeches, and presentation of a sword to Capt. Jacob Jones of the *Wasp*.

In October of 1812 there was even more cause for jubilation, for the frigate *United States*—captain, Stephen Decatur—sailed triumphantly into port with the British frigate *Macedonian*, which she had captured after a stand-up, drag-down fight near faraway Madeira. It was the most decisive example yet of American fighting skill, for the *Macedonian* lost 104 killed and wounded, the *United States* only 11.

Although many New York ship-owners and merchants opposed the war, they found some cause for rejoicing once it came. With no fleet capable of contesting Great Britain for naval supremacy, the American navy was used to harry British commerce. Even this would have been little more than a nibbling nuisance were it not for the private men-of-war, the privateers, which took to the sea in droves to provide more guns and audacity.

Privateering was a very profitable business and many a fortune was made with private men-of-war. Shipbuilders profited, too, for a successful privateer had to be fast and heavily armed.

Once this tragic war was over, America turned its attention at once to trade horizons all over the world.

Although Salem had a strong hold on the India trade, New York began competing. It entered this trade in 1815 when the ship *Emily* sailed for Calcutta with a miscellaneous cargo to exchange for sago, sugar, indigo, straw matting, and other goods. Imports from India were not to change much for a hundred years.

Salem was a leader in the East Indies trade, but New York ships, too, steered for Sumatra and the other spice islands of the Indies.

Daring and bold as they were, the merchants of Salem and Boston had to admire the "get up and go" of their New York cousins. And cousins they

Capt. Stephen Decatur commanded the United States *in her triumphant capture of the British frigate* Macedonian *in October of 1812 near Madeira. It was the most decisive example yet of American fighting skill. Reproduced from a painting by Chappel.*

often were, for many of the far-ranging New Yorkers were expatriate Yankees who had come south for better opportunities in the world of commerce. They could see that New York was to be the port of the future: a great shipping, trading, and financial center.

The city already was fast becoming very cosmopolitan. Its merchants were English, German, Scotch, Irish,

A grateful Congress awarded this dress sword to Stephen Decatur for bravely burning the captured ship Philadelphia *off Tripoli before pirates could retaliate.*

24

Left, On March 28, 1814, frigate Essex, commanded by Capt. David Porter, was attacked by the British frigate Phoebe and the sloop Cherub. Hampered by the loss of her main-topmast in a squall, Essex was repeatedly raked by the enemy. Porter attempted to beach and destroy her, but was finally compelled to surrender. The Essex was flying a banner which said: "Free Trade and Sailors Rights," the basic reason for the War of 1812.

The capture of the British frigate Guerriere by the Constitution, commanded by Capt. Isaac Hull, was the first important naval victory of the War of 1812. The Constitution was superior in all features such as size, sail area, weight of broadside, and accuracy of fire. Hull's superior seamanship made these factors count.

Dutch, French, and "native" American. Even some Swiss, too. In the restaurants and the coffee houses where merchants and captains gathered to talk of ships and cargoes and trading ventures, the conversation was thick with many accents.

Few names stand out more boldly in the history of the port than that of John Jacob Astor. Runaway son of a German butcher, this ambitious young man worked for a while in London and then sailed to New York with some goods to trade for furs. He built one such modest venture on another until he was a rich man at an early age.

Profits would be greater, he reasoned, if he could establish a fur-trading post at the very center of the fur supply, the Pacific Northwest, with the double advantage of obtaining furs from the Northwest trappers and from the Russians in Alaska and the Aleutians. Once the furs were collected they could be shipped back East or could be carried to China, then a booming market for skins.

To accomplish this, Astor formed the Pacific Fur Company, owned by himself and a number of associates, but with most of the money coming from him.

The company's ship *Tonquin*, twelve guns and a crew of twenty-one, plus thirty-three passengers, all partners or employees of the company, left New York on September 8, 1810, with materials for establishing a trading post, with a prefabricated schooner to use along the coast, and with goods for trade. In command was Capt. Jonathan Thorn, a former naval officer; Astor had been influential enough to have him detached from his regular naval duty station to head up the expedition. Astor also wielded enough power to have the frigate *Constitution* accompany the *Tonquin* for several days to ward off any British warships that might be tempted to stop her and impress her seamen, and thus learn about the venture.

Tonquin finally reached the mouth of the Columbia River after numerous adventures en route. The bar at the mouth of the river was breaking too heavily for entry but not too heavily for the imprudent captain to order the mate and a boat's crew to take soundings. The huge combers capsized the boat and eight lives were lost. It was a tragic prelude to what became a series of tragedies. More men were lost in the same way before the weather calmed and *Tonquin* finally crossed the bar into the river. While the ship's company were trying to build a fort and assemble their prefabricated schooner, several were killed by Indians and a number injured in felling huge trees.

After a small fortified trading post was completed and named Astoria, *Tonquin* set out to cruise north and trade for furs. At one of its stops along the coast an unusually large number of Indians boarded the ship, and before the captain could arm his men and order them off, the visitors pulled out concealed knives and fell upon the crew. Within minutes all but a few were killed or dying. (Several men who escaped in a small boat were captured later and tortured to death.)

And then, with hundreds of Indians pillaging the cargo, the *Tonquin* blew up. More than two hundred Indians were killed or wounded. How the explosion occurred is a mystery, and Indians who witnessed and recounted the event had no explanation.

Twenty-seven of the ship's crew had been killed or mortally wounded, but it is possible that one of them, badly wounded and not wanting to

Few names stand out more boldly in the history of the port than that of John Jacob Astor. In 1810 he formed the Pacific Fur Company and was the main financier of the Tonquin expedition sent to establish a fur-trading post at the very center of the fur supply, the Pacific Northwest.

The Pacific Fur Company's ship Tonquin *embarked on September 6, 1810, and reached the mouth of the Columbia River on March 23, 1811, after a stormy voyage. The bar at the mouth of the river was breaking too heavily for entry but Capt. Jonathan Thorn ordered the mate and a boat's crew to take soundings. Huge waves capsized the boat and eight lives were lost.*

27

be captured and tortured, may have crawled to the magazine, lit a torch, and plunged it into a powder keg.

Another Astor ship, the *Lark*, sent out from New York in 1813 to reinforce the *Tonquin*, was wrecked in a storm near the Sandwich Islands and drifted ashore as a derelict.

Astor's Northwest fur-trading venture turned out to be a disaster financially and in the loss of many lives, and only a man of his wealth could have survived it without bankruptcy. But this bold venture in the port's golden age of postwar expansion demonstrates the willingness of New York entrepreneurs to take big chances for trade wherever it might take them. They played for huge stakes—and sometimes took equally large losses.

It was John Jacob Astor who was influential in opening the South American trade for the port of New York. In 1817 Astor dispatched the *Beaver*, a vessel that had spent many years in the China trade, to the port of Valparaiso, although she had been cleared officially for Canton, China. The subterfuge was to bypass Spanish officials who kept an eye on all vessels trading with Spain's South American dominions, then in a state of ferment and revolt.

The *Beaver* was loaded deep with munitions and other supplies for South American trade, either with royalists or rebels. The ship was captured and interned by royalists and the cargo condemned, but Astor again brought his influence to bear in Washington and the ship was released. It continued to trade along the coast and returned to New York several years later.

Discovery of gold in California in January of 1848 sparked a mad rush for the goldfields, with every ship that could float—from small brigs and schooners to tired old packets and whalers—being hurriedly outfitted and advertised "for California." It was also a gold strike for canny New York shipowners and for merchants who foresaw the tremendous demand for goods that would follow the army of adventurers to San Francisco and who did a big business transporting and supplying the gold seekers and permanent emigrants.

News of the California gold strikes reached New York in September of 1848 and, as one newspaper account of the time described it, "has aroused the spirit of adventure as nothing else within memory and has stirred pulses to fever heat. Nothing else is talked about but the quick fortunes to be made in California."

Some argonauts chose the Cape Horn route, others elected to take ship to Chagres, then cross the Isthmus to the ancient city of Panama and re-embark on the Pacific side for San Francisco. Still others took ships from New York to Nicaragua, crossed to the Pacific by mule, wagon, and boat, and then continued on by ship to the goldfields.

More than two hundred ships cleared from New York for California in 1849.

New Yorker Philip Hone made this entry in his diary for January 26, 1849:

The California fever is increasing in violence; thousands are going, among whom are many young men of our best families; the papers are filled with advertisements of vessels for Chagres and San Francisco. Tailors, hatters, grocers, provision merchants, hardware men, and others are employed night and day in fitting out the adventurers.

As one old hooker left her New York dock, packed from bow to stern with high-spirited young men seeking fame and fortune in El Dorado, someone produced a concertina, another a violin, and a hundred voices roared out this farewell song for those waving on the shore:

I came from New York City
   With my washboard on my knee
I'm going to California
   The gold dust for to see
Oh my darling, don't you cry for me
I'm bound for California
That's the land for me.

Even before the gold rush began, there was established steamship service between New York, California, and Oregon. In 1847 the government had awarded mail contracts to the U.S. Mail Steamship Company for a five-ship line from New York to Chagres on the Atlantic side of Panama by way of New Orleans and other ports, and to the Pacific Mail Steamship Company for a three-ship service from the Pacific side of Panama to San Diego, San Francisco, and Astoria,

Oregon. These lines were in operation well before the end of 1848.

Later, they had competition from the Vanderbilt Line, which ran from New York to San Juan del Norte on the east coast of Nicaragua, from whence passengers traveled overland to San Juan del Sur on the Pacific side and boarded another Vanderbilt steamer for San Francisco.

By 1853, Pacific Mail was operating fourteen steamers, and the U.S. Mail ten, to accommodate the huge demand for passage to California by both gold seekers and more mundane settlers lured by prospects of life in the West.

Whether the travelers went by an established steamship line, by a vessel especially chartered by a company of gold seekers, or by one of the huge fleet of ships, barks, brigs, schooners, and assorted steamboats that headed for Nicaragua, Panama, or Cape Horn, the trip was not inexpensive.

In 1850 a stateroom from New York to Chagres "on the new and elegant double-engine steamship George" cost $100 and a single berth $80. Steerage was $50. A stateroom from Panama to San Francisco was advertised at $300 and a berth in steerage or space to sleep on deck at $100 up. Many a gold seeker waiting at Panama for the next ship to San Francisco was forced to pay as much as $500 for passage. There were twice as many gold hunters waiting for a ship as there were berths to accommodate them.

Fortunes in gold dust and bullion were soon pouring into New York in the strongrooms of returning ships. This is a typical news item from the New York *Times* of June 28, 1860:

The S.S. Northern Light, from Aspinwall [near Chagres] arrived at this port yesterday morning. She brings the California mails to the 5th and $1,500,000 in treasure.

Many of the gold rush argonauts died of malaria and other diseases in Panama and Nicaragua. Others perished in shipwrecks. But most of them reached their destination after often-arduous voyages. There is a large volume of literature in books and magazines describing their adventure.

Starting in 1850 the great clipper

The steamer Hartford, commanded by Captain LeFevre, was one of more than two hundred ships cleared from New York for California in 1849, following the discovery of gold. New York shipowners benefited greatly from the business of transporting the gold seekers and emigrants.

ships (those especially built for the California trade) began leaving New York yards to load up along the East River for the run to San Francisco. They were joined by New York-owned clippers built in Boston and elsewhere, for the most romantic era in the history of shipbuilding and seafaring. Most famous of them all was the great *Flying Cloud*, which left New York on her maiden voyage June 2, 1851, and arrived in San Francisco August 31; eighty-nine days and twenty-one hours from Sandy Hook to the Golden Gate. The gold rush and the clipper era gave New York one of the busiest and most exciting periods in its long history as a great terminal for world trade.

The Latin American trade became very important in the 1820s and has remained so ever since. Cuba, Puerto Rico, and the other islands of the Caribbean figured most prominently in the early part of the century in this trade, being the major suppliers of hides, coffee, and sugar. As Central and South America stabilized after their revolt against Spanish rule, trade increased tremendously. A number of New York merchants specialized in the South American business. New York shipped flour, machinery, textiles, and miscellaneous goods of all kinds, from furniture to butter, lard, boots, and livestock.

The vast industrial and commercial base which has been instrumental in making New York one of the great cities of the world began to take shape after the War of 1812. By 1840 New York had 417 commercial establishments engaged in foreign trade, plus thousands of retail dry goods, grocery, and general merchandise stores, all of which were consumers, to varying degrees, of imported merchandise. Hides were imported for the city's 173 leather factories, rum for its eleven distilleries, sugar for the seven refineries, and various woods for its many furniture factories. This is only a sampling of the growing industrial complex that was, in years to come, to absorb vast quantities of imported raw materials.

Outward bound ships loaded with apples, potash, pickled beef, beeswax, brandy, firkins of butter, candles, cheese, cassia, clover seed, casks of cocoa, cotton, hams and bacon,

dried fish, kegs of gunpowder, lard, lumber, pork, linseed, and turpentine. Also being hoisted aboard ship by human muscle or horsepower were barrels of whale oil, hogsheads of tobacco, rice, puncheons of rum, bags of sugar, chests of tea, whiskey, soap, and rice. What pungent smells a balmy spring breeze must have wafted over ships and shore along the crowded docks of the East River.

There was always an aroma of coffee roasting along the East River, too. Coffee came from Brazil, Cuba, Haiti, Dutch Guiana, and from as far away as Sumatra, Java, Arabia, the Phillippines, and Ceylon. Coffee was both imported and exported here.

In 1821 more than twenty-one million pounds were brought into New York; some nine million pounds were exported. The trade boomed because coffee was duty free, coffee houses were proliferating, and it was becoming an ever more popular drink.

Of the many new shipping ventures that began in the period before the Civil War, one of the most notable was the Cuba Mail Line, which started in 1840 with two schooners and expanded until, in the 1860s, it flew its house flag over a large fleet of steam and sail in the Caribbean trade out of New York. In 1881 this company became the New York and Cuba Mail S.S. Company, the largest ship operator under the American flag.

More than 430,000 tons of shipping were registered in New York in 1840 and close to four thousand ships entered and cleared that year in foreign trade. In addition, there were five thousand arrivals and departures in the coastal trades. More than one thousand vessels were registered in the New York Customs District.

The growth of the port of New York was speeded considerably by construction of the Erie Canal, the largest and most ambitious engineering project attempted in this country at the time of its groundbreaking on July 4, 1817. *Ambitious* is a modest word to describe this undertaking. It might be more appropriate to say *herculean*, for there were no steam shovels or diesel-driven earth movers in those days; no bulldozers, pile drivers, electric cutting tools, or cement mixers.

More than three thousand Irish laborers with shovels, oxen, and horses dug this ditch from the Hudson River to Lake Erie across the state of New York. They worked from dawn to dusk for eight dollars a month.

The route was 363 miles long from river to lake. There were eighty-three locks, each ninety feet long. Boats built to traverse it were boxlike craft about seventy feet long, fourteen feet wide, and drawing four feet of water. They were hauled along the canal by two horses on an adjacent towpath. Once they reached Albany they were towed by tugboats downriver to New York.

"Father" of the Erie Canal and the political force behind its financing was DeWitt Clinton, five times mayor of New York City and thrice governor of New York State. Without his persistence, fiery enthusiasm, and canny ability to maneuver the project politically, it probably never would have been built. Also deserving credit were the young American engineers who faced the challenges involved in building the canal, locks, and feeder systems, and saw it to a successful conclusion.

The canal was put into operation as various sections were completed, with the grand opening of the entire route from Buffalo to Albany celebrated on October 26, 1825.

Cannon had been positioned every ten miles or so along the route and down the Hudson and, as soon as the official opening ceremonies were over at Buffalo, the long line of guns boomed out the message to New York in eighty minutes. Each sound of a gun would mark a substantial boost in

The Erie Canal was built along a 363-mile route from the Hudson River to Lake Erie. This view at Lockport shows one of the canal's eighty-three locks. (Courtesy New York State Library)

30

Five times mayor of New York City and thrice governor of New York State, DeWitt Clinton was considered the "father" of the Erie Canal and the political force behind its financing.

commerce for the New York port in years to come.

First boat to go through was the *Seneca Chief,* carrying Governor Clinton and other VIPs.

There was a welcoming ceremony with appropriate oratory by the governor, the mayor, and everyone else who could get on the program, followed by a parade of gaily bedecked steamboats. All shipping in the harbor, from packets to sloops, were brightly dressed with flags and bunting. More than thirty thousand out-of-towners, including many a country

taking over most of the long-haul business and the canal began to slip into eventual eclipse.

To New York the canalboats freighted cattle, wheat, flour, liquor, lumber, flaxseed, potash, corn, rye, oats, buckwheat, and barley. On the westward haul they carried farm machinery, sugar, textiles, clothing, and manufactured goods of all kinds. There was a brisk business in passengers, too. As many as two thousand a week traveled the canal in its heyday. Hundreds of immigrants arriving in New York continued on to

ceived at Buffalo included 88,296,036 pounds of general merchandise, plus substantial tonnages of dried fruit, furniture, and other goods. Major cargoes eastbound this year were wheat and flour. Traffic over the canal was so important that a number of terminals for the canalboats were built in various sections of the harbor.

It would be very difficult, if not impossible, to pinpoint just how much freight brought to tidewater over the Erie and Champlain canals eventually was transferred to ships in New York for the coastwise or over-

32

bumpkin who rarely witnessed pomp and splendor, poured into the city for this historic occasion.

At Sandy Hook two kegs of Lake Erie water transported by the *Seneca Chief* were poured into the Atlantic to symbolize "the wedding of the waters."

Once the speechmaking and the fireworks were over, the canal began to prove its importance to the port of New York. The canalboats carried 218,000 tons of freight in 1825; 1,417,046 in 1840; and 4,116,082 in 1856, after which the railroads began

future homes in the Midwest via the Erie Canal. Flour brought to New York by canalboats continued on to Spain, Portugal, England, Cuba and other Caribbean islands, and the mainland of Latin America. Considerable amounts of flour also were funneled out from New York in the coastwise trade.

An item in the unique little *Sailors Magazine* of October 1846 illustrates the importance of the canal to the New York port. In 1843, according to this item reprinted from a government report, westbound freight re-

The opening of the Erie Canal on October 26, 1825, was marked by a grand celebration with every ship in the harbor bedecked with flags and bunting.

Canton and California clippers dock alongside Liverpool packets, river steamboats, and ships from all over the world unloading goods from such places as London, South America, or faraway Calcutta and Holland, in this 1828 view of South Street from Maiden Lane.

A view of canalboats docked at Pier No. 1 on the North River gives an idea of the immense traffic of goods and produce along the Erie Canal.

seas trades. But writers of that period refer frequently to the great importance of the canals to the city and its port.

An issue of the *Merchants Magazine* for 1845 emphasized the importance of the new waterways thus:

> After the opening of the Erie and Lake Champlain canals New York enjoyed a vastly increased commercial advantage. The opening of navigable communication from the Hudson to the Lakes gave New York the whole of the direct Lakes trade... and made New York at once the greatest competitor of New Orleans for the trade of the Great West.

One clue to the importance of these canals to port business is a tabulation from the *Merchants Magazine* reporting that 3,256,414 barrels of flour were freighted over the Erie Canal in 1839 and that 800,000 barrels of this total were then transshipped at New York for Great Britain. This, together with the big West Indies and coastwise traffic in flour, could have accounted for half or more of all that coming to tidewater over the two main canals. The total value of canal shipments of flour for that year exceeded $19 million.

Coal was a very important cargo on the Hudson. The coal was barged over the Delaware and Hudson Canal from the Pennsylvania coalfields to Rondout, ninety miles north of New York, thence south on the river to the metropolis. In 1867, some eight hundred canalboats were engaged in hauling coal from the Pennsylvania mines to Rondout and thence to New York, more than one million tons of coal being barged in an average year down the river. At New York, it was unloaded at various terminals around the harbor or transshipped on schooners to Boston and other New England ports.

Many other items that appear in lists of canal traffic paying tolls are also to be found in lists of New York exports, such as hides, tobacco, cheese, potash, bacon, wheat, and furs.

In later years, the Erie Canal, through modernization and improvements, became the New York State Barge Canal.

Trade and shipping went hand in hand. Shipping connections from Manhattan reached out in all directions. In 1820 David Dunham started a coastwise steamship service to New Orleans via Charleston and Havana with the seven-hundred-ton paddle-wheeler *Robert Fulton.* The experiment was unprofitable but, again, it evidenced the willingness of New Yorkers to do things in a bold way.

During the early years of the nineteenth century, New York's foreign trade ran the gamut of commerce. On a day in 1818, Bogart and Kneeland of 70 South Street offered "pistols suitable for the South American market," linen Cambric, demijohns, Russian duck, nutmeg, salt petre, and six thousand Dutch bricks. Kirk and Morcein of 22 Wall Street were selling "elegant books just arrived from England," including Bibles, the Arabian Nights, Milton, and the "compleat works of Cowper."

The ship *Cririe* had arrived from Calcutta with East India sugar, cotton, ginger, block tin, gum shellack, gum copal, goat skins, gunny bags, seine twine, and muslins.

Other cargoes in port and available to buyers included "English bar iron, tin plates, German steel, apothecaries' vials, tobacco pipes, English nails, window glass, German toys, Turk's Island salt, attar of roses from Smyrna, Caracao indigo, port wine" and, of all things, diapers.

Many cargoes were sold at auction; some at the Tontine Coffee House.

In the years before the Civil War the growth of the port kept pace with the expansion of the city as a great commercial center. The 1850s saw the rapid spread of brownstone houses and ornate office buildings. Population increased, and with it came a proliferation of restaurants, stores, and hotels. The city was prosperous and people were spending their money. It was said that Gosling's Restaurant on Nassau Street served more than a thousand people every day. Delmonico's on William Street already was famous as a haunt of gourmets and successful men of the world.

The new Astor House at Broadway and Barclay was "the wonder of the day... the place to stay for those who want the best." It had a glittering competitor in the Saint Nicholas Hotel, built at a cost of $1 million and capable of accommodating eight hundred guests, with steam heat in every room.

A new idea in merchandising also had been introduced in New York— the department store, where milady could spend an hour or a day shopping for bonnets, bustles, or boudoir dainties. Much of the choice merchandise offered in New York stores came into the port as premium cargo in the holds of the packets and their smoke-belching competitors, the North Atlantic liners.

This colorful description of South Street appeared in *Ballou's Pictorial* for March 7, 1857:

> South Street is devoted to the wants of ships and their accommodation. Here may be seen the Canton and California clippers, side-by-side with Liverpool packets and river steamboats, the fast sailing fore-and-after, and fishing vessels. Crowds of these latter craft lay off Fulton Market.... The buildings are devoted to sail-lofts, shipping offices, warehouses of every description, cheap eating-houses, markets, and those indescribable stores, where old cables, junk, anchors, and all sorts of cast-off worldly things, that none but a seaman has a name for, find a refuge.

In November of 1853 an article in *Gleason's Pictorial* proudly proclaimed that New York had 112 piers; 55 on the North River and 57 on the East River and that the city had 92 hotels— "all filled to overflowing."

In New York now you could see ships from all over the world—and as colorful a mix of sailors along the waterfront as you would find in Hamburg, London, or Marseilles.

34

The new Astor House at Broadway and Barclay was "...the place to stay for those who want the best." The top scene is in the ballroom, and below New Yorkers mingle in front of the hotel.

An 1850s wood engraving of Delmonico's, one of many gourmet restaurants to open its doors in the prosperity of a rapidly expanding city.

CHAPTER 3
PIRATES, SLAVERS & PRIVATEERS

P irates, slavers, and privateers—they all played a part in the dramatic and colorful history of New York.

What words can stir up more visions of adventure, romance, infamy, and derring-do? Blackguards and scoundrels the pirates may have been, but they wrote a fascinating chapter in the story of the port. Even worse were the slavers, risking the fevers and hazards of the African coast and the guns of preying privateers to deal in human cargoes.

For pure romance and adventure on the high seas there was no equal to the privateer, the private man-o'-war that roamed the seas looking for enemy ships to take. Privateersmen fought with cannon, muskets, cutlasses, and boarding pikes. They were out to profit from war but, at the same time, they helped in no small way to bring victory to the infant nation in its war with Great Britain. Privateers provided the United States with a navy when the nation had none worthy of the name and, withal, dared to challenge the greatest navy in the world. Many hailed from the port of New York.

The first slaves were landed and sold in New York in 1626. They came from Brazil. There were eleven and their slave names still survive in old records; among them, Simon Congo, Anthony Portuguese, John Francisco, and Paul d'Angola.

That most despicable of all trades, the dealing in slaves, was introduced to New Amsterdam by the West India Company, which furnished slaves to the patroons or big landowners as an inducement to colonization. More slaves were landed in the 1640s and 1650s to help till the fields on large farms as agriculture expanded. Most of them came from Africa, but there were also some Carib Indians from the West Indies and blacks from Brazil. Traders paid about $60 a head for slaves in Curacao and sold them in New York for as much as $150. It was said that a strong male could bring $250.

In November of 1654 the ship *White Horse* of New York left for Africa on a slaving voyage and returned with a cargo of blacks the following year. A slaver named Gideon arrived with several hundred slaves shortly before the British fleet captured the port.

The farms of New Amsterdam were never conducive to large-scale crops and the extensive use of slave labor on the scale practiced in the South, but slaves were used in farm work and as domestic servants. The number of slaves landed and sold in New York was not inconsiderable; by the time of the British occupation it is estimated there were some two thousand slaves here. A census taken in Brooklyn in 1755 showed that sixty-two families owned 133 slaves. The last sale of slaves in Brooklyn was in 1773.

Although the slave trade ended here long before it did in the South, the New York port witnessed a dramatic end to slave trading under the American flag. In 1860 the U.S.S. *Mohican*, on anti-slavery patrol with British ships off the west coast of Africa, captured the ship *Erie* of New York with eight hundred slaves on board. The human cargo was taken to Liberia and released. The captain of the *Erie* was taken to New York, tried, and executed.

After the schooner yacht *Wanderer* was launched at Setauket, Long Island, in 1857, New Yorkers with an eye for a ship admired her clipper bow and rakish lines. After a while *Wanderer* disappeared from the New York scene and when later reported had landed a cargo of slaves in Georgia. Still later, she was said to have been chased by a British cruiser off the coast of Africa, and when the cruiser laid alongside was seen to be flying the flag of the New York Yacht Club, the *Wanderer*'s captain ex-

37

Piracy flourished in the seventeenth and eighteenth centuries due to the almost continual state of war among the nations of Europe. For some years the port of New York courted business with pirates, buying their captured loot at favorable prices.

plaining that he was on a cruise "with a party of prominent New York yachtsmen."

The palmy, sea-lapped isles of the Caribbean and the shores of the Spanish Main would seem a more likely lair for pirates than the mundane shores of Manhattan, but New York had a brief flirtation with those who sailed under the Jolly Roger. Indeed, New York was the home and home port of Capt. William Kidd, the most famous pirate of them all—the most famous but by no means the most nefarious.

Piracy, and its quasilegal cousin, privateering, flourished in the seventeenth and eighteenth centuries, thanks to an almost continual state of war among the nations of Europe. New York being an English colony, the privateers here could sally forth and capture enemies of the Crown, usually French or Spanish.

Privateering, of course, worked both ways. While some New Yorkers profited from it, others lost heavily, for many a New York ship and cargo was taken by French and Spanish privateers during colonial times, and later by the British.

For some years the port of New York courted business with pirates, buying their captured loot at favorable prices and making them welcome along the waterfront.

Some say that New York's first pirate was William Mason, who obtained letters of marque in 1689 authorizing him to operate against the French, then at war with England. He soon exceeded his legal authority and became a pirate, capturing so many rich ships that his crew was paid off with eighteen hundred pieces of eight per man when Mason called it quits after three years, happy to have escaped the hangman's noose.

It is said that one of New York's most prosperous and successful merchants, Frederick Philipse, invested in piratical ventures and bought and sold the captured booty. He sponsored Samuel Burgess, a New York privateersman who wasn't too particular whether he captured enemies of the Crown or neutral vessels that crossed his course.

Burgess had good contacts with pirates who had established a kind of pirate republic on the island of Madagascar, from whence they preyed on rich cargoes in the Red Sea and on ships making for the Cape of Good Hope along the east coast of Africa. He was able to channel Madagascar loot back to New York merchants. Burgess was captured while pirating by a British man-of-war, was taken to England, tried, convicted, and sentenced to the gallows, then was pardoned by Queen Anne. He soon went pirating again and met an early death, the usual end for those who hoisted the skull and crossbones.

The hanging of a so-called pirate on Bedloes Island in July of 1860 was a gala day for hundreds of New Yorkers who turned out in excursion boats and small craft to witness the gruesome affair. The culprit was an Albert W. Hicks, alias Johnson, who was convicted of murdering the captain, mate, and two seamen of the New York oyster sloop *E.A. Johnson*, and of having stolen $1,000 which the captain was taking with him to buy seed oysters in Norfolk. The sloop was found abandoned off Staten Island with pools of blood on deck and in

A sketch of the New York slave market about 1730. The first slaves were landed and sold in New York in 1626. The last sale of slaves in Brooklyn was in 1773.

Slavery was introduced to New Amsterdam by the West India Company, which furnished slaves to the patroons or big landowners as an inducement to colonization. Traders paid about $60 a head for slaves in Curacao and sold them in New York for as much as $150. It was said that a strong male could bring $250.

38

the cabin. Hicks was arrested after he had been reported spending money very freely along the waterfront, and had been identified as having landed on Staten Island in a skiff with a "heavy bundle" on the night the murders were presumed to have occurred. The clinching evidence that hanged him was the watch of the dead captain, found in his possession. The steamer *Red Jacket*, which carried Hicks and the gallows party to Bedloes, also carried six hundred paying passengers, including "every class of persons," as the press described it.

A New York syndicate financed a pirate by the name of John Hoar because of his good contacts with the freebooters on Madagascar. He supplied them with powder, cannonballs, and rum; and returned with silks, silver plate, jewels, and other pirate loot.

Gov. Benjamin Fletcher permitted pirates to land, stretch their sea legs, and sell their cargoes for a fee of one hundred dollars, which he called a bond "for good behavior." By associating with the good people of New York, he explained to London, the pirates would be encouraged to mend their wicked ways. Merchants who bought pirated goods, and citizens who obtained silks, laces, perfume, and silver plate at bargain prices, probably chuckled over the governor's tongue-in-cheek explanation of the port's hospitality to freebooters.

As near as can be ascertained, William Kidd was a respected shipmaster and New Yorker of more than average means when he was commissioned by Governor Bellomont in 1696 to sail as a privateer, with pirates, rather than the French or Spanish, as his prey. Bellomont and several associates invested in this unusual venture, buying a new ship called the *Adventure Galley* and placing Kidd in command. She was a new vessel of 287 tons and thirty-four guns—well-equipped for taking on a piratical adversary. Kidd also invested in the venture, probably a condition of his receiving command.

The expedition sailed from London, where the ship had been purchased and outfitted, but no sooner was the *Adventure Galley* at sea than she was stopped by a ship of the Royal Navy, which probably had been alerted in advance, and which, by the custom of impressment of men needed for His Majesty's service, took off the best of Kidd's handpicked crew. Kidd continued across the Atlantic to New York, taking a French prize en route, and augmented his diminished roster with what he could find on the New York waterfront. He then sailed off to look for ships flying the black flag.

The crew had signed on for "no plunder, no pay" and were not agreeable to sailing the seas indefinitely hunting pirates when easier pickings were to be had. They threatened mutiny and Kidd had trouble keeping his crew in hand when a number of peaceful vessels were allowed to go their way. There was evidence later at his trial that the *Adventure Galley* took several Moorish vessels as it cruised about looking for bigger game.

Although he was commissioned to sail against pirates, Kidd evidently assumed that his sponsors had given him some leeway, whether or not in so many words, and that his commission, or letter of marque, permitted him to attack any enemies of the Crown. And so when he espied a big ship called the *Quedagh Merchant*, Armenian-owned but flying the French flag, he captured her. She turned out to be a rich prize, and Kidd took her over as his own ship and sailed her to the Caribbean, where he learned that the authorities had declared him a pirate. It seems that he then abandoned his treasure-laden ship on the island of Hispaniola (now Santo Domingo), still with much of its rich cargo on board, and sailed home, along with some of his shipmates, in a sloop called *Antonio*. Into it he had crammed silks and chests of plate, coins, gems, and jewels.

Most of the *Antonio*'s crew were put ashore in Delaware Bay, after which Kidd proceeded to Gardiner's Island on the eastern end of Long Island, where he visited with John Gardiner, to whom he entrusted a few Negro slaves, chests full of treasure, and a bag of gold coins. His wife and children visited him before he sailed on to Boston, hoping to clear

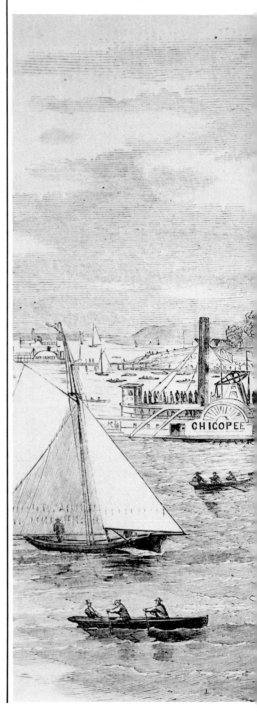

The hanging of a pirate on Bedloe's Island in July of 1860 was a gala day for hundreds of New Yorkers who turned out in excursion boats and small craft to witness the gruesome affair.

himself with Lord Bellomont. But once he landed there, he was arrested by his former partner and dispatched to London for trial as a pirate.

When he was brought to trial another charge was added to that of piracy—that of killing one of his crewmen. This charge was a farce, for in those days the captain was literally master of his ship, in title as well as fact, and the authorities could not have been less concerned how a captain treated his crew. Indeed, for two centuries after that, masters were frequently exonerated of charges of

was intentionally suppressed. In modern parlance, it would seem that Kidd was "framed." He was convicted of piracy and hanged in 1701, still protesting his innocence.

War may have been a disaster for hundreds of peaceful traders on the seas, but it was good business for the privateer.

In the war of 1702 between England and Spain, known in this country as Queen Anne's War and in Europe as the War of the Spanish Succession, some twenty privateers operated against the Spanish out of New York

JOHN ADAMS, President of the United States of America,

To all who shall see these Presents, Greeting:

Know Ye, That in pursuance of an Act of Congress of the United States in this case provided, passed on the ninth day of July, one thousand seven hundred and ninety-eight, I have commissioned, and by these presents do commission the private armed *Ship* called the *Herald* of the burthen of *three hundred twenty-five* tons, or thereabouts, owned by *Ebenezer Preble, & Samuel Parkman of Boston Merchants, & Nathaniel Silsbee of Salem Mariner, all in the State of Massachusetts.*

mounting *Ten* carriage guns, and navigated by *Thirty* men; hereby licensing and authorizing *Nathaniel Silsbee* captain, and *Nathaniel Hathorne 1st & Alexander Anderson 2d* lieutenants of the said *Ship* and the other officers and crew thereof to subdue, seize and take any armed French vessel which shall be found within the jurisdictional limits of the United States, or elsewhere on the high seas ; and such captured vessel, with her apparel, guns and appurtenances, and the goods or effects which shall be found on board the same, together with all French persons and others, who shall be found acting on board, to bring within some port of the United States; and also to retake any vessels goods and effects of the people of the United States, which may have been captured by any French armed vessel; in order that proceedings may be had concerning such capture or re-capture in due form of law, and as to right and justice shall appertain. This commission to continue in force during the pleasure of the President of the United States for the time being.

Given under my Hand and the Seal of the United States of America, at Philadelphia, the *twenty-second* day of *January,* in the year of our Lord, one thousand ~~four~~ *eight* hundred ~~and ninety~~ and of the Independence of the said States, the twenty *fourth.*

John Adams

By the President,

Timothy Pickering Secretary of State.

42

Letters of marque authorized privateers to apprehend foreign vessels trespassing the jurisdictional limits of the United States. Captain Nathaniel Silsbee of the Herald was commissioned in 1800 by President John Adams "…to subdue, seize, and take any armed French vessel…" in his ship's vicinity.

Right, The residence of Capt. William Kidd was on Pearl Street near Water Gate at the east end of Wall. When Trinity Church was being built, from 1696 to 1698, Kidd supplied the block and tackle used for hoisting the wall stones into place

murder or cruelty merely by defending their actions on the need to preserve discipline aboard ship and repel insubordination.

Some authorities suggest that Kidd's offense was in capturing a ship whose cargo actually was owned by English merchants.

To this day many of the circumstances surrounding the trial of William Kidd are a mystery, and there is reason to believe that evidence that would have proved the *Quedagh Merchant* to be a reasonable prize under the "rules of war" at that time

and, when England declared war on France in 1740, a fleet of thirty privateers obtained letters of marque in New York and sailed forth against the king's enemies.

During the war that broke out in 1756 between England and France, New York commissioned 130 privateers. They sent eighty prizes into the port during the first two years of this war, a very profitable business for the owners, the crews, and the city's merchants.

When the colonies rebelled against the mother country in 1776 they were

Before landing in Boston, where he was arrested and dispatched to London for trial as a pirate, privateer William Kidd sailed to Gardiner's Island on the eastern end of Long Island. There he visited with John Gardiner, to whom he entrusted several chests full of treasure and a bag of gold coins. From a painting by the noted illustrator and author, Howard Pyle.

pitted against a nation with the largest and most powerful navy in the world. To exert any semblance of sea power and gnaw the enemy where most effective—at his commerce—the colonies commissioned privateers, privately owned ships with civilian crews, which so harassed British trade routes that many of the king's ships were required to protect convoys and, consequently, were not available for operations against the new nation.

Scores of privateers—from one-gun sloops to swift brigs and schooners—took to the sea during the Revolution to sail and fight with all the dash and fervor of regular naval vessels. They captured hundreds of prizes, not only inflicting vast damage on British trade and commerce but funneling much-needed cargoes into the hard-pressed colonies. In 1778 alone, American privateers took 733 British vessels.

Under almost constant British occupation throughout the war, the port of New York had no privateers at sea, but many a New York seaman sailed in the crews of privateers that slipped through the British blockade from ports in Connecticut and Long Island.

It was a different matter, however, during the War of 1812, when the United States commissioned five hundred privateers to harry British commerce. Many of them, including some of the more successful, were built, outfitted, and sailed out of the port of New York.

Few sagas of the sea are more stirring than the battle between the New York privateer *Prince de Neuchatel* and the forty-gun British frigate *Endymion*. The privateer was a small vessel skippered by a man named Ordronaux, who stood two inches over five feet in his socks. He was small in stature but a giant in fighting spirit.

This privateer was making its way slowly toward New York, towing a recent prize, when it was intercepted by the British ship near Nantucket Island on October 11, 1814. Ordronaux cut away his prize and steered for Nantucket Shoals, where his shallow-draft vessel would have an advantage over the deeper-draft pursuer. In the privateer's hold were

thirty British prisoners, an important cargo because the government offered a bounty for every British sailor brought into port.

Ordronaux's remaining crew numbered a mere thirty-seven, since many had been put aboard prizes and sent home.

The wind died down and *Endymion*, not wanting to venture too close to shoal water, sent five barges with 150 men to capture the privateer. It may have been, too, that the British commander was loath to cannonade a vessel with British prisoners in her hold.

If the barges expected to take the privateer by a mere show of force they were sadly mistaken. As soon as they were within range, the Yankee gunners opened fire. The attack was beaten off. The British licked their wounds and attacked again, only to be even more bloodily repulsed. With the third attack several of the enemy's boats managed to reach the side of the privateer, and yelling seamen climbed over her rail onto the deck, with cutlasses flashing. For a few moments it looked as though the privateersmen would be overwhelmed as the English seamen pressed them along the deck. And then the diminutive Ordronaux, brandishing a pistol, shouted to his crew that he would blow up the ship if they gave another inch. A British cutlass struck him, but he encouraged his men all the more. The crew held and slowly drove their attackers off the deck into the boats alongside. The assault was driven back.

While the British regrouped and decided what next to do, Ordronaux landed his valuable prisoners on the island of Nantucket and, with a breeze springing up, slipped away during the night, but at a cost of seven killed and twenty-four wounded. Only six of the crew were unscathed!

It was America's fleet of privateers, capturing lone British merchantmen, or sometimes several at a time, dashing into heavily protected convoys to cut out a prize and be away with it before protecting warships could reach them, that did as much as anything else to bring a favorable end to the War of 1812. Of course, many American merchantmen were captured by British warships and by

45

During the War of 1812, the United States commissioned 500 privateers to harry British commerce. Many of them, including some of the more successful, were built, outfitted, and sailed out of the port of New York. This engraving by Billings, from The American Cruiser, by Capt. George Little, shows a schooner privateer capturing a British brig.

British privateers. Privateering knew no monopoly.

Most successful and most famous of all these civilian men-of-war was the New York brigantine *General Armstrong*, which cruised from the shores of Europe to the coast of South America, taking ship after ship and making herself "public enemy number one" for British shipowners and merchants. As a privately owned man-of-war, *General Armstrong* carried eight nine-pounders, a twenty-four-pounder, and a crew of some ninety men. Privateers always needed large crews to man the prizes that they took and, it was hoped, bring them safely back to an American port. It was by no means unusual for a meagerly crewed prize to be retaken before it could make its way home.

General Armstrong had created havoc among British shipping, taking twenty-four prizes by the time she arrived in the harbor of Fayal, the Azores, under Capt. Samuel Reid, in 1814. A British squadron learned of her presence there and blockaded the harbor entrance before the *Armstrong* could sail away.

Determined to capture this Yankee nuisance without further ado, the British commander sent a flotilla of barges manned by sailors and marines to board her and have a quick end of it. The attack suffered a bloody repulse from the *Armstrong*'s gunners and sharpshooters. A second attack was launched, this one carrying a force of at least five hundred, enough to storm a ship of the line. The *Armstrong*'s mighty twenty-four-pounder was let loose this time, and the ponderous shot blew more than one attacking boat to bits, along with the

men who manned them. The nine-pounders poured volley after volley of murderous grapeshot into the attackers. They still pressed on and some even managed to climb over the privateer's low-lying hull and reach the deck, only to be run through with pikes and cut down with cutlasses. This time some of the privateer's men jumped down into the British barges before they could pull away, and laid about with their cutlasses.

Despite their frightful losses, the British still were determined to eliminate this privateer, and launched a third attack at daybreak, supported by fire from the British brig *Carnation*. Before this assault also was beaten back the British had lost some three hundred killed and wounded. Tragically, more than a few probably were Americans impressed into the British navy, one of the grievances that had led to the War of 1812.

Seeing that his ship and crew were no longer able to withstand another determined onslaught backed by guns from the *Carnation*, Captain Reid ordered his men ashore and then blew up his ship to prevent its capture.

Few times in the course of naval war has such a small ship put up so determined a battle against such great odds.

46

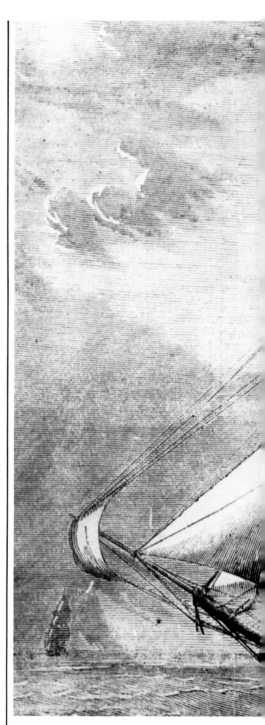

47

The privateer General Armstrong was one of the most successful of all the civilian men-of-war, taking twenty-four prizes before her arrival in the harbor of Fayal, the Azores, under Capt. Samuel Reid, in 1814. A British squadron blockaded the harbor entrance and attempted to capture the Armstrong, but was met by a forceful attack by the privateer. After the third British onslaught, Captain Reid ordered his men ashore and then blew up his ship to prevent its capture.

CHAPTER 4
SHIPS SHIPS AND MORE SHIPS

In the days of New Amsterdam, shipbuilders had the finest of virgin timber right at hand: tall, straight hardwoods of many kinds for stems, knees, keels, frames, masts, spars, and planking. And for almost two hundred years after New Amsterdam became New York, a bountiful supply of timber from Pennsylvania, New York, and New England—plus cypress, live oak, and pine from the southern seaboard—nourished a prosperous wooden-shipbuilding industry.

As wood gave place to iron and iron to steel, New York yards no longer turned out the great wooden sailing ships for which they had become world famous. The carpenter's adze and the caulking iron gave way to metal shears and riveting hammers. Many old skills of wooden shipbuilding became lost arts as steam replaced sail, and other areas—notably Philadelphia—became prominent in iron and steel shipbuilding. Many of the yards that built ships for the age of sail went out of business, their shipways being taken over by warehouses and other commercial enterprises.

New England was the premier builder of ships during the colonial period. A report prepared for the British government in 1770 tabulated the previous year's production of seagoing vessels in the colonies as 137 for Massachusetts, 50 for Connecticut, 45 for New Hampshire, 39 for Rhode Island, and New York 19.

Many factors made New England preeminent in ship construction. Most important was the ready supply of oak and other ship timber close to hundreds of rivers, harbors, and bays. Almost every stream with access to tidewater had one or more shipyards. Three-masted vessels, for instance, were built in towns such as Essex, whose winding, narrow river would seem barely deep or wide enough to float a large sloop. The town of Medford, northwest of Boston, where there is no water of consequence today, was once one of the country's busiest builders of fine ships. The same was true of many other New England towns, where skilled labor was plentiful and men who worked fields in the summer, wielded axes, shapers, and mauls in the winter.

Also, New England's fishing industry needed a large number of ships, and the trade that New England merchants developed with Europe, India, the West Indies, and the Baltic was always in need of new vessels.

According to John H. Morrison's *History of New York Shipyards* (1909), there were three shipyards in New York in 1740. Shipbuilding had been a continuing industry from the Dutch days, but production varied according to demand and the vagaries of colonial economics, which were always affected by the many wars involving England, France, Spain, and the Dutch. Shipbuilding was dependent on fluctuations in trade, on the availability of skilled workmen, and to some extent on the cost of materials that were not produced in the colony: iron, sails, and cordage.

While records are scant on the production of vessels in New York during the Dutch and colonial periods, there is no doubt that small yards turned out the large fleet of sloops and other small craft used on local waters.

One of the earliest products of note to slide down the ways of a New York yard was the U.S.S. *President*, a frigate built by Christian Bergh and launched on April 10, 1800. She sailed from New York on her first cruise, in August of 1800, under Commodore Thomas Truxton to become flagship of the U.S. Mediterranean Squadron. *President* was captured by a British squadron off New York in 1815 while under command of Stephen Decatur.

By the early 1800s New York yards were turning out ships of four hun-

49

An 1873 view of New York Harbor as seen from Brooklyn.

dred to six hundred tons, an average size for those days. At one time in 1824 there were twenty vessels on the stocks and a number of others fitting out. In the year 1826, according to Morrison, local builders launched a prodigious fleet: twenty-three ships, three brigs, forty-nine schooners, sixty-nine sloops, twelve steamboats, fifteen towboats, and nineteen canalboats. Constructing these ships gave employment to thousands of shipwrights, sailmakers, engine and boiler makers, carpenters, joiners, blacksmiths, riggers, chain and anchor

William P. Chappel's 1809 rendering of Bergh's ship yard at Water and Front streets. The U.S.S. President was built by Christian Bergh and launched on April 10, 1800.

50

makers, and others connected with shipbuilding, even to the expert woodcarvers who fashioned the figureheads that graced almost every ship that slid down the ways and sailed off in the deep-sea trades.

By the 1830s no other port in the United States could exceed New York in ship production or in the numbers of craftsmen capable of turning out sailing ships, steamboats, and other craft. In the year 1833 New York yards launched twenty-six ships and barks, seven brigs, thirty-six schooners, five steamboats, and a host of small craft

of many kinds.

Much of this production was for the North Atlantic and coastwise packet trades. Most of the great packet ships that comprised the Atlantic shuttle, forerunners of the majestic liners of the steam age, were New York built. Christian Bergh and his partner, Jacob Aaron Westervelt, launched many of these fine vessels. It is claimed for Westervelt that he built or was partner in the building of at least five hundred ships!

Ship repair was always as important in New York as shipbuilding, though

A ship-of-the-line on the stocks at one of the many shipyards where the great wooden sailing ships were built.

In the early days of New York, ships were built at the foot of Maiden-lane on the site of what, 200 years later, was the heart of shipping activity along the East River.

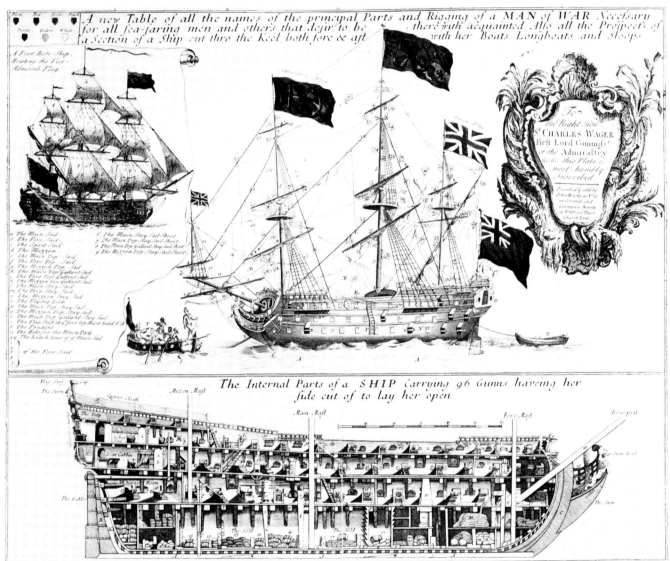

This diagram of the main parts and rigging of a man-of-war dates from 1730 and was designed to educate eighteenth-century seafaring men in ship construction.

it has been overlooked in most maritime histories. All ships, especially in windjammer days, were subject to battering by wind and sea, to strandings, collisions, the strain of fast passages, and the varied other hard knocks of routine use. The North Atlantic was a great ally of the New York ship-repair business, with winter storms sending a continual flow of battered vessels into the yards for new masts, spars, or rigging; the rebuilding of deckhouses swept away by boarding seas; for recaulking, new planking, and re-rigging. And, of course, all ships needed periodic bottom-cleaning and new sheathing. Ship repair capability received an important boost in 1827 when the New York Dry Dock Company opened for business.

The size of ships built by New York yards increased as the demand grew for greater speed, more commodious passenger accommodations, and more space for a payload. During the first half of the nineteenth century, American builders led the world in ship design and construction, and American officers and crews were unsurpassed for ship handling and seamanship. In all of this New York played an important role.

The North Atlantic packet trade, the China trade, and the California trade of gold rush days spurred New York designers and builders to turn out some of the fastest and most beautiful ships ever crafted by the hand of man. It seemed that no sooner did one fine vessel sail away on her maiden voyage to set new marks for size, speed, and appointments, than another was fitting out to challenge her.

If New York yards had never produced anything but clipper ships they would remain justly famous in the history of shipbuilding.

Ship lovers are always disturbed by newspaper-caption writers who describe anything with masts and square sails as a clipper, and just about everything else with canvas as a schooner. The clipper was a distinctive type, the culmination of years of search for the utmost in speed. The term *clipper* had been used for many years to describe an exceptionally sharp or speedy vessel, but the clip-

Early nineteenth century shipbuilding scenes: a. section of Ship's Timbers, stem to stern; b. device for shaping planks by steaming; c. driving iron rings or "Hooping" a mast; d. making sail cloth; e. transverse section view of Ship's Timbers; f. boring "tree nail" holes for pegs; g. manufacturing caulking or Oakum; h. Ship's Timbers in their frame; i. diagonal bracing of a ship; j. making "tree nails" or oak pegs.

By the 1830s no other port in the United States could exceed New York in ship production or in the numbers of craftsmen capable of turning out sailing ships, steamboats, and other craft. This illustration of a sail loft was reproduced from a rare book, Elements of Seamanship, in the Navy Department Library.

52

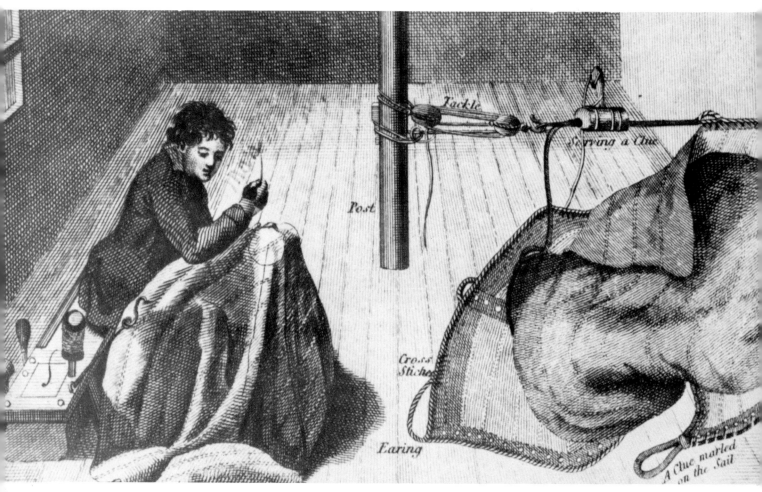

53

per ship, as such, was a product of nineteenth-century American shipyards and, except for a few relics, mostly under foreign flags and cut down in sail spread, had disappeared from the seas before the century was over.

Carl C. Cutler, an eminent authority on clipper ships, says that the lofty, speedy ships developed for the North Atlantic packet trade were "the immediate ancestors of the clipper ship."

"The earliest craft to be generally acclaimed as clippers," he says, "were

lady's boudoir....Her bows are as sharp as the toes of a pair of Chinese shoes."

The clippers shattered all records for speed. Their knifelike sharpness and their vast spread of sail were partly responsible for this. But much credit must go to the captains and the men who sailed these vessels to their fullest potential. Captains were drivers, carrying sail until the last possible moment of safety, often carrying on too long, till the sails blew out of the boltropes and the tremendous force of wind against canvas carried away

Hundreds of clipper-ship sailors who "signed on" by way of a New York waterfront grog shop, woke up bleary-eyed and dazed to find themselves on an outward-bound greyhound. Shanghaiing was common practice.

The N.B. Palmer was one of many speedy clippers operating out of New York. In 1854 the N.B. Palmer charted a passage of eighty-two days from Honolulu to New York, and in 1858 she made a passage of thirty-five days from the Cape of Good Hope to New York.

built primarily for the China trade, but they derived their chief inspiration from the later packets." And with that, New York builders can be said to have contributed to the clipper development perhaps more than any others, for they built many of the finest of the North Atlantic packets.

Cutler describes the great American clippers as the "fastest, loftiest, sharpest sailing ships ever built."

In its description of a newly launched clipper, the New York *Herald* in May of 1844 set these vessels apart from all other sailing ships before or since with this rather lyrical description: "As sharp as a cutter; as symmetrical as a yacht; as rakish in her rig as a pirate, and as neat in her deck and cabin arrangements as a

spars and masts.

Hundreds of clipper-ship sailors who "signed on" by way of a New York waterfront grog shop, woke up bleary-eyed and dazed to find themselves on an outward-bound greyhound, destination Canton or Australia, and hearing some heartless, big-fisted bucko mate rapping on the bulkhead with a belaying pin, shouting some lusty Yankee oaths and yelling, "Turn out, turn out, you Cape Horn stiffs! Rise and shine, you beauties! Up and at 'em! This is no hotel, you lazy plowboys! The last man out gets the end of my boot!"

The hard-driving captain and mates, and the men they drove with boots and belaying pins and all-too-ready fists, made the clipper ship the admiration of sailors all over the

If New York yards had never produced anything but clipper ships they would remain justly famous in the history of shipbuilding. This reproduction of an 1854 Currier & Ives lithograph shows the clipper ship Nightingale getting under way off the Battery in New York.

55

world, and even a hard-driven crew, swearing all the way from New York to Canton that they would "kill that mate" as soon as they found him alone ashore, forgot the hazards of the voyage and swaggered around with great pride in their ship and their calling once the anchor was down and the big ship, with every rope and line coiled, taut, and shipshape, told one and all that she was a Yankee clipper, from her waterline to her main truck.

Tremendous pride went into the clipper ship, from the merchants who owned her to the hundreds of skilled men who built her, to the captains and mates who amazed the world with the speed they got out of her; yes, and from the able seamen who cursed their ships as they fought them into the Pacific 'round the Horn but who swore by them in every port in the world.

While New York yards predominated in the building of North Atlantic packets they shared clipper-ship production with yards in Massachusetts, Maine, Connecticut, and Maryland.

New York's preoccupation with the clipper, while it produced ships of incomparable beauty and speed, may have had a deleterious effect on shipbuilding, for it diverted the attention of New York builders from the advantages of iron in ship construction and gave British builders a lead in iron ship work.

The clippers bore romantic and exciting names. Among the many well-known products of New York builders were the *Celestial*, *White Squall*, *Comet*, *Gazelle*, *Young America*, *Titan*, *Flyaway*, *Hotspur*, and *Intrepid*. Most clippers had short lives, the result of hard driving and over-production of a type of vessel designed to carry premium cargo. Many were sold to foreign flags, and for many fine New York ships there were, after just a few years of useful life, obituaries such as these in the shipping news: "Lost on Paracel's Reef"—"Lost on Belvidere Reef"— "Went ashore on Fire Island while returning from Canton"—"Burned by the Confederate raider Florida"— "Abandoned at sea."

Whether or not they were built in New York, most clippers loaded in New York or returned home here with cargoes from far places, for this port had established itself as the marketplace of North America. Cargoes were financed in New York, bought, sold, and shipped out again from the port of New York.

The yards that built the clippers are all gone now, with not even a marker to recall the great contributions they made to ship design, to trade and commerce. But the names are remembered in maritime histories and perhaps the newly created New York State Maritime Museum will someday do them justice. Their names should be remembered: William Webb; Jabez Williams; Smith and Dimon; Jacob Bell; Jacob Westervelt; Westervelt and Mackey; Perine, Patterson, and Stack.

The New York-built *Sea Witch* is said by some experts on the clipper ship to have been the greatest of them all. She was launched on December 8, 1846, from the yard of Smith and Dimon for the firm of Howland and Aspinwall and was intended for the China trade. A ship of nine hundred tons, measuring 192

Colorful notices were used extensively by shipping merchants to advertise the loading and departure of their ships. During the California gold rush days, the destination of many of the fast clipper ships was San Francisco.

56

The New York ship yard of Smith and Dimon, builder of what was said to be the greatest clipper ship of all, Sea Witch, in 1850, is illustrated in J. Pringle's nineteenth century painting, now owned by the New York State Historical Society.

57

feet overall, she broke many records during her all-too-brief career of ten years.

In 1849, under Capt. R.H. Waterman, *Sea Witch* winged her way from Canton to New York, a span of 14,255 miles, in seventy-four days, fourteen hours. This was a voyage that Cutler called "the most spectacular achievement in the entire history of sail."

Besides turning out staunch and speedy packets for the North Atlantic shuttle, and lofty clippers, New York yards continually were launching smaller sailing vessels, coastwise steamers, and a variety of small craft, from tugs and ferryboats to canalboats, scows, barges, and pilot boats. Scores of fine passenger ships for the deep-sea and coastal trades were produced in New York yards, too.

Because of their reputation for fine ships and their ability to complete them on schedule, the city's yards received many orders from foreign navies. Among early oceangoing steamers built here were the *Lion* and *Eagle*, launched in 1841 by Jacob Bell for the Spanish government. In 1842 William Brown launched the *Kamschatka*, a two-hundred-foot-long side-wheeler for the Russian government. And there were others, too. A total of thirty-eight steamers were launched at New York shipyards up to 1851, showing that the shipbuilding industry here was moving ahead with the times, although these were still the glory days of the sailing ship.

There was a pungent aroma of timber and a soft carpet of wood chips around the building ways of the East River and Greenpoint shipyards. The chip-chip-chip of the sharp-edged adze, shaping out spars, knees, keels, stems, ribs, frames, and side timbers. The swish-swish-swish of the draw knife as lumber was shaped and finished to a rub-down smoothness under the critical eye of the master builder. And then the chock-chock-chock of the caulker's maul as hemp was ironed into the seams of deck and hull timbers and the ship made ready for launching.

A shipyard was a symphony of sound throughout the day, and along with the sounds were the scents and smells: the smell of wood—strong, tough woods for hull and decking;

more delicate woods with soft scents for cabin and saloon interiors. And there was always the sea-like smell of hemp and duck and resin, and of hot tar being poured over new caulking. On launching day the handiwork of the proud craftsmen slid down the ways to an accolade of shouts and cheers, with flags and pennants whipping from mastheads and halyards. For an especially noteworthy launching there might be a band and speeches and a noisy salute from steamboats in the harbor.

There were few rewards or romantic moments for the men who built the ships. In the history books you read that a vessel was "built by Jacob Bell" or by this or that constructor, names that long will be recorded in the history of shipbuilding. But behind the well-known names of designers and yard owners was an army of artisans and apprentices who worked at the hardest kind of manual labor, literally from dawn to dusk six days a week. Few men have worked harder than the ship's carpenter with his draw knife, or the caulker, kneeling for hours on end under a ship's hull or on the staging beside it, maul in one hand and caulking iron and hemp in the other, driving miles of caulking into the seams, day after day, year after year. Their wrists and arms were twice the size of most men's.

The hard lot of the men who built the ships sparked the formation of the New York Journeyman Shipwrights and Caulkers Benevolent Society in 1833. Like most early labor and fraternal organizations, its principal objective was the care of sick or injured workers and their families but, incredible as it may seem in our time, the shipyard workers were seeking a ten-hour working day. Eventually, most of the yards did limit work to ten hours but workers today would shudder at the ten-hour schedule "enjoyed" by New York shipbuilders in the 1840s.

To summon the men to work a large bell was rung at 6:00 A.M. This signaled the start of operations for the day. At 8:00 A.M. the bell rang again to call the men to breakfast, at 9:00 A.M. for resumption of work, at 12 noon for an hour's lunch period, and at 6:00 P.M. to knock off for the day.

The years between 1840 and 1860

have been described as the great age of New York shipbuilding. "In the farthest corners of the world," said one historian of that period, "the Stars and Stripes wave over New York-built vessels."

There were said to be more than thirty shipyards along the East River in the 1850s. In the early morning and evening hours the streets were filled with "the multitude of mechanics going to work in the shipyards or returning."

Best known of these many yards were those of Christian Bergh, Thorn and Williams, Carpenter and Bishop, Ficket and Thomas, James Morgan and Son, Sneden and Laurence, Samuel Harnards, Brown and Bell, Henry Eckford, Adam and Noah Brown, Webb and Allen, Smith and Dimon, James R. and George Steers, William Brown, and Thomas Collyer.

At one time during the Civil War, twenty-five hundred men worked in Greenpoint shipyards, where ships worth $10 million were under construction, mainly for the U.S. government. The A. J. Rowland yard there

Caulkers worked long hours under a ship's hull or on the staging beside it, with a maul in one hand and caulking iron and hemp in the other, driving miles of caulking into the seams.

Construction of the steamer Suwonda in 1865 at a shipyard along the East River between 10th and 11th streets.

specialized in the new iron monitors, the largest of which was the 340-foot *Puritan*, described at her launching as "a perfect marvel of naval architectural strength." The Dry Dock Iron Works at Greenpoint also built monitors.

Some of the world's largest and finest steamships were built by New York yards for the Pacific Mail and U.S. Mail steamship companies and other lines that began to serve the westward migration after the discovery of gold in California.

The *California*, first steamship to carry the American flag into the Pacific, was a product of New York's William H. Webb, with machinery by the Novelty Iron Works. She left port on October 6, 1848, under Captain Cleveland Forbes and arrived safely in San Francisco February 28, making ten stops in between for water, fuel, and passengers. She had accommodations for 150.

Smith and Dimon launched the *John L. Stephens* in 1853 for the Pacific Mail Line. Carrying 350 passengers on her upper or berth deck and 550 in steerage, she was a well-patronized liner on the run between San Francisco and Panama. She boasted bathrooms with hot and cold water.

In the 1860s, New York yards turned out some of the largest wooden ships ever to sail the seas. Henry Steers launched three of them—the sidewheelers *Japan*, *America*, and *Great Republic*, for Pacific Mail's service between the West coast and Far East. They were 380 feet long; iron-strapped and double-planked.

The Henry Steers yard, Greenpoint, unknowingly turned out one of the fastest sailing ships in the navy in 1864. She was the U.S.S. *Idaho* and she was built originally as a wooden steam sloop with twin screws. But she failed to turn the promised fifteen knots, and the navy, making the most of a bad bargain, took out the engines and converted her to sail. As a sailer she was fast but had a short life, being dismasted and nearly sunk in a typhoon off Japan in 1869.

The *Montana*, built in 1865 for the Pacific Mail Steamship Company, was 330 feet long, with a beam of 43. Her keelsons were built up with nine tiers

of heavy timbers. The timbers upon which the ponderous engine rested were sixty feet long, six feet six inches high, and four feet nine inches wide! Used in the construction of this ship were white oak, chestnut, hackmatack, white and yellow pine. The lower hull planking was six inches thick.

It is no wonder that England, which had used up its large ship timber a century before this, beat American yards in iron-ship construction. They welcomed iron because they had long since exhausted their timber resources.

As important as the shipyards were the foundry and engine works which enabled New York to turn out some of the finest steamships, even in the days when sail was still predominant at sea.

Largest and best known were the Allaire Works and the Novelty Iron Works. The former was started by James P. Allaire as a foundry in 1815, but was greatly expanded when he acquired the engine works of Fulton and Livingston at Jersey City and moved them to New York, combining

The launching of the Pacific Mail Steamship Great Republic *before the superstructure was completed and the paddlewheels inserted. It was built at the Henry Steers Yard in Greenpoint, Long Island.*

As important as the shipyards were the foundry and engine works which enabled New York to turn out some of the finest steamships. The Novelty Iron Works was one of the largest iron manufactories in the United States, occupying a large area between 12th and 14th streets in Manhattan, with slips capable of berthing ten large ships at one time.

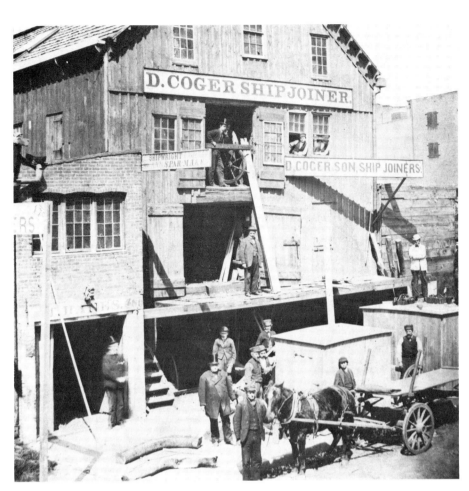

The years between 1840 and 1860 have been described as the great age of New York shipbuilding, and thousands of craftsmen plied their trade here. This advertising photo was taken in 1863.

The 340-foot Puritan was the largest of the iron monitors built at the A.J. Rowland yard in Greenpoint, Long Island.

61

all his operations in a factory at Corlears Hook which employed two hundred men.

Allaire was known for his craftsmanship and his works produced engines for many ships in the early days of steam but, in size, his plant eventually was greatly overshadowed by the Novelty Iron Works, owned by Stillman, Allen and Company. By the 1850s this plant occupied a large area between 12th and 14th streets in Manhattan, with slips capable of berthing ten large ships at one time.

According to an article in the New York *Evening Post* of 1850, the Novelty Iron Works was "one of the largest iron manufactories in the United States." It could do anything in the way of a vessel's machinery and equipment after construction of the hull. Many skills were represented: iron and brass founders, boiler makers, carpenters, coppersmiths, draftsmen, metal-lifeboat builders, hose and belt makers, pattern makers, and riggers. There were 359 machinists. In addition, twenty-one instrument makers produced clocks, thermom-

62

eters, gauges, and other equipment used on board steamships.

Some three hundred tons of iron were consumed in this plant every month, where a battery of furnaces in the iron foundry was capable of melting sixty tons at a time. The average wage for skilled help in those days was $1.50 a day, for work that began at 7 A.M. and ended at 6 P.M.

Naval ship construction was an important phase of New York shipbuilding for more than 150 years. In 1798 the city's merchants initiated a drive to build a warship through public subscription and donate her to the navy. The money was raised and the keel of a thirty-six-gun frigate was laid in August of that year at the yard of Peck and Carpenter. She was launched in April of 1800 and was soon afterward commissioned as the U.S.S. *New York*.

This was the second navy vessel to be named *New York*, the first being a gondola built for General Benedict Arnold's campaign of 1776 on Lake Champlain. There were more *New Yorks* in the years to come.

This proud product of the city's patriotism was 145 feet long, with a 38-foot beam. She carried a crew of 340. *New York* served in the Caribbean and in the Mediterranean to protect American shipping from the Tripolitan pirates. She was burned by the British during their capture of Washington, D.C., in 1814.

The Brooklyn Navy Yard, known variously as the New York Naval Shipyard or New York Navy Yard, turned out a long and distinguished line of ships for the U.S. Navy. This major naval establishment grew out of a small yard at Wallabout Bay, which the Navy Department purchased in 1801 from John Jackson and Brothers for $40,000. There were a few buildings, a small sawmill, and a pond in which ship timbers were stored and seasoned. Jackson and William Sheffield had started the yard in 1781 and had accomplished some substantial work there, including the twenty-eight-gun frigate *Adams* (not to be confused with the Charleston-built frigate *John Adams*). *Adams* was launched at Wallabout Bay in 1799 and took six prizes on her first two cruises to the West Indies during the war with France. She also took part in Mediterranean operations against Tripoli before being laid up for many years at the Washington Navy Yard. The War of 1812 brought her back into service and she took a number of prizes before being blockaded by the British at Camden, Maine, where she was burned by her crew to prevent her capture.

The first man-of-war to be built at the Brooklyn Navy Yard was the seventy-four-gun ship-of-the-line *Ohio*, one of the largest and most powerful warships of her time. Henry Eckford designed her, and the ponderous

The first man-of-war to be built at the Brooklyn Navy Yard was the ship-of-the-line Ohio. *Launched on May 30, 1820, it was one of the largest and most powerful warships of the day.*

Left, Lt. Jonathan Thorn was the Brooklyn Navy Yard's first commandant, 1806-1807.

An 1831 sketch of the Brooklyn Navy Yard, which grew from a small yard at Wallabout Bay purchased by the Navy Department in 1801. The complex then included only a few buildings, a sawmill, and a pond in which ship timbers were seasoned and bent.

63

keel was laid in 1817. She was launched on the 30th of May, 1820, and was immediately put into lay-up as a result of national economies and the vagaries of American naval policies. *Ohio* was refitted and recommissioned in 1838, joining the Mediterranean Squadron under Commodore Isaac Hull. She took part in the siege of Veracruz during the war with Mexico and served with the Pacific Squadron before being sold out of the navy in 1883.

The Brooklyn Navy Yard has turned out almost every type of ship used by the navy: sloops of war, brigs, schooners, steam frigates, transports, ironclads, cruisers, Coast Guard and Revenue Service cutters, monitors, battleships, and aircraft carriers.

Among its more famous products have been the battleship *Maine*, blown up in Havana harbor in 1898; the battleship *Arizona*, launched in 1915 and later sunk during the Japanese attack on Pearl Harbor; the mighty battleship *Missouri*; the carrier *Bennington* (1944); and the 45,000-ton, 963-foot-long supercarrier *Franklin D. Roosevelt* (1945).

More than 18,000 people worked in this yard in World War I, but this was a small force compared to the 71,000 who built and repaired ships there in World War II. Some five thousand naval vessels were overhauled during this war, the work ranging from dented bows and broken propellers to major alterations and repair of extensive battle damage.

After the Navy Yard was declared surplus and sold some years ago, Seatrain Shipbuilding Corporation, an affiliate of the New York-based Seatrain Lines shipping company,

64

Left, A proud Captain Thomas S. Fillebrown stands at his post as commanding officer of the Brooklyn Navy Yard.

The famous battleship U.S.S. Maine, a Brooklyn Navy Yard product, receives a traditional christening.

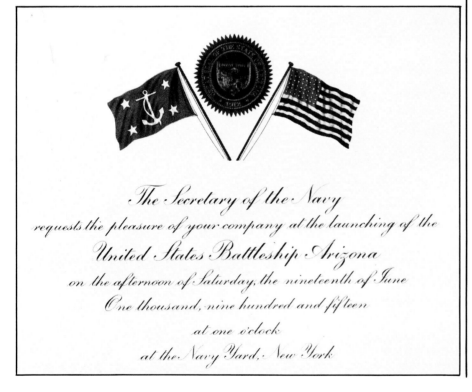

An invitation from the Secretary of the Navy to the launching of the famous battleship Arizona on June 19, 1915 was inscribed with the Navy flag and Arizona state seal.

Fifteen thousand New Yorkers and a host of dignitaries watched the launching of the Maine from the Brooklyn Navy Yard in November, 1890. She was blown up and sunk in Havana's harbor eight years later, sparking the Spanish-American War.

The Brooklyn Navy Yard turned out almost every type of ship used by the navy. Battleship U.S.S. Oregon is seen here during inspection. **65**

took over part of the yard and began construction of the 225,000-ton supertanker *Brooklyn*, largest merchant ship under the American flag. Since then the yard has turned out three sister ships—*Williamsburgh*, *Stuyvesant*, and *Bay Ridge*.

A number of lesser-known yards contributed significantly to New York's role in shipbuilding. One such was the Morris Heights yard of the Consolidated Shipbuilding Corp., on the Harlem River, which built hundreds of small craft from the time it opened in 1887 until it closed in 1955.

This yard launched the 240-foot U.S.S. *Bailey*, one of the world's first torpedo boats, in 1897. It also turned out gunboats, minesweepers, tugs, and hulls for navy seaplanes. Its log of launchings included more than six hundred yachts of all kinds and some ninety-seven small navy ships in World War II.

66

The United States Navy Electrical School's bugle squad stands ready to march at the Brooklyn Navy Yard in New York in 1912.

Under repair at Brooklyn's Navy Yard dry dock, this battleship was one of thousands of naval vessels overhauled during World War I and World War II. The work ranged from dented bows and broken propellers to major alterations and repair of extensive battle damage.

When the 225,000-ton supertanker Brooklyn was constructed, it was the largest vessel in America's merchant-ship fleet. These huge ships no longer slide down the ways when launched; they are floated in dry docks, such as this one at the Seatrain Shipyard in Brooklyn, in 1975.

The Brooklyn Navy Yard was always the scene of great activity as battleships and carriers were loaded and made ready to leave port in World War I. Note the Brownhoist 15-ton locomotive crane.

CHAPTER 5
"FULTON'S FOLLY" AND OTHER PIONEER STEAMBOATS

T he port of New York played a leading role in the steam revolution at sea, in the replacement of sail by paddles and screws.

A number of inventors had a hand in developing the steamboat in America, among them James Rumsey, John Fitch, Samuel Morey, boiler-maker Nathan Read, Elijah Ormsbee, and others.

Fitch built several operable steamboats, demonstrating one of them to members of the Constitutional Convention on the Delaware River in 1787. New Yorkers Robert Stevens and John Stevens were important contributors, too. Robert demonstrated a steam-propelled boat in the harbor in 1804.

But it is Robert Fulton who is honored in most histories as the "father" of the steamboat because he was the first to put this new idea in navigation to practical, commercial use.

A multifaceted inventor who achieved his first success as a miniaturist and portrait painter, Fulton spent many years working on plans for a submarine and trying to sell these concepts to European powers while a resident in France. In 1800 he actually built a submarine and demonstrated it in the River Seine. He also operated a steamboat on the Seine in 1803, arousing the interest of Robert R. Livingston, well-known American landowner and diplomat, and an inventor in his own right.

Convinced that steam could now be advanced from the experimental to the commercial stage, they formed a partnership to construct a steamboat to run between New York and Albany, Livingston to furnish the capital and obtain legislative approval for a monopoly that would protect their investment and insure a profit. In this Livingston was successful, the New York legislature granting the partners an exclusive right to operate steamboats on this run for twenty years.

The hull of the Fulton-Livingston boat was built by Charles Brownne, who had a yard on New York's East River, and the engine by Watt and Bolton in England. It was a single-cylinder machine with a four-foot stroke, using a copper boiler twenty feet long and seven feet in diameter. The machinery moved two paddlewheels with blades four feet long.

This pioneering boat was 140 feet long, with a 16-foot beam and a draft of 28 inches. It was built for commercial use and not as an experimental novelty, and for that reason earned an important place in the history of invention and transportation. Some skeptics said that steam was all right as a plaything for visionary inventors, but would never move a real vessel any distance against wind and current. They predicted a disaster, or at the least a laughable debut, for what they called "Fulton's Folly."

Fulton gave his boat a trial run in August of 1807 and one of the amazed passengers who rode it, Cadwallader D. Colden, later a mayor of New York, said that "nothing could exceed the surprise and admiration of all who witnessed the experiment. The minds of the most incredulous, who had styled the boat 'Fulton's Folly,' were changed in a few minutes. Before the boat had made the progress of a quarter of a mile, the greatest unbeliever must have been converted."

The historic first voyage of Fulton's steamboat received little attention from the press, perhaps because Fulton was too busy getting the machinery in shape to do public relations work with the editors.

New York's *American Citizen* for August 17, 1807, carried this item about the event:

Mr. Fulton's ingenious Steam Boat, invented with a view to the navigation of the Mississippi from

69

New Orleans upwards, sails today from the North River, near the State Prison, to Albany. The velocity of the steam boat is calculated at four miles an hour; it is said that it will make a progress of two against the current of the Mississippi, and if so will be a very valuable acquisition to the commerce of the Western States.

The "Steam Boat" logged a triumphal run from Manhattan to Albany. News of its coming had spread like wildfire. Hundreds of people along the shores stared at this smoke-belching craft in as much awe and amazement as the Indians eyed the *Half Moon*, coursing the same waters two centuries before.

At West Point the entire garrison and corps of cadets turned out to wave their caps and cheer the boat on its way. At Newburgh, according to one passenger's account, "it seemed as if all Orange County had collected there...every sail boat and every watercraft was out on the river." When a boat full of nattily dressed ladies sailed close aboard, Mr. Fulton took off his hat and waved.

70 With its paddles churning bravely against the tide, the boat made the 110 miles from New York to Clermont, the home of Robert Livingston, in twenty-four hours. On the following day it steamed the remaining forty miles to Albany in eight hours. Total time: thirty-two hours.

Those aboard the boat that mild autumn day could not have realized that they were taking part in what was a revolution in water transportation. The boat, later to be popularly known as *Clermont*, began regularly scheduled service between New York and Albany the following month, the trip costing seven dollars for a thirty-six-hour run. Five stops were made en route for passengers and freight. An advertisement promised "good berths and accommodations."

The New York *Daily Advertiser* took notice of the historic first trip with this item on August 22:

We understand that Mr. Fulton's steamboat returned yesterday afternoon about four o'clock—she left New York on Monday about one o'clock—consequently performed the voyage to and from Albany in the short period of four days.

"Fulton's Folly" has become known to history as the *Clermont*, but to passengers and shippers it was advertised as the "North River Steamboat." It is not known for sure what, if anything, she was called at her launching, but Fulton seems never to have referred to her as the *Clermont*. In one of his account books, now in possession of the New York Historical Society, he lists receipts and disbursements for various steamboats, including the *Paragon* and the *Car of Neptune*, but the boat popularly called *Clermont* was referred to by Fulton himself as either "The Steamboat" or "The North River Steamboat."

When the vessel was rebuilt in 1808 she was entered in official documents as *The North River Steamboat of Clermont*.

But the boat was generally known by the name *Clermont* within a few years. Arguing whether or not it was ever officially named *Clermont* may be an exercise for historians, but to hundreds of writers and to millions of readers Fulton's pioneer steamboat is the *Clermont*.

Fulton and Livingston built four more steamers to meet the increasing demand for travel by steamboat, now preferred over the much slower and less comfortable stages or Hudson River sloops. It was clearly evident that paddlewheels were soon to replace sails, at least on inland waters.

As John Morrison points out cogently in his *History of American Steam Navigation*, the construction of these boats was doubly significant. In addition to providing more frequent and faster service on the Hudson, they were the means of training men in engine- and boilermaking and enabled New York to get a jump on all other American ports in the building of steamboats.

By the 1820s, thanks to a Supreme Court decision overturning the Fulton-Livingston monopoly, there were several lines operating on the Hudson; and a trip from Albany to New York had been trimmed to ten hours.

During the years to come, the Hudson River steamboat, along with the passenger vessels on Long Island Sound between New York and New England ports, became the acme of inland-waters design and construc-

Robert R. Livingston, a well-known American landowner and diplomat, formed a partnership with Robert Fulton to construct a steamboat to ply the river between New York and Albany. Livingston furnished the capital and obtained legislative approval for an exclusive right to operate steamboats on this run for twenty years.

On August 22, 1787, an experimental steamboat designed by John Fitch was successfully tried out on the Delaware River, with members of the Constitutional Convention looking on. The engine, built by Henry Voight, a watchmaker, was installed on the small boat to drive twelve paddles, six on a side.

The initial run of the Clermont from Manhattan to Albany was the start of a new age in transportation. The invention was dubbed "Fulton's Folly" but to the passengers aboard, it was an amazing invention. The Battery is in background.

tion. Long, sleek, and speedy, they were the stately, white beauties of river, bay, and sound, providing fast service, fine cuisine, comfortable accommodations, and perhaps more important, inexpensive outings and vacations for millions of city dwellers unable to afford a sea trip on an ocean liner.

New York claims to have had the world's first steam ferryboat, although it is always dangerous to say "first," "greatest," or "biggest," for invariably someone comes up with another "first" to challenge the assertion.

Be that as it may, the city's first steam ferry was built by John Stevens and inaugurated the run between New York and Hoboken in 1811. A service to Jersey City followed a few years later.

Towboat service in New York harbor can trace its beginnings to January 26, 1818, when the bay steamer *Nautilus* towed the ship *Corsair* from the Narrows to the quarantine dock through a harbor filled with floating ice.

The first Brooklyn steam ferry was started by Robert Fulton and William Cutting. "On Sunday last," reported the *Long Island Star* of May 11, 1814, "commenced running the new and beautiful steamboat *Nassau* as a ferryboat between New York and Brooklyn. This noble boat surpassed the expectations of the public in the rapidity of her movements.... Carriages and wagons, however crowded, pass on and off the boat with the same facility as in passing a bridge." It took twelve minutes to cross the East River and the ride cost four cents, although Brooklyn residents held a mass meeting to protest this "exorbitant rate." By 1854 there were to be some forty thousand people riding the Brooklyn ferries every day.

While Fulton has been given the lion's share of credit for developing the first successful steamboat, it is obvious that others had a part in its invention and development. No invention is an entirely isolated stroke of genius or exclusive inspiration. Every innovator contributes ideas and adaptations that eventually become embodied in a successful end product.

Nine years before Fulton's *Cler-* *mont* John Stevens built a steam engine which he placed in a boat and operated on the Passaic River in New Jersey. He later developed a propulsion device similar to the propeller, asserting, quite modestly, that this "invention" was only a further development of an idea conceived by others, including David Bushnell. Stevens also built a twin-screw boat called the *Juliana*, which was given a successful trial run on the Hudson.

Stevens foresaw the revolution to be brought about by steam navigation, predicting that ocean trans-

portation would be revolutionized by "a boiler capable of sustaining high pressure, an engine directly connected to a propeller shaft, and the use of twin screws."

Stevens, termed by one historian "the American genius of steam," deserves an important place in maritime history for building the first steamboat to venture out of protected waters into the open sea. She was named *Phoenix*, constructed on Stevens' designs by John Floyd of Hoboken.

Stevens had intended to use her to open up the New York-Albany run, but was too late in getting his boat finished; and, as the Fulton-Livingston monopoly prevented competition, he decided to employ *Phoenix* on the Delaware River. To do this the little vessel had to navigate the open sea along the New Jersey coast. There was many a wreck of a fine ship in the Jersey sands to show that even this relatively short ocean trip was no cinch, especially with a vessel powered by anything as uncertain as a steam engine.

The Fulton Ferry docked at the foot of Fulton Street in Brooklyn where thousands of passengers boarded the boats that traveled between New York and Brooklyn many times daily. The building was demolished in 1924 and the Brooklyn bridge, shown under construction, was completed in 1883.

Peter Coffee was the pilot of the first steamboat to navigate the Fulton Ferry. "On Sunday last," reported the Long Island Star of May 11, 1814, "commenced running the new and beautiful steamboat Nassau as a ferryboat between New York and Brooklyn. This noble boat surpassed the expectations of the public in the rapidity of her movements."

John Stevens deserves an important place in maritime history for building the first steamboat to venture out of protected waters into the open sea. She was named Phoenix, constructed on Stevens' designs by John Floyd of Hoboken.

73

The historic voyage began on June 10, 1809. Capt. Moses Rogers, later to take the pioneering steamship *Savannah* across the Atlantic, was in command. Robert Stevens, son of the inventor, was the engineer.

These are excerpts from the log of this pioneering vessel on her maiden voyage:

Saturday, June 10—Cast off from the wharf at 11 o'clock A.M. The wind at SSE, a pleasant breeze but foggy. Got our steam up by noon. Anchored at quarantine till fog cleared.

Sunday—Foggy.

Monday—Clear. Got underway, blowing very hard. Anchored in Spermacetti Cove to adjust paddles.

Tuesday—Underway again. More trouble with paddles and had to anchor again. Squally, dirty weather.

Wednesday—Wind blowing a gale. [*Phoenix* still at anchor in the cove.]

Thursday—Awaiting tender [for supplies]. Lightning, thunder, and rain.

Friday—Tender appeared. Rose the steam at 8 o'clock but concluded it rash to encounter the great swell abroad.

Saturday—Got underway again. Weather worsening, so put into Barny Gat. Gale blew all night.

Sunday—Heavy blow and rain.

Monday—Waiting for tender. Weather moderating.

Tuesday—Tender appeared. Had to get more supplies.

Wednesday, 21st—Got underway and past the bar at Barney Gat [sic] at three-quarters past four o'clock A.M., with a smart breeze at NE. Breeze decreased to a light air. Heavy fog. Bore away for the Capes. At 45 minutes past 7 came abreast of Cape May and anchored.

Thursday, 22d—Got underway, first of the flood, wind at south. Foggy. Anchored off New Castle about 8 P.M.

Friday, 23d—Anchored at nine o'clock abreast Market Street wharf, Philadelphia.

On July 10, *Phoenix* inaugurated steam service from Philadelphia to Trenton and, fortunately for its inventor, proved a financial success.

The year 1819 marked an epoch in ocean transportation and the development of steam navigation on the high seas, for in that year the full-rigged sailing ship *Savannah*, with a steam engine and paddlewheels, made the first transatlantic voyage by a steam-powered vessel.

Her detractors sneer at this accomplishment and point out that she used sails most of the time on her crossing, but she was a pioneering vessel and those who financed her were men of vision. There is no doubt that the voyage of the *Savannah* was a "first" and that it did much to accelerate the application of steam propulsion to oceangoing vessels.

Savannah's Atlantic crossing was made from Savannah to Liverpool, but she was a New York-built vessel and after her historic voyage she called here in the coasting trade.

The one-hundred foot, three-masted *Savannah* was being built at Corlears Hook, Manhattan, for use as a packet when Capt. Moses Rogers saw her and thought she would make an excellent vessel for installation of a steam engine and a transatlantic trip. He was the Captain Rogers who had skippered the little *Phoenix*, and that voyage had excited him about the possibilities of steam for ships.

The captain presented his idea to a number of shipowners before the Savannah firm of Scarborough and Isaacs expressed enthusiasm for the project and agreed to finance it.

The machinery was installed, paddlewheels were fitted, and the ship took off for Savannah, from whence she left on May 22, 1819, a date now observed in the United States as National Maritime Day.

The crossing to Liverpool took twenty-nine days, 11 hours, only 105 hours of which were logged under steam, mainly because of the limited coal supply. Early steamers gobbled fuel voraciously.

Savannah created a sensation in England and many a shipowner, who may have belittled the concept of steam for deepwater ships, went back to his office and rethought his prejudices, perhaps made some financial calculations with a *Savannah* of his own in mind.

Captain Rogers continued on to the Baltic to show his vessel there, then went to St. Petersburg, Russia, where the owners hoped that the czar would be intrigued sufficiently to buy her for the Russian navy. The Russians were impressed but they didn't buy,

and a disappointed Rogers had to make the long voyage home empty-handed. The *Savannah* was a failure financially, but she was destined to earn a prominent place in maritime history and the annals of the American merchant marine.

Her engines were removed and the more prosaic *Savannah* was put into the coasting trade as a sailing packet. But her days were numbered. In 1821 she ran aground near Fire Island, New York, and became a total loss.

"The most formidable engine of warfare that human ingenuity has contrived," so a New York paper said of the U.S.S. *Fulton* when it was launched from the East River yard of Adam and Noah Brown on the 29th of October, 1814.

Named *Demologos* (Voice of the People) during her construction, this vessel was truly a novel concept in naval warfare, one of several historic military ships that were to come from New York builders.

The *Fulton*, ex *Demologos*, was the first steam warship in any navy and, like many novel concepts, was years ahead of her time.

In 1813 Robert Fulton made designs for what he called a "steam battery," a kind of floating fort to be used against the British navy in coastal defense. He submitted his plans to President Madison and shortly received approval from Congress to build one or more of these formidable-looking war machines.

Fulton, who supervised construction, named the vessel *Demologos*, but when he died shortly after her launching the navy honored the inventor, entering her on the navy list as the U.S.S. *Fulton*.

By the time she was ready for trials, the *Fulton* represented an investment of $320,000. She displaced 2,475 tons, was 156 feet long, had a beam of 56 feet, and a depth of 20.

The ship was a catamaran, with two hulls, an idea that Fulton had employed in a New York harbor ferry-boat. One hull contained the copper boilers and the other contained the machinery, which was built by the Fulton Engine Works on the North River. She was propelled by a paddle mounted in the long channel between the two hulls.

The year 1819 marked an epoch in ocean transportation and the development of steam navigation on the high seas, for in that year the full-rigged sailing ship Savannah, with a steam engine and paddlewheels, made the first transatlantic voyage by a steam-powered vessel.

The vessel had bulwarks of solid timber four feet high and ten inches thick, pierced by thirty portholes. Added later were two masts, with lateen sails for auxiliary power, as the navy still did not fully trust steam. Old salts must have gasped, or shuddered, at another feature of her rig—a bowsprit and jibs on each end of the ship! There were four rudders so that the vessel could be steered in either direction, like a ferryboat.

Fulton was a floating fort built to repel the most powerful ships of her time. She carried no less than twenty

York in 1824, one of the highlights of his trip was a tour of this great vessel, which he described as a "formidable machine...a floating fortress."

The *Fulton* was set on fire at the Brooklyn Navy Yard, some say in an act of sabotage by a disgruntled crewman, on June 4, 1829. The fire touched off the magazine and the ship blew up, killing or wounding forty-three of the crew.

Although *Fulton* never had an opportunity to prove her prowess in battle, another New York product changed the entire course of naval

Launching of the steam frigate Fulton, *October 29, 1814 from New York.*

thirty-two-pounders and two one-hundred-pounders mounted in the fore and aft "bows." Enough armament to sink a fleet!

She made her trial run in June of 1815 under the well-known Capt. David Porter, but never had a chance to prove her potential, for a treaty of peace was signed before Porter could challenge the enemy.

The *Fulton*, fortunately or unfortunately as the point of view may be, spent her life in lay-up. When the Marquis de Lafayette visited New

warfare and sealed the fate of wooden navies.

In September of 1854 Swedish inventor John Ericsson tried to interest the French in an ironclad vessel, but without success. A mechanical genius and man of many inventions, he had previously developed a steam locomotive and had received a prize of $20,000 from the British Admiralty for a screw propeller.

When the U.S. government ordered a ship to be built in England with Ericsson engines and propeller, the inventor rode the ship to America

In 1813 Robert Fulton made these designs for what he called a "steam battery," a kind of floating fort to be used against the British navy in coastal defense. He submitted his plans to President Madison and shortly after received approval from Congress to build one of these formidable-looking machines.

76

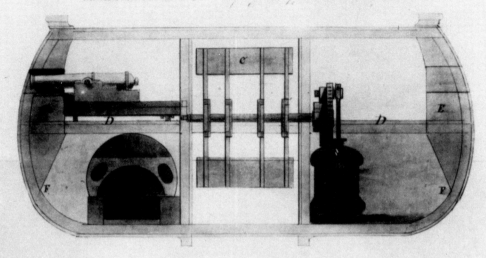

Figure 1.
Scale one quarter of
an inch to ten feet.

Demologos

Transverse section. A her boiler B the steam engine. C the water wheel
D, D gun decks, F, F, her wooden walls 5 feet thick, diminishing to below
the water line as at F F. draught of water 9 feet.

Water line

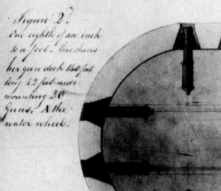

Figure 2.
One eighth of an inch
to a foot. This shews
her gun deck 150 feet
long 42 feet wide
mounting 20
guns. A the
water wheel.

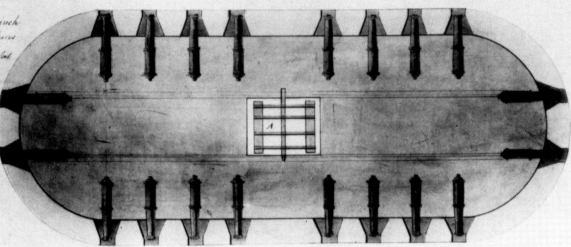

Figure 3.
Side View

Scale 1/8 an inch to a foot

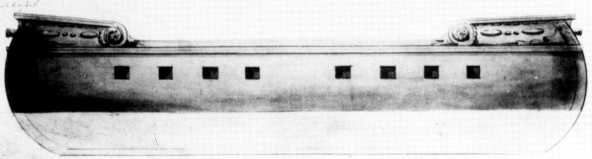

Water line

Robert Fulton
November 1813

and settled in New York, where he became wealthy through ship- and engine-building.

When the Civil War broke out Ericsson went to the Navy Department with his ironclad designs, found receptive ears, and received a contract for construction of a "floating battery."

The keel of the ship, which he promised to deliver in one hundred days, was laid October 25, 1861, at the yard of Thomas F. Rowland in Greenpoint, Long Island, now part of Brooklyn.

The queer craft was launched January 1, 1862, and made her trial run the following month. Total cost to the government was $275,000. Considering the fact that the federal government was chartering transports at rates of $1,000 to $2,000 a day, and that this vessel was destined to save an entire fleet of Union warships, it must have been the biggest bargain in military hardware that this nation ever acquired.

The ship was 174 feet long, with a beam of 41, a depth of 11½, and a draft of 10 feet. She was coal-fired and steam-driven for a speed of nine miles an hour.

The vessel was flat-bottomed and had two iron hulls, the upper one overlapping the lower. Designed to resist the most powerful shot then known, the upper hull was constructed of two-and-one-half-inch white oak covered with six inches of iron plate on the outside and half an inch of iron inside.

Her most distinctive feature was a round turret or revolving cylinder, twenty feet in diameter and nine feet high. This device was constructed of eight thicknesses of one-inch plate

78

bolted together, and it weighed a hundred tons. Inside, with their snouts aimed to fire through two ports, were two eleven-inch Dahlgren guns, the mightiest weapons of their time.

Her name was the U.S.S. Monitor.

Monitor left New York March 6, 1862, on one of the most historic voyages ever made. In command was Lt. John L. Worden. Lt. Samuel Dana Greene was executive officer and Alban C. Stimers engineer. All told, the crew numbered twelve officers and forty-three men.

When the Civil War broke out, Swedish inventor John Ericsson went to the Navy Department with his designs for an ironclad vessel. He received a contract for construction of a "floating battery."

Among the many inventions of John Ericsson was the experimental ship, Destroyer. This photo was taken at the New York Navy Yard about 1890. The U.S.S. Maine is fitting out in the left background.

The Ericsson controllable torpedo was developed during the 1870s and 1880s when the Newport Torpedo Station was experimenting with this type. Although slow, noisy, and impractical, it was the first torpedo to use two counter-rotating propellers mounted on a single shaft.

She steamed into Hampton Roads, Virginia, even as the Confederate ironclad *Virginia* (formerly the U.S. steam frigate *Merrimack*) was wreaking havoc on the Union fleet. Only darkness and the need to rest her crew had kept the ironclad from sinking more ships. The Union fleet was doomed—or so it seemed.

ut what followed is history. When *Virginia* bore up the next morning to complete the destruction of the Union fleet, the strange little *Monitor* steamed out from the lee of the half-wrecked wooden frigate *Minnesota* to offer combat.

For four hours the Union "cheesebox" and the Confederate ironclad thundered and pounded each other at close range, without visible effect. But each shot that bounced off the iron sides was sounding the death knell of wooden navies.

Eventually *Virginia* withdrew, but not for having been completely bested. Conditions for the crews inside these floating forts made it impossible to battle for a protracted length of time. The interior became intolerable because of heat and choking powder smoke.

Each side claimed victory, but *Virginia* did not return to resume the battle and was later blown up to keep her from falling into the hands of advancing Union troops.

Hardly had the sound of the guns died away before the momentous event was being reported to newspapers and admiralties all over the world. To all who witnessed the battle it was startlingly evident that wooden warships were soon to be a thing of the past.

New York builders had contributed significantly to the greatest revolution in naval warfare since invention of powder and gun.

80

The victorious Union gunboat Monitor, *built in New York, changed the course of naval warfare.*

On March 9, 1862 the Union Monitor steamed into Hampton Roads, Virginia, where the Confederate ironclad Virginia was wreaking havoc on the Union fleet. The Monitor offered combat and for four hours the Union "cheesebox" and her opponent thundered and pounded each other at close range. Each side claimed victory, but Virginia did not return to resume the battle and was later blown up to keep her from falling into the hands of advancing Union troops.

CHAPTER 6
PACKETS AND PADDLEWHEELS

In October of 1817 an advertisement appeared in New York newspapers heralding an event that was to open a new era for the port of New York and for ocean transportation in general.

The notice was placed by a new company, later called the Black Ball Line, announcing that one of its vessels would be loading for Liverpool and that it would sail on January 5, 1818, regardless of the weather, the number of passengers that had been booked, or the amount of cargo on board. It would, said the advertisement, be followed by other ships of the same line sailing on regular schedules. The vessels also would leave Liverpool on set dates for the return voyage.

The idea was revolutionary and the boldness of it was exciting to shippers and travelers who, for the first time, could be assured of leaving port on a firm, fixed day of the month. Needless to say, there was no way to set a definite date of arrival on the other side, for the vagaries of wind and weather still determined a ship's progress across the seas. But even a set date for departure was enough to create a sensation in shipping circles.

Hundreds of New Yorkers, most of them probably skeptical about the promised sailing, turned out in a snowstorm to see Capt. James Watkinson, of the ship *James Monroe*, set his sails and drop his lines at the promised hour for departure, to launch a new idea in ocean-freight and passenger service. Later, a large black ball was painted on the Monroe's foretopsail, a symbol of pride and service that would make her owners famous on the oceans as the Black Ball Line for some sixty years to come. For the first sailing there were only seven passengers on board and a small amount of cargo, and the fact that the company dispatched its ship at a financial loss established their good faith with merchants and travelers.

This pioneering venture, which had been formed by four New York shipowners, soon had four vessels on a regular run: *James Monroe*, *Courier*, *Amity*, and *Pacific*. The second Black Baller, the *Courier*, Capt. William Bowne commanding, sailed on January 4, making a forty-nine-day passage against heavy seas and contrary winds.

With this system of scheduled sailings was born the packet ship—the vessel that sailed on a set schedule. It was a New York innovation and one that attracted a great deal of business to the port. By giving birth to the packet the port of New York achieved a significant advantage over its competition in the North Atlantic freight and passenger business. The relation of shipping services to cargo is like the age-old conundrum of which came first, the hen or the egg. Which comes first in building a port: Availability of cargo or frequency of service? The question can be argued ad infinitum.

While the introduction of scheduled sailings brought business to the port, the packet service would not have been economically possible if the business had not been there to warrant it. Other ports tried the same idea but with indifferent success.

The packets made increasingly popular the use of a directive among shippers that was to become the bane of other ports along the Atlantic seaboard: "Ship via port of New York."

It is hard to realize today that many of these trim packets, the pride of the seas in their time, were little more than a hundred feet in length and perhaps no more than thirty feet in width, averaging from three hundred to four hundred tons.

As the years went by the packets became larger, faster, and more commodious. By 1839 there were packets

The packet ship James Monroe *on her arrival in Liverpool on February 1, 1818, 28 days after she initiated Black Ball Line's revolutionary policy of sailing ships on schedule from New York. For the first sailing there were only seven passengers on board and a small amount of cargo, and the fact that the company dispatched its ship at a financial loss established their good faith with merchants and travelers.*

of a thousand tons. One of the largest to be built for the North Atlantic shuttle was the *Amazon*: 215 feet overall, with a beam of 42.

The North Atlantic packets wrote a stirring chapter in the history of merchant shipping. They were skippered by hard-driving masters and their crews were a tough breed of devil-may-care sailors who could claw at half-frozen canvas with bloody fingers and hang onto a royal yard in the face of a howling norwester, with the deck rolling, plunging, and pitching a hundred feet beneath them. Tough they were, and often despised by the even tougher officers who drove them, but no breed of seafarer, with the possible exception of the North Atlantic fisherman, ever pursued a calling as full of hard work and the hostile elements of life before the mast as those who manned the packets sailing the cold and stormy western ocean.

The success of the Black Ball Line, with its dependable departures and usually fast passages, as fast as weather and hard driving would allow, inspired imitators, and within a few years they were competing with the Second Line, the Blue Swallowtail Line, and others. Black Ball remained the most celebrated of them all and has been immortalized in sea song and story.

Packets attracted the premium freight and charged higher rates than other ships. They were preferred by passengers willing to pay extra for better accommodations and faster passages.

Eager to trim every possible hour from an ocean passage, many packet captains drove their ships without mercy. As marine historian Carl Cutler put it, the packets "were driven to the extreme edge of safety at all times....They [the captains] carried sail until it was worth a man's life to go aloft."

Probably the most famous of all the packets was the *Dreadnaught*, built at Newburyport, Massachusetts, in 1852 for the Red Cross Line of New York. She made her first trip in 1853 from New York to Liverpool under Capt. Samuel Samuels. She logged one eastward voyage in thirteen days, eight hours. Her best run from Liverpool to New York was nineteen days.

Some say that the *Yorkshire* was the queen of the western ocean packets. In 1846 she made the trip from Liverpool to New York in sixteen days. Her average time westbound was twenty-nine days, truly remarkable runnning for a ship of that period. This popular packet disappeared on a voyage from New York to Liverpool in 1862, the victim of iceberg, fire, or collision.

Herman Melville, the great writer of tales about life at sea, started sailoring in June of 1839 as a so-called boy, or apprentice, on the packet ship *St. Laurence*, sailing from pier 14, East River. It was experience gained on the *St. Laurence*, a rough introduction to the coarse way of a seaman's life and the rigors of life on the western ocean, that gave Melville material for his novel *Redburn*. *St. Laurence* took almost a month to cross from New York to Liverpool.

Although Melville's books brought him a certain amount of fame during his lifetime, and much more after his death, they brought him little money, and in 1866 he obtained an appointment as an Inspector of Customs in New York. He visited the incoming ships for nineteen years, inspecting their cargoes and assessing the customs charges. His brother, Thomas, was for a long time head of Sailors Snug Harbor, the home for old seamen on Staten Island.

The best of the packets were well built, well manned, and expertly sailed; considering the rugged conditions of the route on which they operated and the number of voyages they made, losses were rare. But losses there were.

The packet ship *Bristol* was returning to New York from Liverpool on her maiden voyage in November of 1836 when she arrived off Sandy Hook and signaled for a pilot. Despite repeated signals, none came off to meet the ship, and the *Bristol*'s captain, fearful of being caught on a lee shore with the wind coming up, stood off to wait for morning. But a thick fog set in, he lost his bearings, and at 4:00 A.M., on the 21st the ship hit on Rockaway Shoals, Long Island.

While distress rockets were being shot off to summon help, seas became heavier and within a few hours it was blowing a gale. Waves carried away the boats and swept the decks. As soon as they could, boatmen put off from shore to aid the stricken vessel and thirty-two passengers were ferried to safety in a daring and courageous rescue effort, but the ship broke up before the others could be saved. Eighty-four passengers and crewmen were drowned. Ship and cargo were a total loss.

More than a hundred were lost when the packet *Mexico*, sixty-seven days out on a stormy voyage from Liverpool, was wrecked on January 1, 1837, at Point Lookout, Long Island. This wreck also was caused by the seeming indifference of pilots who did not come out to guide the vessel safely into port.

In 1849 the packet *Caleb Grimshaw* caught fire in the North Atlantic. Many passengers were rescued, but about one hundred were lost. In 1866 the *William Nelson* of New York burned at sea with a loss of four hundred.

An item in the New York *Herald* of March 4, 1876, was a kind of obituary for the packet era:

News was received in this city yesterday that the large American ship reported ashore on Sable Island, situated ninety miles to the eastward of the Nova Scotia coast, was the well-known Black Ball packet Neptune of New York, belonging to Messrs. C. H. Marshall and Company of this city and commanded by Capt. J. H. Spencer.

According to the owners, the *Neptune* had been a "very lucky vessel," having had only two captains in fifteen years. She had given good service, too, for she had been built for the packet trade in 1855.

By this time the era of the North Atlantic sailing packet was almost over. Even as the tall-masted, white-winged sea queens of the North Atlantic shuttle were setting new records for travel between Europe and America, their days were being numbered. Transatlantic passage by steam, rather than sail, had arrived.

On August 17 of 1833 the 176-foot Canadian-built paddlewheel steamer *Royal William* left Pictou, Nova Scotia, and, after a stormy crossing of twenty-five days, arrived safely and triumphantly at Gravesend, England. While her admirers claim for her the

The packet ship—the vessel that sailed on a set schedule—was a New York innovation that attracted a great deal of business to the port. This reproduction of the Charlemagne, a New York packet ship of the 1830s, is from a painting by Frederic Roux of Havre.

Possibly the most famous of all the packets was the Dreadnaught, *built at Newburyport, Massachusetts, in 1852 for the Red Cross Line of New York. This 1856 Currier lithograph shows her off Tuskar Light, twelve days from New York during her record-making passage to Liverpool.*

honor of being the first vessel to cross the Atlantic entirely under steam power, this claim has to be qualified. Capt. John McDougall stopped his engines for long periods every four days "to clean the boilers of salt." Sails were hoisted to maintain steerageway while this work was being done.

Of much greater significance for the North Atlantic trade and maritime commerce in general was the arrival in the port of New York of the British *Sirius* on April 22, 1838.

By early morning of the night she arrived at anchor off the Battery there were thousands of people along the waterfront and many hundreds more afloat in every kind of boat to get a close-up look at this maritime marvel. *Sirius* was the first steamship to arrive in the port of New York from the other side of the Atlantic.

"The Sirius! The Sirius!," said the New York *Weekly Herald*. "Nothing is talked of in New York but about the Sirius. She is the first steam vessel that has arrived here from England and a glorious boat she is. Lt. Roberts, R.N., commander, is the first man that has navigated a steamship from Europe to America."

No sooner had New Yorkers had a chance to thrill over *Sirius* than another amazing visitor appeared on the horizon.

Only a few hours after Lieutenant Roberts had dropped the hook, a second steamship was sighted coming in from the sea. Marvel of marvels! This was almost too much even for citizens of the nation's biggest city to believe. But it was true. Steaming proudly through the Narrows and streaming a black ribbon of smoke from her coal-fed fires came the British *Great Western*, and within a few hours she, too, was drawing crowds of gaping spectators ashore and afloat, and winning paeans of praise from the city's press, all but overwhelmed by the arrival of two great ships in one day.

Lt. James Hoskens, commander of *Great Western*, had tried desperately to beat *Sirius* for the honor of being first at New York and probably would have had it not been for a fire that delayed the vessel for three days as it headed down the Thames for the

North Sea. This was just enough lead time to enable *Sirius* to be the first ship in, despite a much slower crossing.

After the initial excitement had died down, it was evident to all but the most loyal lovers of sail that a dramatic new day was dawning for North Atlantic travel and for the port of New York.

Owners of the two ships had been engaged in a shipbuilding race to be first to get their ships off across the Atlantic. It was the beginning of a building and a navigation contest that

was to continue unabated for the next hundred years.

Junius Smith, an American who was the driving force behind the new British and American Steam Navigation Company, had conceived the idea of an England-New York steamship service but before his new ship, the *British Queen*, could be completed, he was upstaged by the equally new Great Western Steamship Company. Their *Great Western* was first to take the water; and seeing that his competitors were about to stage a coup, Smith chartered the *Sirius*, a

steamer used in home waters, to carry his house flag first across the Atlantic into the port of New York. The contest was like something out of a Hollywood cliff-hanger, and in true heroic fashion the glory of being first went to the dogged little *Sirius*, which was so determined to beat her more pretentious rival that there was not one shovelful of coal left in the bunkers after she dropped anchor off Manhattan. Another hour and she would have had to be towed into port.

Great Western stole much attention from the *Sirius*, for she was by far the more impressive of the two, being 236 feet long and sporting four masts.

Reporters wrote lyrically about the two ships, but especially about *Great Western*, "a wonder of the sea." Her interior accommodations, said one account, "are in the highest degree tasteful and elegant, and the saloon might vie with the clubhouses of London in luxury and magnificence." She carried three hundred passengers and crew.

Great Western had two 225-horse-power engines and cost $125,000. She was designed by the famous Isambard

The best of the packets were well built, well manned and expertly sailed; considering the rugged conditions of the route on which they operated and the number of voyages they made, losses were rare. But losses there were.

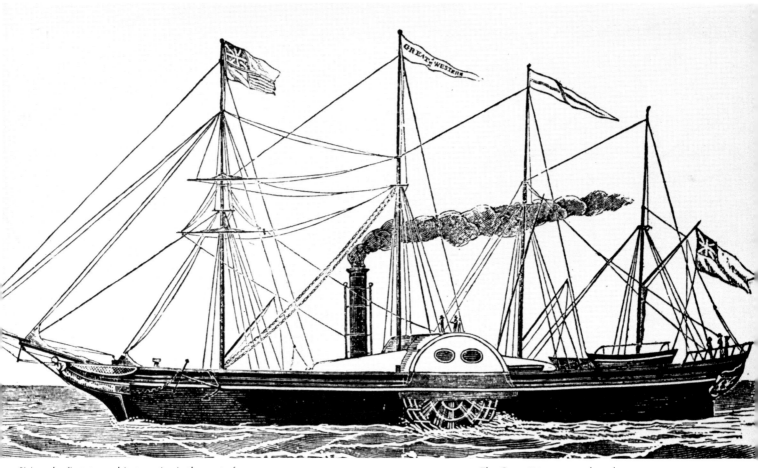

Sirius, the first steamship to arrive in the port of New York from the other side of the Atlantic, was greeted by a thrilled and jubilant crowd of New Yorkers. "The Sirius! The Sirius!," said the New York Weekly Herald. "Nothing is talked of in New York but about the Sirius. She is the first steam vessel that has arrived here from England and a glorious boat she is."

The Great Western made a desperate attempt to win the race to New York despite a fire that delayed the vessel for three days.

Brunel, who was to be heard from again on the North Atlantic.

Philip Hone, a former mayor of New York and an avid diarist, said that "the passengers on board the vessels speak in the highest terms of the convenience, steadiness, and apparent safety of the new mode of conveyance across the ocean. Everybody is enamored of it—that for a while it will supersede the New York packets, the noblest vessels that ever floated in the merchant service, and steamers will continue to be the fashion until some more dashing adventurer of the go-ahead tribe shall demonstrate the practicability of balloon navigation."

On April 27 city officials, editors, and other VIPs were hosted by officers of the two ships at a gala dinner aboard *Great Western* at anchor off Pike Street.

Mr. Hone had this to say of that stirring occasion: "The lovely Queen of Britain was toasted with enthusiasm equal to any which warm the hearts of her own subjects. Long may these feelings continue!"

88

He also made this cogent prediction: "All that is now wanting to confine to steam vessels the patronage of all the passengers going to Europe is the assurance of safety, and that will be obtained by one or two more passages across the Atlantic."

The voyage of *Sirius*, it developed, had been especially commendable because Captain Roberts' crew threatened mutiny and wanted to return to port when the first heavy storm came up, for they doubted the ability of such a novelty, especially since she had been used only on short runs around the British Isles, to withstand a North Atlantic blow. With the help of a brace of pistols, Roberts had encouraged them to change their minds.

These excerpts from her log show the kind of weather she had battled in the race against *Great Western*:

> 6th April—strong breeze and squally weather
> 7th April—storm and gale; very high seas
> 11th April—heavy gale and great swells
> 16th April—fresh gale and heavy seas

17th April—heavy gale with sleet and snow

Although *Sirius* had been overshadowed to some extent by her larger rival, New Yorkers turned out by the thousands to wish her crew and her forty-seven passengers bon voyage when she left on the return trip.

Said one paper:

> They expressed their farewell wishes for a prosperous voyage to the gallant bark in loud and oft-repeated cheers. These were an-

swered by a salute of several guns from the Sirius, after which she made a sweep up the river and upon returning struck gayly off toward the ocean at the rate of nine miles an hour.

New Yorkers were getting somewhat accustomed to steamships by the time the *Royal William*, a former Dublin steam packet (not the Canadian *Royal William*) arrived in July of 1838, followed by the *Liverpool*, a two-stacker, in November. Both flew the house flag of the Transatlantic Steamship Company. *Great Western* had become a regular visitor by the end of this year.

Junius Smith and his British and American Steam Navigation Company soon replaced *Sirius* with their *British Queen*, which the owners were sure was "the most splendid and commodious steamship." She was 275 feet long and had engines of 700 horsepower, having been enlarged in size and power from the original plans. A full-length figurehead of a queen carrying a scepter graced her rakish bow. She sailed from Spithead July 11, 1839, and arrived in New York

thirteen days, eleven hours later. She was given "a boisterous reception." A sister ship, the *President*, entered the New York run in 1840.

Splendid though she was, *British Queen* could not make money. This, coupled with the tragic loss of the *President* in 1841, put the company out of business. The Transatlantic Steamship Company fared no better and hauled down its flag in 1840. Great Western Steamship Company learned that fame didn't pay bills and sold out in 1847. Owners discovered at this early date that it took a government's financial help to compete with expensive passenger ships on the Atlantic.

The ill-fated *President* left New York for England on March 11, 1841, with many distinguished passengers, including the well-known Irish actor Tyrone Power. There were 136 people on board.

A day or so later, another ship saw the *President* east of Cape Cod, laboring heavily in tremendous seas. Nothing was ever seen of her again.

On May 3, Junius Smith wrote to his nephew: "I suppose the President is lost. I have slight hopes of ever hearing of her again."

"What sighs have been wafted after that ship," wrote Washington Irving. "What prayers offered up at the deserted fireside of home! Alas! Not one memento shall ever return for love to cherish. All that shall ever be known is that she sailed from her port—and was never heard of more."

Newspaper reporters of the day wrote lyrically about the Great Western, "a wonder of the sea." Her interior accommodations, said one account, "are in the highest degree tasteful and elegant, and the saloon might vie with the clubhouses of London in luxury and magnificence." She carried three hundred passengers and crew.

Opposite, The ill-fated President left New York for England on March 11, 1841, with many distinguished passengers. In the inquiry before the British Consul, June 5, 1841, Captain Cole of the packet ship Orpheus, stated that when he last saw the President on the 12th of March she was rising on the top of a tremendous sea pitching heavily and laboring tremendously. It was also his belief that all perished before sundown on the 13th or in less than twenty-four hours after he last saw her, most probably in the terrible night of March 12, 1841.

The owners of the British Queen were sure she was "the most splendid and commodious steamship." She was 275 feet long, and a full-length figurehead of a queen carrying a scepter graced her rakish bow.

90

CHAPTER 7
THE GOLDEN DOOR

The advent of the packet ship coincided with the great surge of emigration from northern Europe to the United States. Packets enjoyed a large share of this business. Of some five-and-a-half million immigrants who arrived in the United States between 1820 and 1845, close to four million came to the "promised land" through the port of New York.

Quite obviously, it required hundreds of ships making hundreds of voyages to transport such a mass migration. Ships of all kinds and conditions were employed in this trade—from old bluff-bowed whalers that could never do ten knots in a gale of wind, to crack packets of the Black Ball class.

And much of America was built by the hardy and courageous people who made the arduous journey.

Andrew Carnegie, the multimillionaire steel magnate and philanthropist, came to America from Scotland with his parents in 1848 on a converted whaler. The voyage took seven weeks.

The average immigrant ship sailing for New York carried from five hundred to six hundred men, women, and children jammed into every available foot of space. For most immigrants cabin passage was an impossible luxury. They slept in large dormitory-style spaces that afforded little if any privacy, were ill-ventilated (and not ventilated at all in bad weather), and stank from unwashed bodies and the mass effects of mal-de-mer. Toilet facilities, which were on deck, were minimal. Often, immigrants provided and cooked their own food on community stoves, when the weather was favorable and their stomachs could endure it. Most immigrants, needless to say, were miserably seasick as their New York-bound ships rolled and pitched their way across the western ocean.

Tragically, many immigrants lived through the miseries and dangers of a transatlantic passage and saw the long-awaited shores of America only to perish before they could land and begin a new life.

In 1854 the *Powhatan*, bound from Le Havre to New York with two hundred German immigrants, was driven ashore on the coast of New Jersey near Atlantic City. By the time those on shore could summon a lifesaving crew with a surf boat and other equipment, the angry waves had battered the ship to pieces. All on board were drowned.

91

The symbol of America to all the world, The Statue of Liberty, as we know her, was conceived at a French dinner party in 1865 and unveiled in New York harbor twenty-one years later. A topic of controversy in the United States, there were many uneven attempts to build her. Designed by Auguste Barthold, the form was hammered out of thin copper sheet and supported on an elaborate wrought iron truss. Liberty Enlightening the World (her original name) was completed in the Paris workshops of Gaget, Gauthier et Cie and shipped in sections to her final site on Bedloe's Island.

The very first immigrants to America had no trouble entering the new land. There were no immigration laws or restrictions. Most of them were sponsored by religious groups, or agencies, such as the Dutch West India Company or the Massachusetts Bay Company. Quite a few eighteenth-century immigrants to America were indentured servants obligated to work for a period of years to repay the cost of their passage. One authority estimates that "as many as two-thirds of all European immigrants south of New England were 'colonists in bondage,'" which explains how many of Europe's debt-ridden tradesmen were able to pay their way to America.

Early waves of immigration in the eighteenth century included more than 200,000 Germans, Scots, Irish, and French Huguenots fleeing religious persecution in France. Figures on immigration for this time are sparse and incomplete, but it is estimated that well over a million Europeans entered this country between 1783 and 1847. This was only

92 the beginning. The peak years of

Andrew Carnegie, the multimillionaire steel magnate and philanthropist, came to America from Scotland with his parents in 1848 on a converted whaler. America was largely built by men whose beginnings were quite inauspicious and who lived the American dream of success.

White Star Line advertised, "The steerage accommodation in these steamers is one of the very highest character, the rooms are unusually spacious, well lighted, ventilated, and warmed, and passengers of this class will find their comfort carefully studied."

WHITE STAR LINE

UNITED STATES   MAIL STEAMERS.

BRITANNIC.   CELTIC.   GERMANIC.   ADRIATIC.   BALTIC.
REPUBLIC.   OCEANIC.   GAELIC.   BELGIC.

THESE WELL-KNOWN, FAST MAIL STEAMERS SAIL FROM

LIVERPOOL TO NEW YORK,

EVERY THURSDAY,

GERMANIC,	Thursday, Aug. 31	BRITANNIC,	Thursday, Oct. 26
CELTIC,	" Sept. 7	GERMANIC,	" Nov. 9
BRITANNIC,	" 21	CELTIC,	" 16
GERMANIC,	" Oct. 5	BRITANNIC,	" 30
CELTIC,	" 12		

Calling at QUEENSTOWN on the Following Day.

These splendid, full-powered, First-class Iron Screw Steamers are among the largest and most powerful vessels afloat, and are distinguished for the shortness and regularity of their passages, and the completeness and comfort of their passenger accommodation.

SALOON PASSAGE, 15, 18, AND 21 GUINEAS EACH BERTH,

According to State Room selected, all having equal Privileges in Saloon. Children under Twelve Years, Half-Fare. Infants Free.
Return Tickets, available for one year, issued at Reduced Rates.

These rates include a Liberal Table and Steward's Fee, without Wines or Liquors, which can be obtained on board. £5 Deposit is required to secure Cabin Berths, the balance to be paid the day before sailing. Luggage will go on board with the Passengers in the Tender that leaves the Landing Stage for the Steamer on the day of sailing.

STEERAGE FARE to NEW YORK, BOSTON, or PHILADELPHIA,

Six Guineas (£6 6s.) including a plentiful supply of cooked Provisions.
Children under Eight years Half Fare, and Infants under 12 months £1 1s.

The Steerage accommodation in these Steamers is of the very highest character, the rooms are unusually spacious, well lighted, ventilated, and warmed, and passengers of this class will find their comfort carefully studied.

Passengers will be provided with Berths to sleep in, each adult having a separate berth; but they have to provide themselves with a Plate Mug, Knife, Fork, Spoon, and Water Can, also Bedding—all of which can be purchased on shore for about 10/-. MARRIED COUPLES, WITH THEIR CHILDREN, WILL BE BERTHED TOGETHER. FEMALES will be Berthed in rooms by themselves.
BILL OF FARE.—Each Passenger will be supplied with 3 quarts of Water daily, and with as much Provisions as he can eat, which are all of the best quality, and which are examined and put on board under the inspection of Her Majesty's Emigration Officers, and cooked and served out by the Company's servants.
BREAKFAST AT EIGHT O'CLOCK—Coffee, Sugar, and fresh Bread and Butter, or Biscuit and Butter, or Oatmeal Porridge and Molasses.
DINNER AT ONE O'CLOCK—Soup and Beef, Pork, or Fish, according to the day of the week, with Bread and Potatoes, and on Sunday Pudding will be added.
SUPPER AT SIX O'CLOCK—Tea, Sugar, Biscuit, and Butter. Oatmeal Gruel will be supplied at 8 p.m. when necessary
LUGGAGE.—TEN CUBIC FEET will be allowed for each adult Steerage Passenger, and 20 cubic feet for each adult Saloon Passenger, free; for all over that quantity a charge of 1s. 6d. for each cubic foot will be made. Steerage Passengers must have their luggage ready to go on board the Steamer on the morning of the day of sailing.
Passengers are landed at the Government Depot, Castle Garden, New York, where they can purchase Tickets for, and receive every information respecting the departure of Trains, Steam-boats, &c.
These Steamers run in connection with the Erie Railway from New York—the shortest and best route to the West, North and South-Western States; and Passengers are Booked through at low rates, to all parts of the States, Canada, Aspinwall and San Francisco, also to Australia, New Zealand, China and Japan, by the Pacific Railway and Mail Steam-ship Company.
All passengers are liable to be rejected, who, upon examination, are found to be lunatic, idiot, deaf, dumb, blind, maimed, or infirm, or above the age of 60 years; or widow with a child or children, or any woman without a husband with a child or children; or any person unable to take care of himself (or herself) without becoming a public charge, or who from any attending circumstances are likely to become a public charge, or who from sickness or disease, existing at the time of departure, are likely soon to become a public charge. Sick persons or widows with children cannot be taken, nor lame persons, unless full security be given for the Bonds to be entered into by the Steamer to the United States Government, that the parties will not become chargeable to the State.
ALL STEERAGE PASSENGERS embarking at Liverpool must be at the Office of the Agents, 10, Water Street, Liverpool, not later than 6 p.m. of the day before the advertised date of sailing, when the balance of the passage-money must be paid, or the deposit forfeited.
All Steerage Passengers embarking at Queenstown must be at the Office of the Agent at Queenstown (Cork) not later than Six o'clock p.m. of the day before sailing when the balance of the passage-money must be paid, or the deposit forfeited, and all Passengers will have strictly to conform to the Rules laid down by the Company
In order to meet the requirements of the Government Emigration Officer, Contract Tickets will be issued for the Noon of the day previous to the advertised date of sailing
AN EXPERIENCED SURGEON IS CARRIED BY EACH STEAMER.
STEWARDESSES IN STEERAGE TO ATTEND THE WOMEN AND CHILDREN. NO FEES OR EXTRA CHARGES
Passage can be engaged and Tickets obtained from any Agent of the "White Star" Line, or by sending name, age, and occupation, together with a deposit of One Pound on each berth, to

Wells & Holohan, Railway Agents,

It is estimated that well over a million Europeans entered this country between 1783 and 1847. This was only the beginning. The peak years of immigration were from 1905 to 1914. More than 1,285,000 came in the year 1907 alone.

For most immigrants cabin passage was an impossible luxury. They slept in large dormitory-style spaces that afforded little if any privacy.

immigration were from 1905 to 1914. More than 1,285,000 came in the year 1907 alone.

Prior to 1883, immigrants came mostly from the British Isles, Northern Europe, and Scandinavia. The great famine of 1846-47 in Ireland impelled a great surge of immigrants, although many Irish, of course, had come here prior to that. During a period of seven years in the 1840s, more than a million and a half Irish emigrated, most of them to the United States through the port of New York.

"The rush for ships was so great," says one historian, "that emigrants were crowded almost to suffocation in miserable quarters without privacy or sufficient provisions."

Prior to 1847, immigrants landing in New York were essentially on their own. There were no impediments to immigration except for the general quarantine restrictions. The federal government favored a policy of unrestricted immigration.

Often newcomers were sick or destitute and to keep as many as possible from becoming public charges, the New York State legislature in 1847 established the New York State Immigration Commission, which administered the Castle Garden Emigrant Depot and the hospitals on Staten Island and Ward's Island.

Formerly a huge theatre used for such events as the American debut of singer Jenny Lind and the public reception for General Lafayette, Castle Garden was leased by the Commissioners of Immigration in 1855 and fitted out for processing immigrants. It was a busy place. On one day in 1873 just one ship, the S.S. *Egypt*, brought 1,767 steerage passengers to New York.

An article in *Harper's Weekly* in 1865 reported that this facility "has afforded a haven of security for immigrants....Besides having a place of safety for the landing of his effects, the emigrant is relieved from the exploitation of runners and of the sellers of bogus railway tickets." There was an office for buying railroad tickets from authorized agents, an inquiry room where newcomers could meet friends or relatives, an employment office, and a writing room where they could write letters

94

or have letters written for them.

Castle Garden and, later, Ellis Island received their people from the steerage (cheapest quarters) of North Atlantic liners and other ships used for the emigrant trade. First- and second-class cabin passengers did not have to go through the immigration stations, it being assumed, with some logic, that those who could afford to ride across in style, were most likely to be people in good health and with enough money that they would not become public charges.

Steerage passengers in the 1890s

Formerly a huge theater used for such events as the American debut of singer Jenny Lind and the public reception for General Lafayette, Castle Garden was leased by the Commissioners of Immigration in 1855 and fitted out for processing immigrants.

and early 1900s paid about $20 to $25 for the trip to America. The cost of steerage passage on the *Furst Bismarck* from Hamburg to New York was only $18 for a seven-day voyage of three thousand miles! This is the answer to the question of how so many poor people could afford to make the voyage. By selling everything they had, they were able to raise money for a trip to the nearest seaport and buy the low-cost ticket to America. Many were helped financially by relatives who already had come to America and found jobs.

An emigrant trip in the 1890s was graphically described by M. Phelps Whitemarsh in the *Century Illustrated Monthly* of February, 1898. He was an English journalist who made the voyage as an emigrant to see and feel the rigors of a steerage passage.

The steerage passengers for Whitemarsh's ship were assembled on a pier in Birkenhead, England, then taken by boat to their ship, which lay at anchor in the harbor. Cabin passengers were embarked at a dock. It was the custom of most lines to embark the steerage or third-class trav-

A scene near Castle Garden in 1890, where over a thousand immigrants were processed every day.

Steerage passengers were allowed only a small amount of deck room, which was blocked off from the cabin-class spaces and was too limited for all to enjoy sun and fresh air at the same time, even in good weather.

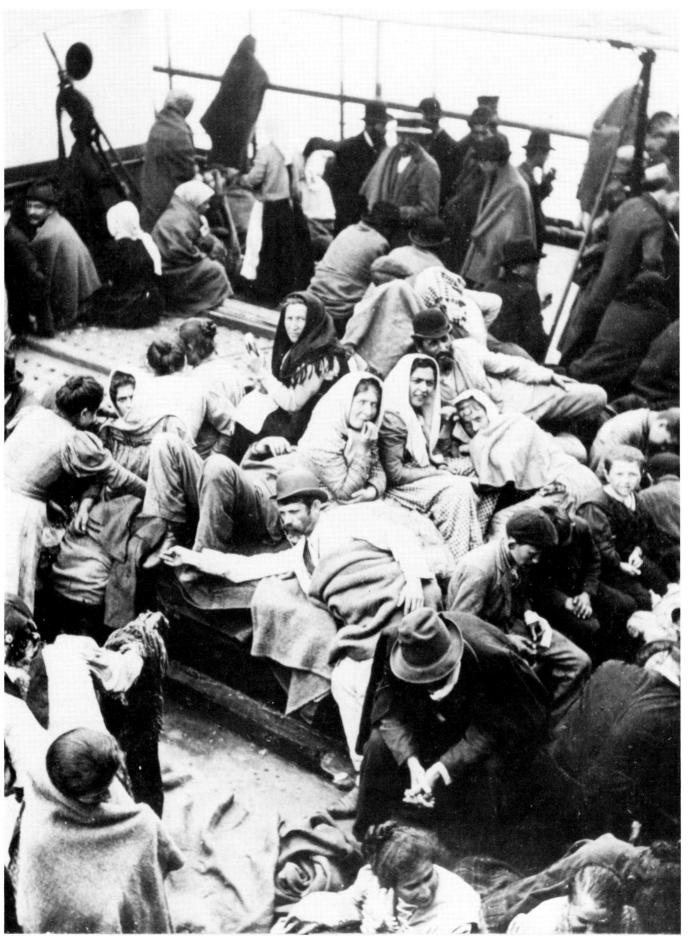

elers first because there were usually so many more of them and the problem of getting them settled in their quarters, with the multiplicity of languages involved, took time.

There were more than 300 of us," said Whitemarsh. "Opposite me in the boat was a Welshman, his wife, and five children. Pretty, dark-eyed little tots but oh, so dirty! On my left were two Irishmen, one old and beery, the other a strapping young fellow with clean-cut features from Tyrone. Close by huddled a family of Finns, the woman comely and scrupulously clean."

There was no polite "welcome aboard" for these steerage folk, but only a gruff "step lively there... watch where you're going...hurry up now!"

This ship, which Whitemarsh did not mention by name, had steerage quarters in the forward part of the vessel, below the main deck.

"Steerage number one," he said, "was in the eyes of the vessel and ran across from one side to another without a partition. It was lighted entirely by portholes, under which were narrow tables with benches. The remaining space was filled with iron bunks, row after row, tier after tier, all running fore and aft in double banks. A thin, iron rod is all that separated one sleeper from another. In each bunk was placed a 'donkey's breakfast' (sailor's name for a straw mattress), a blanket of the horse variety, and a battered tin plate and panniken, a knife, a fork, and a spoon. This completed the emigrant's 'kit,' which in former days had to be provided by himself." This section of the steerage, which held 118, was reserved for English-speaking males.

There were similar compartments for foreign-speaking males, for single females, and for families.

"To the credit of the ship," said Whitemarsh, "every thing was very clean. Sweet smelling it was not. Spotless, scrubbed decks and scrubbed paintwork could not hide the sour, shippy, reminiscent odor that hangs about steerages, one and all."

The emigrants came aboard lugging carpetbags, brown paper parcels, cans of cooked victuals, fruit, bird cages, and "sundry loud-smelling bottles." The Scandinavian women wore every petticoat they possessed, a practical way of saving baggage. Everyone also had some antidote for the much-dreaded seasickness—from lime drops to patent medicines and raw onions. It was later to be proved that "not one of these antidotes had the slightest effect."

Before the ship got under way, the steerage passengers were mustered for medical inspection, being kept standing for several hours before the doctor showed up and began his duties, which consisted mainly of a quick look at tongues and eyes.

After the ship had proceeded to a dock to load its cabin passengers and finally sounded its long, solemn blasts of farewell to the shore and the well wishers on the dockside, there was much cheering by the men and waving of handkerchiefs by the ladies on the top decks—those in first and second cabin. But there wasn't much cheering or waving among the emigrants, and for a good reason. "With every ship that sails from England," said Whitemarsh, "how many there are who leave their friends for ever."

First- and second-class cabin passengers did not have to go through the immigration stations, it being assumed, with some logic, that those who could afford to ride across in style were most likely to be people in good health and with enough money that they would not become public charges. This group is part of the 1000 marriageable girls that arrived on the Baltic in 1907.

"The rush for ships was so great," says one historian, "that emigrants were crowded almost to suffocation in miserable quarters without privacy or sufficient provisions."

An article in Harper's Weekly in 1865 reported that Castle Garden "has afforded a haven of security for immigrants......
Besides having a place of safety for the landing of his effects, the emigrant is relieved from the exploitation of runners and of sellers of bogus railway tickets."

Once the ship was at sea and feeling the ocean swells, it was not long before the English journalist was forced to the open deck "by the stifling atmosphere, the stench, and the unearthly noises of the sick."

Steerage passengers were allowed only a small amount of deck room, which was blocked off from the cabin-class spaces and was too limited for all of them to enjoy sun and fresh air at the same time, even in good weather. After the onslaught of seasickness had worn away, there was much jollity and camaraderie, for all were sharing a great adventure. There were flutes, violins, and accordions, with singing, dancing, and romancing, thanks to some twenty or so "very pretty young Irish girls" with lively feet and sparkling eyes. Females were ordered to their quarters at 9 P.M.., but this rule was frequently evaded and many a romance bloomed as the ship plunged westward.

Steerage passengers on this ship were fed plainly but amply. For breakfast there was oatmeal, coffee, bread, and butter. Dinner consisted of soup, meat or fish, potatoes, bread, and pudding. For supper there was bread, butter, and tea.

In steerage there were no waiters. Food was placed on the tables in big containers, with the call to "help yourself." Too many immigrants, according to one traveler, "dug into the meat and potato pots as though they had never eaten before in their life."

Whitemarsh's companions included English, Irish, Norwegians, Swedes, Finns, Welsh, and Germans, with one Frenchman, and one Bohemian. Most of them told of having relatives in America, the relatives being the ones who had paid the fare for those who could not afford it on their own.

S ome steamship companies, it should be mentioned, had a reputation for treating their steerage passengers well, considering that the fare and food cost less than a penny a mile.

The Inman Line, for instance, was started by William Inman in 1850 partly with the aim of providing better accommodations for immigrants in a fleet of new, fast ships. Steerage tickets cost $40 in those days, and in one year the Inman fleet ferried more than eighty thousand steerage passengers to America. As ships got bigger and competition for immigrants increased, fares were greatly reduced.

A steerage passage sometimes had its amenities. The French Line advertised wine at all meals for steerage folk and special dinners for holidays. A steerage passenger on a Cunard ship in 1889 reported "very ample meals" with oatmeal or porridge with molasses for breakfast and "coffee in plenty," with rolls and butter. For

dinner there was soup, beef or pork or fish, and potatoes. And for supper, rolls and tea. On Sunday, roast beef and plum duff.

Starting in the 1870s, the federal government became active in the immigration process. In 1882 Congress passed the first general law on immigration, barring the admission of idiots, lunatics, convicts, and persons likely to become public charges. The New York Commissioners had blamed various authorities in Europe for paying steamship companies to ship such undesirables to the United States to get rid of them. Ellis Island was set up in order to enforce the new federal immigration laws.

E llis Island! To the more than twelve million immigrants who passed through it on the way to a new life in America it was a golden door. To the many thousands who were turned away and sent back home, or separated from their families, it was an "island of tears."

From the time it opened in 1892 until its closing in 1954, Ellis Island was an "open sesame" to America for people from every nation in Europe.

It served the country during the flood tide of immigration, when some 70 percent of all newcomers to America passed through its doors. Officially, it was known as the Ellis Island Immigration Station.

Ellis Island has a colorful history going far beyond its immigration days. It was called Gull Island by the Indians, who fished there, and it was used as a base of operations by Dutch oystermen. Its first owner was Capt. William Dyre, a collector of customs in the 1670s.

It acquired the name Gibbet Island

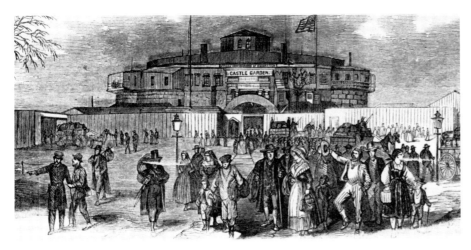

Before the Ellis Island Station was opened, emigrants were processed through Castle Gardens. Here is an 1865 scene depicting the transfer of emigrants to the various boats to and from Castle Gardens.

Ellis Island! To the more than twelve million immigrants who passed through it on the way to a new life in America it was a golden door. It served the country during the flood-tide of immigration, when some 70 percent of all newcomers to America passed through it.

99

From the time it opened in 1829 until its closing in 1954, Ellis Island was an "open sesame" to America for people from every nation in Europe.

after a pirate named Anderson was hanged there in 1765. Another pirate met his end there on the scaffold in 1769, and during the 1830s two men accused of a murder and robbery on a ship were executed on Gibbet Island. In 1814, when it was one of several harbor fortifications, a soldier was executed there for allegedly trying to kill his superior officer.

The present name comes from an owner named Samuel Ellis, who acquired it about the time of the Revolution.

Originally, the island was only 3.3 acres in extent, but was enlarged by fill over the years to its present 27.5.

The federal government purchased the island in 1890 for an immigration station, which was built at a cost of $500,000, outfitted with frame buildings, and opened in 1892. On June 14, 1897, the buildings were destroyed by fire and, until the present facilities were completed in 1900, immigrants were processed in crowded quarters in the Barge Office at the Battery.

The new facility on Ellis Island included a number of handsome three-story brick buildings in the French Renaissance style. The "great hall" was 385 feet long and 165 feet wide. A high, vaulted ceiling and large windows helped to brighten an otherwise frightening experience for the hundreds of tired people who filled its benches, waiting their turn to be interviewed and then inspected by doctors.

There was a clinic where those who failed to pass the initial physical examination were taken for further tests, special dormitories where detainees were kept, and the big dining room where they were fed prior to final admittance or deportation. In its later years the dining room served ethnic foods, including kosher meals. No less important were the bath houses, a luxury which many immigrants in those years had never known before. The island also had a crematorium. Those with fatal illnesses often died on the island, and it is said that approximately three thousand despondent people committed suicide there after learning that they were not to be admitted.

Certain to be barred were those with contagious diseases—especially trachoma—the insane, paupers, prostitutes, and criminals. Anarchists were deported, too. It was not unusual for families to be separated for any one of these reasons.

Most common of all the stories told about Ellis Island is how some immigrants, especially Russians and Polish, would enter with one name and leave with another. Unable to understand a name as the newcomer pronounced it, the inspector would list him under a name which sounded phonetically similar and thus the immigrant would officially enter America.

Immigrants usually had about $10 when they arrived at Ellis Island. A report made in the early 1900s said that Russian Jews landed with the most money, an average of $25; and that the Italians had the least, many of them with almost nothing.

An immigrant coming in with no money, no job, and no friends faced possible deportation unless he could convince a board of examiners that he could "make it" on his own in the new country. The then-current economic conditions had much to do with how the board decided appeals.

Immigrants who were turned down by doctors or interviewers had the right to appeal to this board at Ellis Island for a final decision. With sometimes thousands of people to process in a day's time, it is not surprising that overworked immigration agents often seemed callous or indifferent to newcomers and that Ellis acquired a reputation as a "hard place."

December 17, 1900, was a typical day, with the Station receiving 2,251 arrivals from the steamers *Vincenzo Florio*, *Umbria*, and *Kaiser Wilhelm II*. With so many to be processed in one day, agents had no time for social amenities. New arrivals were herded through.

The island was a magnet for crooks and sharpies who preyed on the newcomers, most of whom knew no English and many of whom were illiterate. They were cheated on foreign exchange, sold fake citizenship certificates, and otherwise swindled and bamboozled. When President Theodore Roosevelt ordered a drastic reform at the station he was horrified to learn that the dining room didn't even bother to wash its dishes. De-

Upon arrival at Ellis Island, immigrants were interviewed and then given a physical exam by doctors. Certain to be barred were those with contagious diseases—especially trachoma— the insane, paupers, prostitutes, and criminals.

100

Children arriving at Ellis Island with contagious diseases were denied admission and sent back to their homeland. If the parents did not have the money for their own passage, they remained and the children returned alone. Parents who were not granted entry due to illness made the trip back alone leaving the children behind if they could not afford passage.

Thousands of immigrants awaiting final admittance or deportation at Ellis Island were served hot nourishing meals in the big dining room.

101

tainees ate on dirty dishes or didn't eat at all. He ousted political hacks and appointed an honest and diligent administrator, a New York lawyer named William Williams who ran the station honestly and efficiently. The same policy was followed by President Taft.

No more immigrants are processed at the port of New York now, although close to half a million legal immigrants come into the United States every year under the quotas and by special acts of Congress. Legal immigrants are now processed in American consulates in their native lands.

Today the world-famous facility in New York harbor is a national monument administered by the National Park Service.

The impressive brick buildings of the now-deserted Immigration Station may be restored and outfitted as a national museum of immigration. Plans for this are being developed by the Park Service, but preliminary estimates suggest it will take at least $100 million just to restore the buildings, which are now in a sad state of disrepair. Meanwhile, since 1976, thousands of visitors have taken the boat from Battery Park at the foot of Manhattan to the island for a guided tour of the empty buildings, and bright young guides offer a historical discourse about the role Ellis Island played in the nation's history.

At the start of each tour the guide asks how many had parents or relatives who passed through the station and always, they say, a number of hands are raised. When the guide asks what country these relatives came from, the answers are usually Russia, Rumania, Italy, Poland, Serbia, Hungary, Greece, or some other nation of Eastern Europe, for in the great tide of immigration, which Ellis Island was intended to accommodate, the majority came from Middle and Eastern Europe.

Silent, decaying, and empty, the buildings on Ellis Island today are a stark reminder of that epic era when New York was port of entry for millions of new Americans. The very emptiness of the spacious halls, with the peeling plaster, faded paint, the bare corridors, and the echoing footsteps along the tiled floors creates an

awesome atmosphere for those to whom a tour has special meaning. It is not unusual to see some older visitor drop back from the guided group and stand with eyes closed, wrapped in memory, or in the contemplation of what these rooms must have meant to parents or relatives starting a new life in America.

Top, *An immigrant coming in with no money, no job, and no friends faced deportation unless he could convince a board of examiners that he could "make it" on his own in the new country.*

米國へ入國を許さるゝ前に何人
も讀書力試驗に合格せざるべからず
されば貴方の讀書力を示す爲に
兩方の手のひらを机の上に伏せて
檢査官に貴方の行く先の地名
を告げなさい

(Japanese-Kanji.)

Every applicant for admission must demonstrate his ability to read. To prove that you can meet this test, place both hands upon the table before you, palms down, and tell the inspector in what city you expect to live.

Above, *Each immigrant was administered a literacy test during admission procedures. The applicant had to demonstrate his ability to read and comprehend either English or his own language.*

Left, *A group of hardy immigrants arrives on dock at Ellis Island after a long and arduous journey across the sea.*

Opposite, *With all their worldly belongings in bags and baskets, arrivals to Ellis Island in 1912 gaze across to Manhattan full of hopes and dreams of the future.*

THE AUGUSTUS F. SHERMAN COLLECTION

Some of the most vivid and poignant records of the great waves of immigrants entering America at the turn of the century lie in a set of 135 photographs taken by Augustus F. Sherman, Chief Clerk of the Ellis Island Station.

Sherman lives on through his photography which testifies to his compassion and artistic sensibilities, but the man behind the pictures remains in the shadows. Little is known of his life away from the Immigration Service. His associates remembered him as a kind, popular gentleman whose passion for photography never interfered with his regular duties. He joined the service in 1890 and was at Ellis Island from its inauguration in 1892. Sherman never married. His death certificate states that he came from Pennsylvania and was 59 when he died in 1925.

Thousands of men, women, and children arrived daily at Ellis Island frightened and poor but hopeful about their futures. Through Sherman's photographs the expressions of despair, hope, fear, and exhaustion that marked the faces of the new arrivals are frozen in time.

Sherman kept no surviving records apart from notations concerning countries of origin but the photographs themselves speak eloquently of the high emotion of the era.

Augustus F. Sherman

109

112

CHAPTER 8
CUNARD, COLLINS & COMPETITION

In 1845 the Postmaster General of the United States invited bids for U.S. flag mail steamship services from New York to Liverpool, Le Havre, Southampton, Bremen, and other European ports.

At this time the Post Office Department was paying foreign lines, principally Cunard, to carry the transatlantic mails, and it pricked national pride to see the American merchant marine plodding an inferior position on that most important ocean highway, the North Atlantic.

A Mr. Edward Mills of New York, a man with no prior shipping experience, submitted the low bid for a Southampton-Bremen service and was granted a subsidy of $400,000 a year for such an operation, with New York as the home port. He organized the Ocean Steam Navigation Company and contracted with the New York builders Westervelt and Mackey for two large paddlewheelers.

First to come off the ways was the S.S. *Washington*, rigged as a three-masted auxiliary bark, for no one trusted steam completely in those days and, not infrequently, it was the provision for sail that brought a ship in when cylinders cracked, drive shafts broke, or coal ran out. She made her first voyage in June of 1847, with 120 passengers. The *Hermann* followed her a few months later, logging the run to Southampton in eleven days, twenty-one hours. After some ten years on the North Atlantic ferry, both ships were sold for use in the Pacific. The *Hermann* was lost with approximately two hun-

dred lives near Japan in 1869.

The New York and Havre Steam Navigation Company began operations with the New York-built ships *Franklin* and *Humboldt*, which started running in 1850 and 1851, respectively. They did a fair ten and a half knots on the run between New York and Le Havre, France, but had short lives, *Humboldt* being wrecked on the coast of Nova Scotia in 1853 and *Franklin* on Long Island in 1854. There was enough of the *Franklin* still visible during World War II that the navy used the wreck for target practice.

Coincident with these ventures was an attempt to establish an American flag steamship service between New York and Liverpool by Charles H. Marshall and Company, owners of the Black Ball Line. They had William H. Webb of New York build the paddlewheeler *United States*, a very heavily constructed vessel that had no less than five layers of huge pine keelsons, plus a clipper bow and four masts for auxiliary sail. She had accommodations for 148 passengers and four hundred tons of cargo.

As with all of her kind, much potential cargo space was used for coal bunkers because the inefficient engines of that time gulped coal at a great rate. The *United States* carried eight hundred tons and burned about fifty tons a day.

The ship lost money, was unable to lure passengers from Cunard, and made only a few trips. The Black Ball Line sold her to the German government for conversion into a warship; they, in turn, sold her to the British for transport duties in the Crimean War, and when this task was done she became the flagship of a new and short-lived passenger service from Ireland to New York.

The advent of American competition prompted Cunard to ask for—and receive—a substantial boost in his mail subsidy so that he could add New York to his schedule. If the *Washington* and *Hermann* did nothing else, they speeded Cunard's entry into the port of New York and thus provided the Cunard organization's dependable service on the North Atlantic ferry for a century to come. With Cunard here, it was inevitable that others would follow.

A quiet, reserved man of consid-

115

In 1840 Samuel Cunard formed the North Atlantic Royal Mail Steam Packet Company, later to become the famous Cunard Steamship Company and the Cunard Line.

erable imagination and business acumen, Samuel Cunard, a Halifax shipowner, appreciated the possibilities of ocean steam navigation and won a transatlantic mail subsidy from the British Post Office despite the fact that several competitors already had steamships in the Atlantic service.

In 1840 he formed the North American Royal Mail Steam Packet Company, later to become the famous Cunard Steamship Company and the Cunard Line. For the new service he ordered four ships from builders on the Clyde: the *Britannia*, *Acadia*, *Caledonia*, and *Columbia*. With these he established his regular mail service from Liverpool to Halifax and Boston, a city which received his ships with tremendous enthusiasm and with visions of becoming the most important port in North America.

It did not take Cunard long to realize that the fast-growing New York metropolis should be the western terminus for his Atlantic operations and, when the *Washington* and *Hermann* entered the North Atlantic run, Cunard ordered four more ships especially for a New York service. They were close to being sister ships, all about eighteen hundred tons, with engines developing two thousand horsepower for a speed of ten knots, and with accommodations for 140 passengers.

The first sailing of a Cunard ship for New York was made by the ten-knot, 248-foot *Hibernia* in December of 1847.

By 1850 a British paper could describe the Cunard Company as having "a magnificent fleet preeminent among ocean steamers." The claim could hardly be disputed, but contenders were soon to come along.

In 1847 the United States Post Office had again invited bids for a transatlantic mail service, the emphasis being on a New York to Liverpool run to compete directly with Cunard. The winner was E. K. Collins, a New Yorker with long and successful experience in ship owning and operating. Collins had inaugurated the first line of New York-New Orleans packets in 1832, and in 1835 had started the successful Dramatic Line of transatlantic sailing packets out of New York.

Collins's contract with the government called for the construction of five fast steamers to maintain a regular service to the United Kingdom, with a subsidy of $385,000 a year. The signing of this contract was aptly described at the time as "a contest with England for the supremacy of ocean steam navigation." As it turned out, only four of the specified five ships were built; construction costs were much higher than expected, and the government agreed to eliminate one vessel from the contract.

Collins incorporated the U.S. Mail Steamship Company, better known as the Collins Line, and opened what was to become one of the boldest— and most tragic—chapters in American maritime history.

The Collins fleet comprised the steamers *Atlantic*, *Pacific*, *Arctic*, and *Baltic*, all constructed in New York. These sister ships were twenty-eight-hundred-ton paddlewheelers measuring three hundred feet overall, with a forty-five-foot beam. They introduced a number of amenities in ocean travel, including separate bathrooms, a smoking room for men, and steam heat in the public rooms. The main saloon was sixty-seven feet long and twenty feet wide, with satinwood, holly, and rosewood paneling, and with much bronze, stained glass, and paintings in the decor.

Atlantic was the first to put to sea, leaving for Liverpool on April 27, 1850, with a hundred passengers and the mails. Drift ice along the Grand Banks of Newfoundland and generally bad weather prevented her from doing her best speed, but she made up for this coming west, logging a passage of ten days, sixteen hours to New York. She beat the best Cunard time by twelve hours.

Atlantic was followed into service by *Pacific*, *Arctic*, and *Baltic*.

An account of the departure of the *Arctic* on March 20, 1852, was written by a passenger, John S. C. Abbott, and appeared in *Hunt's Merchants Magazine*. Here are some excerpts from that story:

At precisely seven minutes after 12 o'clock today, the steamer Arctic left New York for Liverpool. Our whole ship's company, passengers and crew, amounted to one hun-

The American steamship Washington, *rigged as a three-masted auxiliary bark, made her first voyage in June of 1847.*

Until the 1850s the U.S. Post Office Department was paying foreign lines, principally Cunard, to carry the transatlantic mails from New York to Liverpool, Le Havre, Southampton, Bremen, and other European ports. A British paper described the Cunard Company as having "a magnificent fleet preeminent among ocean steamers."

dred and eighty. The day was clear and cold. A strong north wind swept from the snow-clad hills over the rough bay. Icicles were pendent from the paddle wheels and the spray was freezing upon the decks. As the majestic steamship left the wharf, the crowd assembled there gave three cheers and two guns were fired from on board. With the engines in active play, and our sails pressed by the fresh breeze, we pressed rapidly down the narrows.

Transatlantic travel is undertaken almost casually today, but not in those early days of the Atlantic ferry. Passengers were all too conscious of the hazards to be met from storms, fire, and collision—and of the many ships that had run aground in trying to make a landfall on a fog-shrouded coast.

Author Abbott observed:

"No one can thus leave his home, to traverse weary leagues of land and sea, without emotion. Images of the loved, who may never be seen again, will rush upon the mind.

After some time in his cabin, where he had second thoughts about this ocean voyage, he returned to the deck.

118

It was swept by a bleak wintry wind. Taking a stand in the shelter of the enormous smoke pipe, so vast that twenty men could with perfect convenience cluster under its lee, we watched the receding shores.

At half past three o'clock the gong summoned us to a sumptuous dinner. Again returning to the deck we watched the dim outline of the land until it disappeared beneath the horizon of the sea. At seven o'clock we were again summoned to the tea-table. Returning to the deck, we found dark and gloomy night brooding over the ocean. The wind, though piercingly cold, was fresh and fair. The stars shone brilliantly through black masses of clouds. Our ship rose and fell as it plowed its way over the majestic billows of the Atlantic.

It didn't take long for the Collins and Cunard ships to begin competing intensely for the fastest passages across the "big pond."

In the contest for speed between Collins and Cunard, the Collins ships were dramatically dominant. In 1851, the *Pacific* set a record from New York to Liverpool of nine days, twenty

hours, ten minutes; and in 1851 the *Baltic* crossed from Liverpool to New York in nine days, eighteen hours.

In August of 1852, the *Baltic* set a new record from Liverpool to New York of nine days, thirteen hours. This was to be the last blue-ribbon record crossing by an American flag liner until the American superliner *United States* shattered all records a century later, in July of 1952.

There was an even more intense competition to provide the utmost in luxury and passenger comfort. Cu-

E.K. Collins, a New Yorker with long and successful experience in ship owning and operating, incorporated the U.S. Mail Steamship Company, better known as the Collins Line, and opened what was to become one of the boldest and most tragic chapters in American maritime history.

In August of 1852, the U.S. mail steamship Baltic set a new record from Liverpool to New York of nine days, thirteen hours. This was to be the last blue-ribbon record crossing by an American flag liner until the American superliner United States shattered all records a century later.

Paddlewheeler Arctic, one of four Collins Line sister ships, introduced steam heat in the public rooms, a smoking room for men, and the luxury of separate bathrooms.

nard countered Collins with its *Arabia*, which typified the increasing size of the Atlantic liners. She had accommodations for 180 passengers and 750 tons of cargo. She boasted a nursery and a library.

In 1854 the *Arctic*, commanded by Capt. James Luce, collided with the small French steamer *Vesta* in a fog sixty miles south of Cape Race. Concern was for the little freighter, which was soon lost to sight in a fog bank, but before long it was apparent that the *Arctic* herself was the ship in dire peril. Water poured in through the shattered planking faster than the pumps could handle it. Captain Luce headed at full speed for Cape Race, but never arrived. The ship went down with the loss of 318 passengers and crew. Among them were Collins's wife and two children, returning from a vacation in England.

As if this were not calamity enough, the *Pacific* left Liverpool for New York in January of 1856, but failed to arrive. It was assumed that she hit an iceberg and went down with all hands.

The ship had sailed about the same time as the Cunard steamer *Persia* left from Liverpool for New York. *Persia* hit an iceberg near Newfoundland and stove in her bow, but limped safely into port. This ship in 1856 became the blue ribbon queen of the Atlantic, with a crossing from New York to Liverpool of nine days, one hour, and forty-five minutes.

Burdened and saddened by both personal and business tragedies, Collins nevertheless persisted in his attempt to make the American flag dominant on the Atlantic, ordering the *Adriatic* from the George Steers yard in New York.

It was a bold and gallant effort. The penultimate wooden paddlewheeler to be built for the Atlantic ferry, *Adriatic* was 351 feet long, with a normal beam of 50 feet, and a beam over the paddle boxes of 79. She carried 316 passengers in first class and 60 in second, with appointments far more luxurious than any other ship afloat.

Adriatic made a ten-day eastward crossing on her maiden voyage in November of 1857, not usually a month for setting speed records on the stormy North Atlantic. No sooner, however, was the *Adriatic* winning

plaudits on both sides of the ocean for her speed and luxurious accommodations than Congress cut the Collins mail subsidy in half. By 1858 the company was out of business and its ships were sold at public auction in New York. *Atlantic* and *Baltic* became transports during the Civil War, the latter vessel eventually being de-engined and converted to sail. She was active until 1880.

The last transatlantic paddlewheel liner was the *Vanderbilt*, constructed for Cornelius Vanderbilt's attempt to regain American supremacy on the

Atlantic with his Vanderbilt European Line to New York, Southampton, and Le Havre. Completed in 1857, this ship joined his fast steamers *North Star* and *Ariel* on a service that was extended to include Bremen. The *Vanderbilt* was a fast ship, making a trip from Southampton to New York in nine days, five hours. These ships might have been the nucleus for another serious American challenge to Cunard, but any dreams that Vanderbilt entertained for this were changed by the Civil War.

America's bid for supremacy on the Atlantic ended with the last Collins Line sailing in 1858. The Civil War soon diverted the nation's interests and resources, and after the war came a period of western expansion and preoccupation with internal industrial growth. The sea held little interest for Americans and what there was of a deep-sea merchant marine was manned largely by foreign seamen. Not until World War I did the nation again turn to the sea with enthusiasm.

While increasing competition between the United States and Great

Britain for passenger ship dominance made the North Atlantic an international maritime arena in the period before the Civil War, probably the most dramatic event on the Atlantic ferry was the appearance of a nautical colossus, the *Great Eastern*.

Colossus — leviathan — giant of the sea. These were appropriate appellations for a vessel that excited the wonderment of the world, attracted thousands of visitors to New York when she docked here for the first time, and has fascinated maritime writers ever since.

An 1868 sketch of the Adriatic, which was built for the Collins Line by the George Steers yard, and was the penultimate wooden paddlewheeler to be built for the Atlantic ferry. She carried 316 passengers in first class and 60 in second, with appointments far more luxurious than any other ship afloat.

The last transatlantic paddlewheel liner was the Vanderbilt, constructed for Cornelius Vanderbilt's attempt to regain American supremacy on the Atlantic with his Vanderbilt European Line to New York, Southampton, and Le Havre. This photo of Vanderbilt was taken by famed Civil War photographer Matthew Brady.

Larger than any liner launched until the turn of the century, *Great Eastern* was conceived by the engineering genius Isambard Kingdom Brunel, well described by one biographer as "the most daring engineer of the 19th century." He had to be a daring engineer, as well as a super-salesman, to design such a ship, obtain the financing, and successfully complete a monster that required materials and components on such a grand scale.

Brunel conceived *Great Eastern* as a cargo-passenger liner on the run between the United Kingdom and Australia; a ship large enough to make the voyage without stopping for bunkers en route and, if need be, to make a round trip without refueling.

Shipowners thought Brunel must be daffy—or dreaming—when he revealed the dimensions of his colossus. But when the keel was laid at the new Scott Russell yard near London, they learned that it was no fantasy. The vessel was to be 692 feet overall, with a beam of 83 feet, and a prodigious width, over the paddle boxes, of 120 feet. She was to be of 27,384 tons displacement.

122

Brunel intended to make her the safest ship afloat, with both transverse and longitudinal bulkheads and a double bottom. There were six masts and a vast spread of sail for use when winds were fair, for additional speed or in case of an emergency.

There would hardly be any need for the ship to use sail to reach port, however, for there were two systems of propulsion, both paddlewheels and propeller. Before the introduction of twin screws in Atlantic liners, one propeller was insufficient to move the great iron mass at the desired fifteen knots, so the tried-and-true paddlewheel was incorporated, too. There were separate power plants for screw and paddles.

Statistically, the ship was mind boggling. She carried ten anchors, the larger ones weighing more than fifteen thousand pounds each. The propeller shaft was 160 feet long. It took six boilers to supply steam for the propeller engine and four for the paddle engine. The bunkers held thirteen thousand tons of coal, enough to fill two average-size tramp ships of the 1920 era.

There were accommodations for eight hundred passengers in first class, two thousand in second class, and twelve hundred in third class, plus a crew of four hundred. For a passenger liner, this was a very low ratio of crew to passengers, who, apparently, were not expected to receive much personal attention.

The owners went broke before *Great Eastern* was completed, and refinancing had to be arranged. So ponderous was the great ship that it took three months and an expenditure of $500,000 to launch her, which caused another financial crisis and another refinancing.

Before her launching it was decided to enter the ship into the transatlantic trade instead of to Australia, and when the leviathan finally dropped her lines and stood down the Thames for her maiden voyage on June 17, 1860, it was toward the port of New York that she headed. What other port, the owners reasoned, could financially support such a huge ship and help recoup their endangered investment?

Colossus—leviathan—giant of the sea. These were appropriate appellations for the Great Eastern, a vessel that excited the wonderment of the world, attracted thousands of visitors to New York when she docked here for the first time, and has fascinated maritime writers ever since.

For months the port had been expecting the *Great Eastern*, and the numerous delays had made New Yorkers wonder if the ship was real or if it would ever appear.

In an editorial entitled "The Coming Monster," the New York *Times* of June 7, 1860, said:

The sweet uses of adversity have found a fortunate illustration in the history of the Great Eastern. There is very little reason to doubt that had the great ship visited America last autumn [1859] the visitation would have resulted in a very serious popular disappointment. On no topic had sensation writing so exhausted itself. The dimensions of the monster, its ponderous machinery, its stupendous shafts and wheels and screw, its vast vistas of saloons, its steadiness, its speed, its manageability had all been the subject of exaggerated statements and of pictorial effort which far exceeded all possibility of realization."

Be that as it may, the *Times* went all-out editorially when the "monster" did appear. The entire front page of the edition for June 29 was devoted to "The Great Eastern—A Complete Account of the Trip—from our special correspondent." Most of an inside page also was exclusively *Great Eastern*.

Word spread like wildfire that the "monster" had finally arrived. It seemed as though ditches, drays, desks, lathes, kitchens, and counting-houses had been deserted and that everyone had turned out to see the "maritime giant."

Said the *Times*:

No description could do justice to the scene of animation and enthusiasm which surrounded the steamer as she approached the Narrows. Steamers of all sizes and descriptions swarmed about her, crowded with ladies and gentlemen cheering and waving their salutations. The yacht squadron was out in force... conspicuous in the brilliant procession, darting gracefully in and out like white-winged birds, about the moving leviathan.

The U.S. Revenue cutter *Harriet Lane* brought the Collector of the port alongside, fired a welcoming salute, and was saluted in return while her crew stared in awe up the mountainlike side of the incoming leviathan.

The Staten Island ferryboats were jammed, as was the Staten Island shore, with thousands straining for a look at the huge visitor as she came through the Narrows.

According to the *Times*:

At a few minutes after 3 P.M., the Great Eastern was dimly discerned in the foggy distance of the Lower Bay. An hour passed before she had finished with the official greetings and business of arrival, finally steaming through the Narrows and into the Bay...proceeding rapidly up the harbor.

With an uncontrollable impulse, a shout arose from the vast crowd on the Quarantine grounds and Bern Gardens. Opposite Fort Hamilton she stopped and the fort gave her a rousing salute of cannon.

As she passed the shores of the Island [Governors], with the smoke of her cannon mantling about her, and partially obscuring her magnificent proportions, she announced herself as the leviathan of the Bay....Spectators were madly enthusiastic in their praise.

The Battery, the piers along the North River, and the housetops as far as the eye could reach were filled with spectators....It was a continual ovation.

There was one note of distraction. Visitors to the ship, and especially seamen, were surprised at the "neglected condition of her decks, which appeared as though they had neither been cleaned, scraped, holystoned, or varnished since she was launched.... There is a generally dirty appearance," said a *Times* reporter, "about the whole outside of the ship."

Perhaps the ship was just too huge for good housekeeping with a small crew. But this did not keep her from becoming the marvel of the day—a floating Barnum, Bailey, and Ringling Brothers extravaganza that was to amaze thousands of city folks and thousands more of their country cousins who poured in by all manner of conveyance to see this floating marvel.

The ship was docked at the only place that could accommodate such a monstrosity—a three-block-long lumber pier at West 11th Street.

The owners tried to recoup some of the financial loss of the first Atlantic crossing by turning the ship into a showboat and by running excursions.

All kinds of hawkers and peddlers set up shop in the area, selling everything from lemonade to beer and oysters. After a few days of primping and scrubbing, *Great Eastern* was open to public visiting at a dollar a head. Despite this stiff assessment, more than fifteen hundred awestruck New Yorkers paid their way on board that first day, July 3.

The British visitors were unacquainted with an American accoutrement known as the spittoon, and with the unpleasant American proclivity for chewing tobacco and shooting a mouthful whenever it was convenient to do so. Ship's officers were horrified at the amount of tobacco juice expelled aboard ship that first day and prepared for the influx on July 4 by liberal doses of sand, which, they hoped, the American visitors would use for lack of spittoons.

More than two thousand toured *Great Eastern* on Independence Day and carried away so many souvenirs in the way of anything removable that representatives of the owners wondered if the money made from admissions would pay for the vandalism. When admission price was lowered to fifty cents, a horde of sightseers all but sank the ship.

After a month or so of showboating, there were two excursions, the first to Cape May and return, and the second to Baltimore. Two thousand tickets were sold for the first jaunt. The ship ran out of food, and those who had to sleep on deck were sprinkled with soot from the ship's five huge funnels, the largest number in Atlantic history. On the Baltimore trip President Buchanan was as awed and amazed as the rawest country bumpkin.

By the time the *Great Eastern* left New York for home, with a handful of passengers and a meager cargo, there were no ovations and no fanfare. New Yorkers, it seemed, had become indifferent to bigness.

Bigness in ships, however, was to become commonplace for the world's largest port in the years to come. New York was to become the western terminus for the biggest ever built.

Larger than any liner launched until the turn of the century, Great Eastern was conceived by the engineering genius Isambard Kingdom Brunel, well described by one biographer as "the most daring engineer of the 19th century."

The Great Eastern was conceived as a cargo-passenger liner on the run between the United Kingdom and Australia, a ship large enough to make the voyage without stopping for bunkers en route and, if need be, to make a round trip without refueling. Shipowners thought Brunel must be daffy—or dreaming—when he revealed the dimensions of this colossus. But when the keel was laid at the new Scott Russell yard near London, they learned that it was no fantasy. The vessel was to be 692 feet overall, with a beam of 83 feet, and a prodigious width, over the paddle boxes, of 120 feet.

CHAPTER 9
THE LUXURY
LINERS

Sirius and *Great Western* started the century-long race along the North Atlantic and it lasted until there were no longer any of the great sea queens left to compete.

Almost from the beginnings of steam travel on the western ocean, competition for the speediest passages between Europe and New York transcended competition between companies to become a matter of national pride. It was a race between governments as well as ships and steamship lines. The prize was national prestige.

This speed race created the great North Atlantic liner, the acme of marine engineering and big-ship architecture in steam, as the clipper ship was in sail. The North Atlantic liner was designed, built, and navigated to carry people from Europe to America in speed and comfort, and America, for the most part, meant New York. These majestic sea queens were married to Manhattan. The largest, fastest, and most luxurious of them made New York their destination on this side of the "big pond."

The success of Cunard piqued America's national pride and the result was the enterprising but short-lived Collins Line. Many years passed before the United States, whose maritime interests and commitments fluctuated greatly between the Civil War and World War I, made a serious bid for a prominent place on the North Atlantic ferry. Meanwhile, the race was mainly a contest between British companies, then between the

British and the Germans. After World War I it was a multinational contest, with British, Germans, French, and Italians in a seesaw rivalry for honors, the United States making only a feeble effort among the more ambitious competitors. But it was an American ship, the liner *United States*, that finally became the fastest passenger ship ever to ply the North Atlantic and fly the blue ribbon, the honorary symbol of speed supremacy on the North Atlantic. It was an almost anti-climactic triumph in the fading hours of the North American passenger trade.

Luxury on the North Atlantic came about from the intense competition among the various lines to entice the cream of the travel trade.

When Charles Dickens came to America on the *Britannia* in 1842 he described his stateroom as being so small "it would hardly hold my baggage...had a hard, slab-like seat covered with hair, while the bunks, of which there were two, boasted a very flat quilt covering, a very thin mattress, spread like a surgical plaster, on a most inaccessible shelf."

A radical improvement in passenger accommodations was initiated with the sailing of the first Collins liner, the *Atlantic*, in 1850. Collins introduced many of the amenities of comfort and style that became standard features on ships yet to come. His vessels featured larger cabins and were furnished with rich carpets, marble-topped tables, expensively upholstered chairs and sofas, a profusion of gilded mirrors and other costly ornamentation not exceeded in the best hotels.

In *McClure's* magazine of March, 1895, an anonymous writer gave a colorful account of "Life Aboard an Ocean Flyer," the *Furst Bismarck*, flagship of the Hamburg-American fleet. He was impressed by the seemingly endless broad sweep of decks, "where swarms of people wander as comfortably as on city streets...by the wide doorways, opening into great halls and grand staircases descending into vast depths...the hugeness and magnificence of the vast, iron-hulled cavern."

Passengers on the *Furst Bismarck* were fed in princely style. And while, as on all the North Atlantic flyers,

127

The Europa, *which won the blue ribbon by cutting time on the westward run to four days, seventeen hours, and six minutes, is given a traditional launch from her dock.*

most cabins were fairly small and shared by more than one person, passengers had the free use of "all the rich luxuriousness of dining and smoking and music saloons, of library and writing rooms."

The *Furst Bismarck* had "a noble dining hall... with ornate ceilings and generous mahogany tables surrounded by comfortable chairs." Broad divans ran the length of the hall. Port holes were draped in silk and lace, while "chandeliers gave forth a flood of tempered light."

The chef had a score of cooks and "an army of carvers and scullions." The chief steward had eighty-four men and women to assist him. There were three separate and complete kitchens and dining rooms for each of the first, second, and third classes.

The traveler soon found that "everything about the ship has a true German military air. The stewards file in regular order and when a change is made all march out keeping time to the band and making, with their neat uniforms and white gloves, a goodly sight to see."

128 In 1891 a North Atlantic traveler reported that "no well-ordered vessel is without a library, a piano, and an organ." At this time North German Lloyd introduced the ship's band, which played for the first-cabin clientele at dinner and for a concert on deck at night, weather permitting.

Each line was eager to offer some new attraction for the Atlantic trade. In the 1890s the French Line inaugurated the "Captain's dinner" on the last night before arrival, a gala affair with champagne, music, and endless toasts to America, France, officers, crew, and lovely ladies.

The *Olympic* of the White Star Line, biggest ship in the world when she was launched in 1910, introduced the first swimming pool, or "plunge" as it was called. More sedate passengers were shocked at mixed bathing and some of the daring bathing attire.

Aboard Cunard ships on Sundays the captain read the Church of England service attired in full uniform, flanked by his officers, also in formal dress—a bit of pageantry that impressed travelers for its religious solemnity and dignity. By now, all the liners were celebrating patriotic occasions such as the Fourth of July and

royal birthdays. These were occasions to dress ship, with pennants and bunting whipping in the breeze fore and aft.

Those recovering from mal-de-mer could stay in their cabins and the room steward would call half a dozen times a day to ask what they wanted to eat—crackers, bouillon, tea, or dainty tea sandwiches to tempt an uneasy palate. For those who liked to stay on deck in the fresh air, the deck steward was always on hand to bring an excellent dinner without extra charge.

The regular dinner on *Furst Bis-*

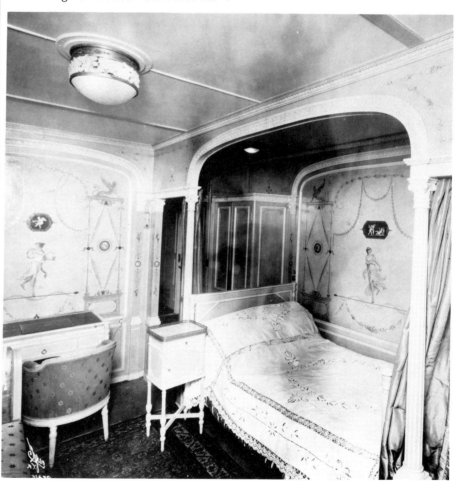

Typical of the elegant accommodations available on luxury liners at the turn of the century is this suite aboard the SS France.

marck consisted of from seven to ten courses and took a full two hours to enjoy. In addition to the regular meals there was 8 P.M. tea, with sandwiches, and at 9 P.M. a band concert with Hamburg beer and pretzels.

Ship decor followed the changes in fashion and style, but there wasn't much over the years that the companies could do to make travel more lavish for their first-cabin customers until the introduction of elevators, moving pictures, dance orchestras, beauty shops, and swimming pools.

A bill of fare from a Cunard liner of the 1890s evidences the elaborate table provided for first-class travelers. Second-cabin people ate bountifully, though less elaborately. A traveler who wanted to get his money's worth could hardly make the voyage without letting out a notch or two in his belt.

Soups
Turtle and Spring Chicken

Fish
Scotch salmon
with sauce Hollandaise

Life aboard ship was luxurious, with little to do but dine, dance, and drink. A luncheon menu from the Laconia testifies to the culinary delights that were available.

Luncheon.

.★.★.★.★

Herrings Le Sardine   Norwegian Anchovies   Tomatoes—Vinaigrette
Westphalia Ham   Table Celery   Potted Shrimps
Salami, Lyon, Liver and Cervelet Sausage
Salade Russe   Egg Mayonnaise
Queen and Stuffed Olives
SPECIAL: SAUMON D'ECOSSE FUME

Consomme Julienne   Potage Marigny

Fried Fillets of Plaice—Remoulade Sauce   Lobster—Mayonnaise

To order—Fines Herbes or Nantes Omelettes—(10 minutes)

SPECIAL DISH:
Pepper Steak—Manhattan

Roast Quarters of Lamb—Mint Sauce
French Beans   Dressed Cabbage
Baked Plain, Mashed and Lyonnaise Potatoes

Spaghetti—Neapolitaine

TO ORDER FROM GRILL (15 minutes)
Spring Chicken—French Fried Potatoes   Calf's Liver and Bacon

COLD BUFFET—
Roast Sirloin & Ribs of Beef   York Ham   Roast Lamb
Galantine of Turkey   Rolled Ox Tongue
Veal and Ham Pie   Pressed Beef

Salad—Lettuce   Tomatoes   Beetroot   Allemande
Thousand Island, Russian, French, Roquefort and Mayonnaise Dressing

Tapioca Pudding   Fresh Rhubarb Pie
Ice Cream and Wafers

CHEESE Stilton   Kraft   Cheshire   Gruyere   St. Ivel
Gorgonzola   Roquefort   Young American   Chilvern Cottage
American   Camembert   Pasteurized   Cheddar

Dessert
Tea   Coffee

CUNARD

Entrees
Blanquettes de Poulet
aux Champignons
Filets de Boeuf à la Bordelaise
Cailles sur Canapés

Joints
Saddle of mutton and jelly
Beef and Yorkshire pudding
York ham and Champagne Sauce

Poultry
Roast Turkey and Truffles
Spring Ducklings

Vegetables
Pommes de Terre Duchesse
Asparagus   Potatoes   Parsnips

Sweets
International Pudding
Rhubarb with Custard
Strawberry Jam   Tartlets
Sandwiches

Pastry
Genoese Pastry
Marlborough Pudding
Gooseberry Soufflés
Lemon Cream

Desserts
Seville Oranges   Hamburg Grapes
English Walnuts   Madeira Nuts
Cantaloupes
Café Noir

A typical dinner in second class would include soup, fish, mutton, roast beef, baked potatoes, mashed turnips, rice pudding, apple tarts, pastries, biscuits, cheese, tea and coffee, and a variety of fruits for "nibbling."

A German liner of these days stocking up in New York for the eastward crossing would lay in a supply of pineapples, plums, cherries, strawberries, raspberries, watermelons, oranges, peaches, apples, pears, and muskmelons. All pastry-making was done on board and some of the finest chefs in Europe were hired for this baking.

In 1907, Laurence Sperry, writing in the magazine *World's Work*, described a voyage from Hamburg to New York on the German liner *Amerika*: "From the moment he [the traveler] leaves Europe, nothing will occur to disturb the illusion that he is living in a perfectly appointed hotel."

V oyagers with fat pocketbooks could enjoy an entire apartment, with bedrooms, parlor, bath and toilet, en suite. The suite would be furnished with brass beds, mahogany tables, chairs and desks in rich designs, silk and damask draperies, and velvet carpets, along with electric heaters and reading lights and even electric curling-iron heaters for the lady. A luxurious suite would cost from $600 to $1500 depending on its location and the size of the ship.

Besides its regular dining rooms, the *Amerika* had a number of restaurants. Its café featured an Austrian string band. There was a gymnasium, a massage room, and a smoking room "modelled in the style of the hunting room of an Elizabethan manor house ...the walls of solid oak, hand-carved." A fire of real logs burned in the fireplace. Waiters stood by to supply anything that might be wanted; literally, from "soup to nuts."

"Throughout the vessel," Sperry wrote, "there are grand staircases, libraries with thousands of volumes, cozy corners, music rooms; everything that could occur to the mind of the most exacting."

It is hard to tell from old news stories just when the term *blue ribbon* first came to be mentioned in connection with the fastest ship. But competition for this honor might well be dated from the time that the Inman Line's new *City of Paris* captured speed honors from Cunard's S.S. *Russia* in 1867. The *Paris's* record was broken, in turn, by another Inman liner, the *City of Brussels*, the first ship to cross in less than eight days. In 1872 a new competitor for the blue ribbon, the White Star Line, appeared on the scene and became supreme with its liner *Adriatic*.

Germany's most determined bid for the blue ribbon came with the launching of the *Kaiser Wilhelm der Grosse* of North German Lloyd in 1897. This huge four-stacker set a new westbound record in 1898 by steaming from Southampton to Sandy Hook in five days, seventeen hours, and twenty-seven minutes.

While the Germans were sharing the blue ribbon among a succession of great ships, Cunard countered with two of the most famous liners ever to ply the Atlantic. They were the illustrious *Mauretania* and her sister-ship, the ill-fated *Lusitania*, sunk by a German submarine off the Irish coast on May 7, 1915, with a loss of 1,198 passengers and crew. Both ships had the newly developed turbine engines in place of the traditional reciprocating engines.

L usitania took the blue ribbon from the Germans on her second voyage in October of 1907, crossing from Queenstown to New York—2,780 miles—in four days, nineteen hours, fifty-two minutes, at an average speed of 23.99 knots.

Fifty thousand patriotic Britons cheered *Mauretania* off from Liverpool on her maiden voyage in November of 1907, with a full passenger load and $10 million in gold bullion from the Bank of England to the United States Treasury. Heavy gales prevented a record crossing, but she claimed the blue ribbon on her return from New York to Queenstown in four days, twenty-two hours, twenty-nine minutes. On her maiden voyage, 324 firemen and coal passers fed nine hundred tons of coal into her furnaces every twenty-four hours. Taking speed honors was expensive in manpower and fuel consumption.

After jousting with *Lusitania* for a year or so, *Mauretania* remained the speed queen of the North Atlantic until beaten by the German liner *Bremen* in 1929. During World World I, *Mauretania* carried more than thirty thousand troops from New York to Liverpool and repatriated some twenty thousand after the war.

Of all the luxury liners few were more beloved of travelers than *Mauretania*. This touching salute to her was written by her captain, Sir Arthur Rostron, when she made her last trip—to the wreckers in Scotland:

"She gave of her best, served the Cunard Company well, was an honor and credit to her builders, to her owners and to Britain, was loved by all who ever served in her and admired by all who crossed in her."

The great *Mauretania*, considered by many to be the most illustrious of all the speed queens, held the blue ribbon for no less than twenty-one years. That a ship could maintain such a record even in her older days is not only a tribute to her builders, owners, seamen, and engineers but emphasizes the relatively slim margin of

Germany's most determined bid for the blue ribbon came with the launching of the Kaiser Wilhelm der Grosse of North German Lloyd in 1897. In this photograph the ship's crew undergoes preparation for lifeboat drill.

Captain of the Kronprinz Wilhelm stands at the helm of the North German Lloyd owned liner.

advantage that competitors were able to squeeze out of ships and engines in the heyday of this dramatic ocean rivalry.

White Star's answer to the *Mauretania* and *Lusitania* were the sister ships *Olympic, Titanic,* and *Britannic.* They were four-funneled monsters measuring 883 feet overall, with triple screws that gave them a speed of twenty-three knots. *Titanic,* as any reader of sealore well knows, hit an iceberg on her maiden voyage and sank on the night of April 14, 1912, with the loss of 815 passengers and 688 of her crew.

Titanic's sister ship, the 45,000-ton *Olympic,* was the largest ship in the world when she visited New York in 1911, but she never attained the blue ribbon. The 48,000-ton *Britannic* never had a chance to show what she could do on the Atlantic. She went into war service as a hospital ship soon after completion in 1915 and had a very brief career, being sunk by a mine in the Aegean Sea in 1916.

Olympic figured in another Atlantic tragedy when she rammed and sank the Nantucket lightship in May of 1934. She served as a troopship in World War I, ferrying thousands of Yanks to the European war zone, and was finally broken up in 1935.

The 54,000-ton German liner *Vaterland* of Hamburg America Line was tied up in New York on her maiden voyage soon after the outbreak of World War I and was extensively sabotaged by her caretaker crew being commandeered by the U.S. government in 1917. Repaired, and renamed *Leviathan,* she became a troop transport and carried more than 100,000 American fighting men to England and France. Put into the Atlantic liner run after postwar conversion, *Leviathan* never won the blue ribbon, but made many fast passages and had a steady following among Americans for whom luxury and American cuisine were more important than top speed.

Laid up in 1934 as unprofitable, this grand old lady of the liner lanes ended her career at the hands of Scottish ship breakers in 1938.

The greatest of all the French contenders, the magnificent *Normandie,* broke all records on the Atlantic ferry in June of 1935 when she sped across the western ocean in four days, three hours, and fourteen minutes. Measuring more than one thousand feet overall, she became the largest of all the blue ribbon queens. Her funnels were 160 feet around, larger than the overall length of the pioneer Atlantic steamship *Savannah. Normandie's* main dining room was three hundred feet long and three decks high. She probably had a greater ratio of crew to passengers than any other passenger ship anywhere: 1,350 crew for 1,972 paying guests.

The Atlantic speed queens were received with enthusiastic welcomes in their "second home port" of New York, regardless of politics or nationality. The city's feeling for the *Normandie* and for her "sisters of the sea" was expressed in this editorial in the *Herald Tribune* of June 4, 1935.

It is a pleasure to welcome this queen of floating palaces and congratulate her makers and owners and the nation whose flag she flies on her beauty and her might. New York is by no means unmindful of the flattery of her presence, which is

White Star Line sister ships Titanic and Olympic tower majestically above their builders' heads. These four-funneled monsters measured 883 feet overall, with triple screws that gave them a speed of twenty-three knots. Scene in the Harland & Wolf Shipyards in Belfast, 1910.

The mighty Mauretania, queen of the North Atlantic, held the blue ribbon for no less than twenty-one years.

133

simply one more proof that no matter where the latest thing in liners may originate, it enters the service of this port.

Normandie burned and sank in New York harbor in World War II, and, after being raised in a multi-million-dollar salvage operation, she was written off as unusable for further service and sold for a paltry $161,000. She cost $60 million to build, the most expensive of all the blue ribbon contenders up to that time.

Queen Mary was not only Britain's answer to French speed supremacy but an ambitious means of providing work for British shipbuilders during the worldwide economic depression of the 1930s. She eclipsed the *Normandie*, making the run from Bishop Rock to Ambrose lightship in four days and twenty-seven minutes at an average speed of 30.14 knots.

For those who wonder why so many hundreds of millions of dollars were invested in a very small number of ships to compete for a symbolic and often ephemeral honor, this description of the *Queen Mary's* departure from Southampton for her

Right, *View of the USS* Lafayette, *formerly the* Normandie, *as smoke rose from her hull and deck February 9, 1942. Some of her workmen were reported trapped between the blazing decks of the big ship.*

The largest ship in the world, the French liner Normandie, *which on her maiden voyage across the Atlantic broke all records, is pictured pulling into her dock in New York City, June 3, 1935. The Atlantic speed queens were received with enthusiastic welcomes in their "second home port" of New York, regardless of politics or nationality.*

134

Rudolf Valentino posed for this photograph aboard the Leviathan in 1925. Put into the Atlantic liner run after postwar conversion, Leviathan never won the blue ribbon, but had a steady following among Americans for whom luxury and American cuisine were more important than top speed.

Center, USS Lafayette undergoes salvage operations after she burned and sank in New York harbor during World War II.

Bottom, Steaming up the North River in New York, the USS Leviathan returns from France with 8,000 troops on December 16, 1918.

maiden voyage to New York provides one answer. From an Associated Press report in the New York *Herald Tribune* of May 28, 1936:

> At 3:45 P.M. the gongs of stewards mingled with the cries of 'all ashore that's going ashore' and the gangplanks were pulled up. With three deep blasts of her siren the giant liner—Britain's hope for a record Atlantic crossing—was edged away from the dock and the first test had begun.
>
> Bands blared 'Rule Britannia,' the thousands of sightseers screamed from rooftops and shore points, and planes droned overhead while tugs faultlessly nosed the Queen Mary from her dock.
>
> The Queen Mary pointed her bow toward the English Channel amidst scenes of public enthusiasm that transformed Southampton harbor into a vividly exciting welter of sound and color. More than 500,000 spectators blackened docks and the roofs of buildings and overflowed to vantage points along The Solent. Thousands of motorboats, tugs, and excursion craft swarmed like so many chips in a pond about the giant.
>
> Ships in the harbor broke out their flags and bunting. Factory and ship sirens screamed a farewell, with the Queen Mary's siren, audible for ten miles, lifting clearly above the rampage of noise.

In New York the great ship was given a queen's welcome. A flotilla of 150 boats escorted her from the Narrows to her Hudson River pier.

Queen Mary, as a newspaper story reported it, "received every last bit of the hoarse, shrill, exciting welcome that the world's greatest seaport reserves for the world's greatest ships."

The *Queen Elizabeth* was launched just before the outbreak of war and, with *Queen Mary*, spent the war years as a troopship, carrying as many as fifteen thousand GIs in a single trip from New York to the war zones, always running solo—without convoy. She went back into peacetime liner service to New York in 1946, but never captured the blue ribbon.

In June of 1952, the 990-foot, 53,000-ton superliner *United States* became the flagship of the American merchant marine when she sailed on her shakedown voyage from the builder's yard at Newport News,

King Edward receives an enthusiastic welcome from hundreds of workmen after a tour of inspection aboard the giant Queen Mary in March, 1936.

Numerous excursion boats, tugs and harbor craft of every description, trail in the wake of the Queen Mary, as Britain's pride of the sea steams majestically from Quarantine to her North River pier to discharge her passengers and cargo, June 1, 1936.

136

Army nurses wave and cheer from the pier at the Queen Elizabeth, bringing 12,719 U.S. Army servicemen and Netherlanders to the States, docks in New York on August 11, 1945.

Virginia, to her home port of New York, where she was given a tumultuous reception.

Largest merchant ship ever built in the United States, she had accommodations for two thousand passengers and, as the United States Lines proudly put it, "in a style that surpasses even the most luxurious hotels."

On her first voyage she took the blue ribbon from *Queen Mary* with a record time of three days, ten hours, and forty minutes, but this did not prevent the British people from giving her a lavish welcome.

The *Herald Tribune's* marine editor, Walter Hamshar, who was on board for the maiden voyage, described it in these words:

The English people gave a dramatic display of international sportsmanship today by greeting the superliner United States with one of the greatest spontaneous welcomes ever tendered to a ship in any port.

As the new ocean queen steamed across the English Channel from Le Havre to her terminal berth in Southampton, thousands turned out in everything that would float to escort the vessel into port. Other thousands lined the quays and docks to cheer the big ship that had taken the blue ribbon from the Queen Mary in her recordbreaking voyage.

On the westward run, the newly crowned queen of the Atlantic logged a passage of three days, twelve hours, and twelve minutes from Bishop Rock to Ambrose lightship. It was just a little more than a century before that another American ship, the *Baltic* of the Collins Line, had taken speed honors with a crossing of nine days, thirteen hours.

When *United States* approached her home port after breaking the Atlantic record twice on her maiden trip, passengers sang the national anthem and the ship's orchestra struck up "God Bless America," followed by "The First Lady of the Sea," a song especially written for the ship.

A forty-foot-long blue pennant waved from the foremast as the pride of America's merchant marine steamed through a harbor haze to a welcome that few ships have ever received here before.

It was the last time that the port of New York was to roar out a "welcome and well done" to a winner of the blue ribbon. *United States* was the last of the majestic speed contenders. Airliners and the soaring cost of ship construction had made them almost obsolete.

Even this great ship, which had finally won the speed trophy for America, was to have a fairly brief career. In 1969, after holding the blue ribbon of the Atlantic for seventeen years, she was laid up, paced out of the port-to-port passenger trade by air travel, unsuitable for costly conversion to the cruise-ship trade. Idle and aging, the fastest of all the North Atlantic speed queens seems destined for an eventual trip to the wreckers after many years of lay-up.

United States was the last to hold the blue ribbon but not the last of the huge luxury liners. This honor belonged to the S.S. *France*, which measured 1,035 feet from her rakish stem to her graceful stern, aptly described as "the French Line's $80-million gamble in the jet age."

Although the *France* plied the North Atlantic ferry for about a decade, the cream of the trade was being siphoned off by the airlines and she became the last of her kind. She was intended to amortize her cost in twenty-five years, but was laid up as unprofitable long before that and finally was sold for use as a floating hotel in the Middle East.

France logged thirty-five knots during her sea trials but never tried to take the blue ribbon from the *United States*. The French Line figured, quite logically, that the *United States* had never opened up her engines full speed and that a speed race would cost more than it was worth.

Emphasizing comfort rather than speed, the *France* was equipped with four stabilizers to reduce roll and had winglike devices on the smokestacks to swish away soot from promenading passengers.

There were even unusual comforts for canine passengers. On board were fifty-two carpeted kennels in first and tourist class. First-class canines received four kinds of dog food every day.

New York sensed that the *France*

138

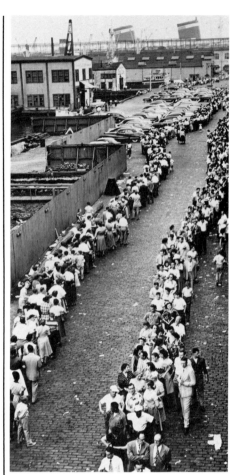

In a line that stretched from 46th Street to 37th Street and doubled back up to Hudson River Pier 86, New Yorkers paid respects to United States as the liner held open house June 29, 1952.

Opposite, Top Right, Super-liner United States leaves her New York pier for Southampton. Such scenes were daily occurrences in the New York waterfront's former years.

The SS France, which measured 1,035 feet from her rakish stem to her graceful stern, was aptly described as "the French Line's $80-million gamble in the jet age."

139

might be one of the last of the great liners and gave her an unusually warm reception, with a fleet of fifty tugs, Coast Guard craft, and fireboats escorting her into the harbor. As a token of his appreciation, Captain Georges Crosile saluted the city a dozen times or more with the ship's booming horn as the *France* progressed up the Hudson and dipped the French flag to the Statue of Liberty, with a prolonged blast from the horn as a kind of hail and farewell for all the great ships that had passed Miss Liberty in the century before.

What was to be the last of the North Atlantic liners, Cunard's 65,000-ton *Queen Elizabeth II*, went into service in 1969 but has never vied for the blue ribbon. Nor is she strictly a member of the old North Atlantic ferry fraternity, or "sorority," as purists may prefer, for *QE2* spends much of her time in the cruise business. But speed considerations aside, the great *QE2* is queen of the New York liner fleet, an impressive member of the city's maritime scene.

140

The blue-ribbon contenders and their queenly sisters were the darlings of the sea; proud, majestic, and lordly. They made news every time they docked or sailed. Their pictures appeared in the papers almost as often as those of society matrons, tycoons, kings, dukes, duchesses, and debutantes. The dreams of millions of workaday stay-at-homes sailed with them every time they dropped down the river and boomed out their deep-throated farewells.

But these great North Atlantic leviathans represented only a few of the passenger ships that served the port of New York over a span of many decades and made this city the greatest passenger-ship port in the world.

Some names may be remembered still, such as *Evangeline, Independence, Veednam, Kungsholm,* and *Robert E. Lee.* Many more, though very well known and much beloved of travelers in their day, are now only names in the "arrivals and departures" columns of the shipping news in musty old newspapers.

But, one and all, they served the port well, providing passenger, mail, and express cargo service to coastal points and many other parts of the world. Their forte was regular, dependable service rather than speed records, but hundreds of thousands of people rode these ships to Scandinavia, Northern Europe, the Middle East, Africa, Latin America, and the Caribbean, in addition to coastal ports.

Over the years New York was home port for a host of fine, small passenger ships in the coastwise services and, for a while, in the intercoastal runs, too. A large fleet of coastal passenger ships was operated out of New York

by Clyde Mallory Line, Merchants and Miners Transportation Company, Morgan Line, Eastern Steamship Company, and the Old Dominion Line.

What better example of the importance of the lesser-known liners could there be than this line-up of passenger ships, all at dock in the port of New York one day in 1934:

Oriente—Ward Line—for Havana
Evangeline—Eastern S.S. Co.—for Yarmouth, Nova Scotia
George Washington—Old Dominion Line—for Norfolk

Cameronia—Anchor Line—for Glasgow
American Merchant—American Merchant Line—for London
President Hayes—Panama Pacific Line—for San Francisco
Seminole—Clyde Mallory Line—for Jacksonville
Virginia—Panama Pacific Line—for Havana, San Diego, and San Francisco
Kosciuszko—Gdynia-America Line—for Gdynia
Southern Cross—Munson Line—for Havana
Morro Castle—Ward Line—for Havana

Add to these a number of famous transatlantic liners in port that day, among them the *Saturnia, Scythia,* and *Adriatic.*

In addition to passenger ships as such, New York was also home for many combination ships that carried from fifty to one hundred or so passengers, plus freight. Typical of these was Grace Lines' *Santa Barbara,* which had accommodations for fifty-two guests on the run to Valparaiso, or a number of ships in the United Fruit Company's "Great White Fleet,"

The staterooms of the Ile de France in 1928 represented the epitome of luxury travel. Among her many passengers in 347 crossings were J.D. Rockefeller, Arturo Toscanini, Gloria Swanson and Will Rogers.

Opposite, Luxury and comfort were foremost aboard the SS Ile de France during the 1930s. This view of the first class dining salon represents the apex of travel.

Sensing that the SS France might be one of the last of the great liners, New York gave her an unusually warm reception with a fleet of fifty tugs, Coast Guard craft, and fireboats escorting her up the Hudson and into the harbor.

which had accommodations for ninety-nine out of New York to Caribbean and Central American ports.

The New York-Mediterranean passenger service was very important for the port of New York because of the large number of Greek- and Italian-Americans traveling back and forth on visits to the homeland. Many fine ships operated on these runs, among them the Italian liners *Vulcania* and *Saturnia* of the Cosulich Line. They were among the world's largest motor ships.

Described by the *Herald Tribune*'s maritime writer as "a beautiful vessel in every sense of the word," the 24,000-ton *Saturnia* and her sister ship, the *Vulcania*, arrived in New York for the first time in 1928.

Not out to break any speed records, these ships, like a host of other passenger vessels calling here, "provided comfortable but inconspicuous service," as one writer described it.

Vulcania made more than one hundred calls in New York, carrying many thousands of passengers, between 1928 and her last voyage in 1940, when Cosulich transferred her to their South American routes.

It wasn't only the *Mauretania*, the *Leviathan*, and their like for which New Yorkers developed a fond affection. When the *Vulcania* sailed from a North River pier on her last trip, there were many moist eyes in the large crowd of well-wishers who waved goodbye. The big ship chugged from her pier "with the band playing and the white superstructure gleaming in the sunlight."

When the Germans swept into Trieste in 1940, the crew of *Saturnia* hurriedly got their ship underway, nosed out of the harbor, and sped full tilt down the Adriatic before the Nazis realized what was happening. When they finally did, bombers were sent out to sink her, but the Italian captain zig-zagged so expertly that the bombs missed and *Saturnia* made an eight-hundred-mile escape to Malta, where the crew turned her over to the British. She was later taken to Gibraltar, thence to New York for conversion into the U.S. Army hospital ship *Frances Y. Slanger*, named for the first U.S. Army nurse to be killed in the European theater of war.

Soon after the war, *Saturnia* was turned over to the Russians.

There are scores of fine passenger ships, many with colorful histories, that should be mentioned, but an entire book could be devoted to this large part of the American merchant marine, and New York was home port for most of these ships. Very few of them returned to service after the war. Some were sunk. Others had become obsolete and their replacement was financially impossible under the more stringent building standards prevailing since 1936.

A number of new liners joined the roster of New York passenger ships after World War II. Especially noteworthy among these were the sister ships *Constitution* and *Independence* of American Export Lines. These 26,000-tonners were 683 feet long and had a speed of twenty-five knots. Carrying a thousand passengers and a crew of 578, they were very popular on the run from New York to Mediterranean ports.

The North Atlantic liners were the "speed merchants." While their exploits were making the headlines, small items in the shipping news would tell of recordmaking voyages by the many other less-renowned passenger ships serving the port.

A one-paragraph note on the shipping page of the *Herald Tribune* in 1925, for instance, told about the *George Washington* of the Clyde Line setting a new speed record from Miami to New York of fifty-four hours, twenty minutes, and the *Shawnee* of Clyde Mallory steaming from Jacksonville to New York in 1934 in the record time of forty hours, forty-one minutes. And there was a record-making run of the *Drottingholm* of the Swedish-American Line from New York to Gothenburg in 1923 of eight days, sixteen hours, and twenty-nine minutes. The *Minnewaska* of Atlantic Transport Line, carrying 238 passengers, set a new record for a one-class ship of seven days, eighteen hours from New York to London in 1923. This was the second *Minnewaska*, the first having been torpedoed by a German submarine off Crete in World War I.

Every route had its speed contenders, with honors going to many a proud ship whose name and exploits,

though once well known on the New York waterfront, have now been long forgotten.

One of the many passenger ships that served the port of New York in years past was the 10,518 ton, twin-screw mail steamer *Bermudian* of the Quebec S.S. Company, offering weekly sailings from pier 47, North River. The *Bermudian* advertised "cabins de luxe with private bath" and, apropos of the *Titanic* disaster, "sufficient lifeboats to carry all passengers and crew." Many handsome liners operated on the New York-Bermuda run.

Sooner or later all of the fine, old Atlantic liners slacked their fires, lowered their colors, and were towed into bone yards or sent to the wreckers.

Such was the fate of the once-proud *Leviathan*. A sad sight she was as workmen prepared her at a Hoboken pier for the voyage to Rosyth, Scotland, for scrapping in 1938.

"Three years of idleness and exposure," said a story in the *Herald-Tribune*, "had coated the Leviathan with grime and soot-stains on her black steel flanks and once-white superstructure, but the luxurious interiors were even more distressing. Dust and gloom were everywhere.

"The four-room royal suite, once occupied by Queen Marie of Rumania, was a welter of disordered furniture and rolled-up rugs. Its private sundeck was hardly visible through the grimy windows. The spacious library was water-soaked in one corner from a bursting steam pipe. In the grand salon the set of four huge paintings by Gerard de Lairesse had grown dim with dust.

"The swimming pool, the biggest and most luxurious ever built into a ship, was a blank space of mud-soaked tile and corroded bronze."

Sic Transit Gloria.

143

A number of new liners joined the roster of
New York passenger ships after World War II.
One and all, they served the port well, providing dependable passenger, mail, and express cargo service to coastal points and many
other parts of the world.

CHAPTER 10
THE UNSUNG THOUSANDS

Imposing and romantic though they were, the great North Atlantic queens and their smaller sisters on the other liner routes were no more important to the port of New York than were the cargo ships—the berth-line (regularly scheduled) freighters, the tankers, the bulk carriers, and the humble, homeless tramp ships, the hardworking cargo droghers that roamed the seas of the world, taking cargoes wherever they could be had and delivering them anywhere that the consignees wanted them unloaded. It was the cargo ships of all kinds that freighted most of the tonnage in and out of New York port.

Look at the shipping news of years past and you will see them listed by the hundreds. Ships that seldom made the news, plowing their routine ways across the ocean tracks to and from New York and just about any port you could mention around the world. There were ships named *Ruby Castle, Roxen, Castella, Kansan, Tai Yin, Nordfarer, Minnetonka, Black Tern, Yamazoto Maru, Malayan Princess, Waukegan, West Arrow, Ruth Kellogg, Marga, Nerissa, Luna,* and *Darlington Court*. Ordinary, hardworking cargo carriers, freighting everything from oil and lumber to burlap, coffee, and ores; from canned tomatoes, rubber, and tea, to mica, machinery, wheat, and paper pulp.

The freight ships remained anonymous except when something happened.

In May of 1920, for instance, the Spanish Royal Mail liner *Cristobal Colon* was outward-bound at a slow speed in a thick fog when it slammed into the British freighter *River Orontes*. The *Cristobal Colon*, which had a thousand passengers on board, was only slightly damaged, but the thirty-nine-man freighter was badly holed and settled onto the mud along the Bay Ridge channel in Brooklyn. For the first time in its career, it had made more news than its usual two-line, six-point notice in the shipping columns. The pilot on the freighter, incidentally, was J. E. McCarthy. His brother, J. F. McCarthy, was piloting the Spanish liner.

Passengers on the Staten Island ferry would see them at anchor in the roads, steaming upchannel toward a pier, or heading for the Narrows, outward-bound, riding down to their marks; next stop, Rotterdam, Cape Town, Melbourne, Singapore, or Callao.

At one time there was also a large fleet of coastwise coal barges operating out of New York to New England points. They loaded in New Jersey, then sat at anchor off the Brooklyn shore waiting for tugs to tow them, usually three at a time, up the coast to Providence, Fall River, Boston, and Portland. Millions of tons of coal moved out of New York over the years by tug and barge. It was a colorful phase of maritime activity that is given no mention in histories of the port. The coastwise lumber trade was important, too, up to World War II, and it was once a common sight for ferry commuters to see schooners coming into the harbor with their decks piled high with lumber from Canada, Maine, or southern ports.

The great liners carried only a limited amount of "rush" cargo. Liners which did not have to vie for speed records could carry less fuel and more cargo, but even then they were not primarily cargo carriers. Their freight consisted mainly of baggage and the mails. It was the all-cargo freighter that made New York the biggest port in the world as far as tonnage was concerned, and gave employment to thousands of longshoremen and others on the waterfront.

And it is those people—and countless others—who have made the port of New York. The story of the port is a chronicle of nameless men, all of

145

Very much like their modern brothers, these early stevedores bent their backs to unload a ship in the middle of the nineteenth century.

whom have contributed to its drama, its color, progress and prosperity.

In earlier times there were the bold merchants who ventured fortunes on the uncertainties of trading voyages to hostile and uncharted shores; seamen, with their tattooed arms and salt-bleached dungarees; and the painstaking mechanics who machined the moving parts for engines of great ships that made New York builders famous.

There were the longshoremen, sweating puncheons of rum, crates of machinery, lumber, and bales of cotton from ships' holds with straining muscles and iron hooks. No less memorable were the harbor pilots, guiding in and out those thousands of ships with their passengers and cargoes from all over the world. There were the U.S. Customs inspectors; the immigration officers; the U.S. Public Health Service people, who visited every ship to protect the nation against the importation of contagious diseases; and the agents of the Department of Agriculture, enforcing regulations on the importation of fruit, meat, and vegetables.

The story of the tugboatmen would make a book in itself. And there were the crimps, the tattoo artists, the shipping masters, and even the dance hall girls. They all had a share in the colorful history of the harbor.

The men who sail American ships in and out of New York today are not only well paid but enjoy excellent food and accommodations, paid vacations, liberal retirement, and other benefits that seamen could not even have dreamed of a century ago. On the newest American ships, as well as on many of the foreign vessels calling here, each seaman has his own room, as spacious and comfortable as most hotel rooms on shore. Sailors on foreign ships also enjoy pay and other conditions immeasurably improved from those of even a few decades past.

New York was always a popular port for seamen "on the beach"—men in need of a job. If there was any port in the world where a man could ship out—catch an outward-bounder—it was the port of New York. Great depressions affect all trades and there have been periods when seamen walked the waterfront here by the hundreds trying to find berth, but in normal times a good man could always find a ship in New York.

In the days before maritime labor unions controlled hiring with their own hiring halls, crews were hired by shipping masters or supplied by boardinghouse keepers. Some captains preferred to hire their own men "off the dock." There were seamen's homes which ran informal employment services and in some cases the larger companies had their own shipping offices.

In the 1920s and 1930s there was a big black man from Barbados who could always be found along South Street. He hired men for the lumber schooners and the few square-riggers still left in those days.

And, of course, there was always a list of ships and their berths in the shipping news so that a man wanting a berth could go down to the ship bound for a part of the world he preferred, climb aboard, look up the mate, the chief engineer, or the steward, and ask for a job.

A century ago the sailor's life was one of danger, hard work, poor food, poor pay, and often-miserable living conditions when afloat. When ashore, the sailor was the target of every harpie along the waterfront. Worst of these were the crimps, the boardinghouse keepers and their runners, who besieged every crew of an incoming deepwater ship to induce them into patronizing the various sailors' boardinghouses, and also acted as shipping agents, obtaining crews for outbound ships. After the sailor had carelessly spent his hard-earned wages from a long voyage, the crimp not only shipped him out for a fee which was paid by the captain, but obtained an advance against the poor sailor's wages to pay for bills which the sailor had run up at the boardinghouse for food, drink, and lodgings. The sailor was thus in debt to the ship before it ever sailed. It was all legal, until eventually forbidden by law.

Numerous organizations sprang up here and elsewhere to help the seaman and keep him out of the clutches of saloonkeepers, thugs, crimps, and prostitutes. Some of these groups were primarily concerned with saving

The small, but powerful, tugboats, docked along the East River in the early 1900s, stood ready to tow and push the majestic liners, berth-line freighters, and tankers through the New York harbor.

The Marine Exchange where sailors signed up for berths on ships bound for any part of the world and collected their hard-earned wages after a long voyage.

New York was always a popular port for seamen "on the beach"—men in need of a job. Many a seaman got a berth on an outward-bounder through the maritime labor union's hiring halls.

the seaman's soul and did more preaching than extending practical help and services. The sailor was exhorted to reform, warned not to sail on the Sabbath, and pressed with enough religious tracts to fill a sea chest.

One of these organizations, however, developed a practical approach toward the mariner and became well known to seamen all over the world as well as a famous landmark along the South Street waterfront.

Now known as the Seamen's Church Institute, it began in 1834 as the Young Men's Auxiliary Missionary and Education Society. In 1844 it launched a floating church, which was tied up at Peck's Slip in the heart of South Street shipping.

To combat the evil influence of the sailors' boardinghouses, the Society expanded its program to include "the lodging and entertainment of seamen and boatmen in the port of New York for the purpose of caring for their moral, spiritual, mental, and bodily welfare."

Several missions with lodgings and other facilities were opened. Brooklyn's Erie Basin and Atlantic docks were "home port" for thousands of seamen, so the Society opened the Breakwater Hotel for Seamen on Atlantic Avenue, Brooklyn, in 1907. At the same time it changed its name to Seamen's Church Institute of New York.

In 1913 it built a thirteen-story Seamen's Home at 25 South Street in Manhattan, a building which became known as "The Institute" and was a home away from home for untold thousands of seafarers and a home for those who had no home but a ship. Here the sailor could get lodgings in a dormitory or private room, meals, storage for his baggage, and a place to receive his mail. There was an employment office, a library, writing rooms, and a Missing Seamen's Bureau which, over the years, has located thousands of men for shipmates, families, and friends.

Today, the Institute continues its work geared to changing times and a new breed of sailor. Its headquarters are now in a high-rise building adjacent to the Battery, with a branch near the container terminal at Port Newark.

It is inconceivable today, but New York papers as late as the 1870s and 1880s recounted tales of brutal treatment of seamen on American ships.

Typical of these was the case of the clipper ship *Crusader* on a voyage from New York to San Francisco. The captain and first mate took a dislike to a slow-witted Norwegian seaman named Seifert Nelson and subjected him to daily beatings. They lashed him to the jibboom during a winter passage around Cape Horn so that he was kept cold and wet while the vessel ploughed its way through stormy seas.

Even worse was the case of the ship *Sunrise* on a voyage from New York to San Francisco in 1873. No vessel more deserved the term "hell ship." Even the most hardened crimps on the San Francisco waterfront were horrified at the looks of the crew and the tales of ill-treatment they had to tell when the *Sunrise* dropped anchor there. Three of the crew had jumped overboard, preferring suicide to continued beatings and sadistic treatment. The case of the *Sunrise* so aroused San Francisco that the captain was sentenced to a year in jail and the sadistic first mate to four years.

Such ships were, of course, the exception. Many vessels treated their crews well, at least as well as would be expected in their time.

But ill treatment was common enough that it was one of the reasons for the seamen's labor union movement. Other stimulants toward unionization were the generally poor food, poor pay, poor accommodations, and conditions of employment which made the sailor little more than a serf with no legal recourse in the courts. Having to put to sea in unsafe ships also stirred the seamen's ire.

There were attempts to form unions as early as the 1850s in the port of New York, but the first effective organization came about on the Great Lakes and the West coast in the 1870s and early 1880s. In 1892 the National Seamen's Union of America (later known as the International Seamen's Union) was organized in Chicago and included the Atlantic Coast Seamen's Union. Other Gulf and East Coast seamen's groups affiliated with it.

One of the founders of the seamen's labor movement in the United States was a tall, gaunt Norwegian square-rigger sailor named Andrew Furuseth, who devoted a lifetime to union organization and to national legislation improving the lot of the merchant sailor. For years he was the voice of the seaman in Washington. Along with Sen. Robert LaFollette he fathered the historic Seaman's Act of 1915, the "magna carta" of the American merchant sailor.

It is difficult to conceive now but,

Mrs. Janet Roper was "Mother Roper" to thousands of seamen as director of the Missing Seamen's Bureau for more than fifty years. She united "missing seamen" with their families.

148

This light tower was dedicated by the Seamen's Church Institute in April of 1912 to those who lost their lives in the Titanic disaster. It originally opened in 1913 at 25 South Street and the tower now stands at South Street Seaport.

The good work of the Seamen's Church Institute is legendary. Here, in 1916, some sailors are being taken on a day trip. In the background is their popular "home away from home."

prior to 1914, longshoremen were paid twenty-five cents an hour for day work and thirty-five cents for night work. During World War I their pay jumped to forty cents an hour on day shifts and sixty cents for night work, with a bonus for Sunday work that gave longshoremen an unheard-of eighty cents an hour. All harbor wages went up, from longshoremen to the deckhands on lighters, to towboat crews and coal handlers at the bunkering docks.

Unions for unlicensed seamen were only partially successful until

150

the great maritime strikes of the 1930s, which resulted in the formation of the National Maritime Union and the Seafarer's International Union, both of which are headquartered in New York and which now represent the bulk of unlicensed seamen on American vessels. These unions, together with several seamen's unions on the West Coast, won the wages and working conditions which today make the American sailor the envy of seamen all over the world.

In the earliest days of the port seamen also unloaded the cargoes but, as commerce increased, the dock worker—the longshoreman—took over this job. Like the seaman, his hours were long, his work was hard, the pay poor, and employment often spasmodic.

Longshoremen tried for many years to improve their lot by unionization, the first recorded dock worker's strike dating back to 1836. The first major strike by dock workers occurred in 1874 when eight thousand men walked off their jobs here to protest a reduction in wages. This

strike collapsed after five weeks because the men could not afford to go without an income longer than that.

There was another big strike in 1887 to protest an effort by the employers to set a flat pay rate of twelve dollars a week in place of the prevailing twenty-five cents an hour. This strike was ineffectual, too, as were several others to follow. But the effort for improved pay and working conditions finally resulted in the formation of the International Longshoremen's Association in the 1890s. The ILA became strong enough by 1914 to obtain the first portwide collective bargaining agreement with New York employers and has been the dominant labor group for longshoremen here ever since.

The longshoreman has been called "the man with the hook" because of the sharp-pointed steel hook which he always carried in his belt and with which he manhandled the crates, bales, and other cargo in the holds of ships. The hook is still useful for some cargos but for longshoremen working containerships it is now more of an antique than a useful tool. Containerized cargo is handled by huge cranes and most general cargo now moves in containers.

No group of harbor workers has a more dramatic history than the Sandy Hook pilots, a history going back to colonial times. The first official provision for pilotage in New York dates from 1694, when the city's Provincial Council decreed that incoming vessels must be guided by pilots. One of the earliest acts of the New York legislature was a law regulating pilotage of vessels into the port.

By 1837 there were twenty-three pilots on the Sandy Hook station, plus a group of pilots who guided ships through the treacherous Hell Gate on the busy East River. By 1860 there were seventeen New York pilot boats in service, manned by forty-two pilots, and four New Jersey boats with thirty pilots. There once were thirty pilot companies competing for business and they sent their sleek, yacht-like schooners one hundred miles and more offshore looking for incoming ships. Not infrequently, several schooners would sight an inbound ship at the same time and it

The longshoreman has been called "the man with the hook" because of the sharp-pointed hook which he always carried in his belt and with which he manhandled the crates, bales, and other cargo in the holds of ships.

Left, Andrew Furuseth, a Norwegian who had sailed the square-rigged ships, devoted the rest of his life to the betterment of sailors' working conditions and was a co-author of the Seaman's Act of 1915.

The coffee booths were little restaurants that abounded along the waterfront in the second half of the nineteenth century. Here a policeman tells a woman and child to move along; a newsboy and coatless girl stare at the door, lacking the few cents that would buy a meal while a warmly dressed man leaves. 1871.

The 1911 seamen's strike was just one of the efforts to protest the long hours, hard work, and poor pay common to seamen and longshoremen for many years. It is difficult to conceive now but, prior to 1914, longshoremen were paid twenty-five cents an hour for day work and thirty-five cents for night work.

was up to the sailing skill of the master and crew to reach the vessel first and get the business.

The years between 1838 and 1860 were a sad period for Sandy Hook pilots, no less than fifteen boats being lost in storms and collisions.

The Sandy Hook Pilots roll of honor includes such entries as these:

Pilot Robert Mitchell: froze to death when the pilot boat *E.K. Collins* went ashore in 1856.

John Campbell: lost when the *Ariel Patterson* was sunk in 1883.

Four pilots were drowned when the *Enchantress* went down during a roaring blizzard in March of 1888.

Six more were lost when the pilot boat *Warren* disappeared at sea in 1895.

Altogether, some sixty-five Sandy Hook pilots have been lost in line of duty.

Pilots now use motorboats to go to and from ships off Ambrose Light, but for many years they were ferried in a pulling boat from the pilot vessel to the ship. Picking up the pilot off the lightship was always an exciting occasion for passengers of incoming liners. They would line the rails to watch the tiny yawl leave the often-heaving pilot ship and brave its way through seas and swells to the ship's side, where the pilot would make a leap for the Jacob's ladder, the rope ladder thrown over the ship's side, and up it, rung by rung, the pilot would climb to the main deck, where he was welcomed like an honored guest.

One traveler wrote that "the pilot came aboard like a visiting admiral. No sou'wester, oilskins, or seaboots for this gentleman. He wore a top hat and a frock coat and a four-in-hand tie. He was every bit a seagoing dandy. The captain met him at the rail like a long-lost brother and escorted him to the bridge."

Today all pilotage here is handled by the Sandy Hook Pilots, an association administered by the New York and New Jersey Board of Pilot Commissioners. The pilots have their headquarters and communications center on Staten Island and operate the pilot boats *New York* and *New Jersey*, which alternate on station near Ambrose Light.

Pilots, incidentally, have occasionally become unexpected passengers on transatlantic liners. During a storm in 1888, pilot John Hall could not get off to the pilot ship on an outbound liner and got a free ride to England. His son, pilot John Hall, had a similar vacation in 1929 when a storm prevented his leaving the liner *Reliance*. He rode her all the way to Hamburg.

This has worked in reverse, too. In 1932 pilot James Lynch could not get off the liner *St. Louis* at Cobh, Ireland, and received a free trip to New York and back in a fine stateroom.

In January of 1945, 112 Sandy Hook pilots set an alltime record by guiding 243 ships in and out of port in twenty-four hours. A ship passed through the Narrows every six minutes on that wartime day.

Probably the most unusual assignment that a Sandy Hook pilot ever had was in 1860 when one of them was sent to England to pilot the *Great Eastern* on her maiden voyage. It was thought that, with a New York pilot on board, there would be less chance of her being lured at the last minute into going to Boston or some other port instead.

The work of customs inspectors in

152

Captain Electus Comfort poses for a photograph in his working clothes, a top hat and frock coat. No group of harbor workers has a more dramatic story than the Sandy Hook pilots, a history going back to colonial times.

Picking up the Sandy Hook pilot was always an exciting occasion. Often passengers would line the rails to watch the tiny yawl leave the often-heaving pilot ship and brave its way through seas and swells to the ship's side, where the pilot would make a leap for the Jacob's ladder, the rope ladder thrown over the ship's side, and up it, rung by rung, the pilot would climb to the main deck, where he was welcomed like an honored guest.

Pilot liner SS City of New York *as she moves through the ice to pier 84. The first official provision for pilotage in New York dates from 1694 when the city's Provincial Council decreed that incoming vessels must be guided by pilots.*

153

the port of New York has been well spiced with excitement, too. They have been hunting contraband aboard ship since the earliest days of the port.

While customs agents can't find everything that's smuggled into the port, they do uncover things in the most unlikely places—like finding 195 pounds of opium hidden in the hollow base of the foremast on the S.S. *Ruby Castle*, or one hundred quarter-bottles of brandy cached in the water drum of a boiler on the S.S. *Christina*. They have even dug through tons of coal to uncover contraband hidden in coal bunkers.

Before the popularity of marijuana and cocaine, the favorite drug for smugglers was opium, especially on ships from the Far East. Vessels coming in from the Orient always received a special shakedown from customs agents.

Soon after the *Southern Prince* docked at pier 4 in Brooklyn in November of 1925, inbound from China and Hong Kong, agents gave her more than the usual going-over. Perhaps they had been tipped off in advance that there was opium on board, but they worked their way from the crew's quarters in the bow, through the cabins and galley amidships, to storerooms in the stern. Finding nothing there, they progressed to the food-storage lockers below decks, a favorite place for secreting illegal merchandise.

One of the agents chanced to look into a dark, narrow space in back of the big meat refrigerator and noticed that a section of paneling there seemed to be loose. Suspicious at this, he ripped off the loose board and discovered a small space filled with sawdust, part of the refrigerator's insulation. He felt around and found a small can with a label in Chinese characters and on opening the lid he found it to be full of opium. Further probing uncovered 442 additional cans—with a street value of half a million dollars!

During Prohibition days, customs inspectors were given a merry time by liquor smugglers.

It was a favorite ploy of rumrunners on outbound liners to secrete the contraband, which had been brought in from Europe, and then sneak it ashore during the last-minute excitement of sailing time.

A few minutes before the hawsers were to be let go from the liner *Paris* one day in 1928, customs men noticed a small barge pull up on the waterside of the big ship. Moments later, hands began shoving packages out of portholes into waiting hands on the barge. The customs officers called police but the men on the barge did not intend to surrender their contraband without a fight. Shots were fired before the fleeing barge was captured; the customs men counted forty-five sacks of cognac and champagne.

There was a touch of somewhat tragic humor in one of these Prohibition-time searches.

Tipped off that a fishing schooner at the Fulton Fish Market had brought in liquor along with its cod and haddock, customs agents descended on the ship with drills and augers, figuring that the contraband was in a false compartment under the main hold. They probed the bottom of the ship so assiduously in this hunt for smuggled goods that they drilled into the river, water spouted up through the drilled holes, and the little ship sank at her dock.

There are thousands of such stories told of the times when South Street was one of the most colorful areas of the city.

The port of New York no longer has a "sailor street" as it did in the days when South Street was lined with bars, sailors' outfitters, and various places doing business with ships. The modern seaman is no longer distinguishable by his tattoos and his dungarees. Good pay has enabled him to dress like anyone else along the waterfront and to patronize the best establishments if he has a mind. The ships are gone from South Street, but the ghosts still remain for many a sailor who remembers when lower Manhattan on any one day was the port of a hundred ships, their masts and booms like a forest along the harbor side, their booming whistles a haunting call for the seaman tired of the shore and eager to see far places.

Above, *A scene of total confusion as customs officers inspect the great steamer trunks of passengers in 1890.*

In order to fit the ship into its berth at South Street, the jib boom of this unidentified clipper has been folded back, as has the dolphin striker, so that its immense length will not interfere with the street traffic. If it were full length it would have reached the building across the street.

CHAPTER 11
LADIES OF THE SOUND

The great ocean liners have been pictured as the glamour girls of the New York maritime scene. Impressive they certainly were, imperious and queenly symbols of power, wealth, and majesty at sea. But for the average New Yorker or New Englander who would never see London or Paris, and wanted an inexpensive escape from summer heat and city sidewalks, the "great white ladies of the Sound" were argosies of romance and adventure.

Any maritime history of New York that overlooks the Long Island Sound and Hudson River lines would be omitting one of the most memorable and glamorous chapters in the history of the port. The passenger liners that plied these inland and coastal waters provided cheap, fast, and comfortable transportation and vacations for millions of travelers for more than a century, not to mention employment for many thousands of ship and engine builders, seamen, longshoremen, office workers, and those in other maritime trades. Many of these great steamers were built in New York yards and afforded an opportunity for the city's craftsmen to employ their skills in elaborate accommodations and decor.

It is no exaggeration to call these ships *great*—in their size, their engines, speed and appointments, and the skill with which they were navigated on almost trainlike schedules through fogs, squalls, and heavy traffic on berth-to-berth runs.

In 1863 the Hudson River liner *St. John*, built by John Englis of Brooklyn, was the second-largest ship in the world, exceeded only by the *Great Eastern*. She cost $600,000 to build and sported a grand staircase of Santo Domingo mahogany that in itself cost $25,000. Her furnishing, it was claimed, was as elaborate as those of the North Atlantic liners of her time. *St. John* ran between New York and Albany for twenty-one years. The ship was destroyed by fire in New York in 1885.

It wasn't long after the *Clermont's* pioneering trip that Hudson River steamboats had become sizable vessels. The *Albany* (1826) was 212 feet long, and the *DeWitt Clinton*, built in 1828, was 233 feet in length. The *Novelty* of 1830 had twelve boilers and poured a blanket of smoke over Hudson waters from her stacks as she raced upriver with freight and passengers.

In 1826 there were sixteen steamboats on the Hudson, and by 1840 there were close to a hundred. The number of operators proliferated, too, and competition was so keen at times that fares were almost a giveaway to lure passengers. Runners were employed at some landings to "steal" passengers from rival boats, sometimes by hustling their baggage on board before the surprised traveler could protest that he had a ticket on another steamer.

Of the many lines that served this river, the Hudson River Day Line was justly the most famous and best remembered, for it began in 1863 and hoisted its house flag for the last time in 1948.

It was bought out by the Hudson River Steamboat Company, which operated as the Hudson River Day Line, Inc., and kept the river service alive until 1971 with the famous *Robert Fulton* and *Alexander Hamilton*, both of which could carry more than three thousand passengers on regular runs and excursions. A long tradition of steamboating on the Hudson was ended when the *Alexander Hamilton* made the last run for the Hudson River Day Line, Inc., in 1971.

The use of the Hudson as a great river highway for shipboard passengers and freight has been ended by trains, trucks, planes, buses, and

157

The passenger liners that plied the inland and coastal waters provided cheap, fast, and comfortable transportation and vacations for millions of travelers for more than a century. Courtesy Harper's Weekly, September 28, 1878

motorcars, although tugs and barges, of course, still ply the Hudson and the New York State Barge Canal. Deep-sea ships also use the port of Albany.

Probably no other waterway in the world, the English Channel included, offered more glamorous and luxurious short-haul passenger service than was enjoyed by generations of travelers between New York and New England points on Long Island Sound and its adjacent bays and rivers.

It was no exaggeration to say, as did one newspaper account of the 1850s, that the Sound steamers were "remarkable specimens of American naval architecture." They were an American type, as much as cigar-store Indians, clam chowder, and the Model T.

Old scenes of the port of New York almost invariably picture one or more of these stately Long Island Sound steamships knifing through harbor waters, long and lean, with gleaming white superstructures, tall stacks, gilded paddle boxes, and wind-whipped banners. They were the special pride of the port.

158   The 134-foot *Fulton*, built by Robert

Passengers travel up the Hudson River aboard the Alexander Hamilton *in 1924. For the average New Yorker or New Englander who would never see London or Paris, and wanted an inexpensive escape from summer heat and city sidewalks, the "great white ladies of the Sound" were argosies of romance and adventure.*

The Hudson River Day Line's Robert Fulton *could carry more than three thousand passengers on regular runs and excursions.*

It wasn't long after Clermont's pioneering trip that Hudson River steamboats had become sizable vessels. The DeWitt Clinton, built in 1828, measured 233 feet in length.

Fulton shortly before his death, inaugurated service between New York and New Haven in March of 1815, making the run in eleven hours. In 1816 the *Connecticut*, captain, E. S. Bunker, opened steamship service between New York and Norwich and was joined by the *Fulton* the following year in a regularly scheduled passenger and freight operation.

Boats increased in size, speed, and comfort. When the *President* went into service between New York and Providence in 1829 it advertised 137 berths, including private staterooms and separate cabins for ladies. The Providence *Journal* wrote glowingly of this ship: "What further improvements remain to be made in steamboats we cannot imagine; to us in our generation she unites comfort and convenience with safety, elegance and unrivalled speed. She is a floating palace."

But the *President's* elegance was only a taste of what coastal voyagers were to enjoy in the years ahead.

In 1846 the *Merchant's Magazine* reported that the new steamer *Atlantic* "seems to have reached the very acme of perfection." Largest steamer built in the United States up to that time, *Atlantic* was 320 feet long and had a beam of 64 feet over the paddle boxes. A unique innovation was a six-inch-thick watertight bulkhead of heavy oak some forty-four feet aft of the bow to keep the ship afloat in event of collision.

The ladies' saloon, which contained sixty berths, was "richly and tastefully furnished with the most costly Axminster carpets, rosewood and satin damask curtains, gilded cornices, superb mirrors and, in short, everything to gratify the taste and comfort of the fair traveller."

For the utmost in traveling comfort the *Atlantic* offered bathing rooms, "where the passengers may enjoy warm or cold, fresh or salt water showers or plunge baths."

The *Atlantic*, unfortunately, was to have a brief career, for in November of 1846 she went ashore on Fisher's Island near New London, Connecticut, when a main steam line broke and the ship was rendered helpless during a storm. Some thirty passengers and crewmen lost their lives

in this tragedy.

Considering the number of trips they made and their consistent schedule-keeping despite fogs and other inclement weather, there were remarkably few accidents on the Sound runs.

One of the most tragic exceptions was the loss of the steamer *Lexington* on a trip from New York toward Stonington, Connecticut, in January of 1840. When off Eaton's Neck, Long Island, it was discovered that the woodwork around the smoke stack had caught fire. Although buckets of

One of the many fine passenger ships that served the Port of New York in years past was the twin screw mail steamship Bermudian of the Quebec Steamship Company, offering weekly sailings from Pier 47, North River. The Bermudian *had "cabins deluxe with private bath" and due to the Titanic disaster, "sufficient lifeboats to carry all passengers and crew."*

Rate Sheet in Effect January 1st to June 1st, 1913.

Quebec Steamship Co., Ltd.

ESTABLISHED 1867.

GO TO BERMUDA

BY FASTEST STEAMER

(Record Trip 39 hours and 20 minutes)

BY NEWEST STEAMER (Built 1904) EXPRESSLY FOR THE BERMUDA ROUTE

By only Steamer Landing Passengers and Baggage Directly on the Dock in Hamilton Without Transfer.

Twin=Screw S. S. "BERMUDIAN"

10,518 Tons Displacement. Bilge Keels, Double Bottom. Wireless Telegraph, No Steerage. Electric Fans.   SUITES DE LUXE. WITH PRIVATE BATH.   ORCHESTRA.

From Pier 47, North River, (foot of West 10th Street.) New York.

Rates of passenger Fares to Bermuda and return, Including Stateroom, Berth and Meals.

ROOMS	2 PERSONS IN A ROOM Per Berth	3 PERSONS IN A ROOM Per Berth
Promenade Deck.		
1--2	$90	$80
3--4	$80	—
5--6 (Cabins de Luxe with Private Bath)	$120	—
A--B	$90	—
Shelter Deck (Upper Deck)		
7--8--9--10--11--12--14--15--16--17--18--19--20--21--22--23--24--25--26--27. 7 and 8 accommodate 2 persons only.	$90	$75
28--29--30--31--32--33--34--35--36--37--38--39--40--41--42--43 42 and 43 accommodate 2 persons only.	$80	$65
44--45--46--47--48--49 (For 2 persons only)	$60	—
Saloon Deck.		
66--69--70--73--74--79--80--85--86--89--90--93--94--97--98--99--101--103--106--108--110	$70	$60
57--58--61--62--104--107--111--114--118--122--126--130--134	$60	$50
53--54--64--67--68--71--72--77--78--83--84--87--88--91--92--95--96--102	$50	$40
50--51--52--55--56--59--60--75--76--81--82--105--109--112--116--120--124--128--132 . . . . 51--52--75--76--81--82 accommodate 2 persons only.	$40	$35
140--141--142--143--144--145--146--147--148--149--150--151--152--153--154	$30	$25

Most of the Inside Rooms are well lighted and ventilated by means of skylights or ventilating ports opening directly from the upper decks, thus giving much of the advantage of Outside Rooms.

Rate for one person in whole room one-half fare extra.
Intermediate Class, round trip $18.   U. S. Alien tax $4. additional.

ABOVE RATES ARE SUBJECT TO CHANGE WITHOUT NOTICE.

NOTE.—Children under three years of age are taken free, and three to twelve years of age, half the above rates when occupying sofa berth. On the return voyage should there be no berth vacant at the rate paid passengers agree to pay additional for higher rate berth or accept refund if only cheaper berths are available.

SERVANTS IN CABIN—will be taken at $20. rate, berth to be assigned on board or when occupying stateroom with employer at ⅔ of the cabin rate but not less than $25.00.

All Atlantic Lines charge various rates according to location and number of persons occupying a room, and these rates are based on the actual value of each berth or room and their individual desirability. This is the only way of dealing impartially with all our passengers and give each just what they pay for.

160

One of the most tragic accidents on the Long Island Sound run was the loss of the steamer Lexington on a trip from New York toward Stonington, Connecticut, in January of 1840. When off Eaton's Neck, Long Island, the woodwork around the smoke stack caught fire. Terrified passengers and crew retreated to the bow as the flames consumed the midships, eventually jumping overboard into the icy waters. Three of the passengers who clung to bales of cotton from the ship's cargo survived. More than one hundred were lost in this disaster.

THE EXTRA SUN.

Awful Conflagration of the Steam Boat **LEXINGTON** In Long Island Sound on Monday Eve^g Jany 13th 1840, by which melancholy occurrence, over **100 PERSONS PERISHED**

water were poured on the fire, this was unavailing. Even as the pilot headed at top speed for the shore of Long Island, the ship became a raging inferno and captain and pilot were soon driven from the wheelhouse. Boats were launched but immediately swamped because the ship still had too much way on her.

Terrified passengers and crew retreated to the bow as the flames consumed the midships, eventually jumping overboard into the icy waters. Some clung for a while to bales of cotton from the ship's cargo.

It was by clinging to cotton bales that three passengers survived. One, a Captain Hilliard, was in the water for forty-eight hours before being picked up. More than one hundred were lost in this disaster.

Of the many lines which ran from New York up the Sound, the best known and certainly the one that will be most nostalgically remembered was the Fall River Line. Every President from U.S. Grant to Franklin D. Roosevelt rode the Fall River boats, plus tycoons, senators, noted thespians, and other celebrities too numerous to mention.

162

In 1845 a railroad was constructed from Boston to Fall River, Massachusetts, and in 1847 the Bay State Steamboat Company started operations with the *Bay State*, which made the run in about eight hours from New York to Fall River, with a stop at Newport. A waiting train received passengers from New York in the morning and hurried them on to Boston. A train from Boston brought passengers to Fall River in time to make the night boat to New York.

This company operated as the Fall River Line and no steamship service under the American flag, not excluding the North Atlantic liners, was more beloved by the traveling public or more greatly mourned when it was no more.

The ships of the Fall River Line epitomized the pleasure of short trips by sea. Diners enjoyed excellent cuisine and the kind of white-coated, attentive table service that was customary in the best hotels. They had their meals in beautiful dining rooms, feasting on clam chowder, oysters, Yankee pot roast, and apple pie.

BAY STATE LINE.

SUMMER ARRANGEMENT, Between BOSTON and

NEW YORK

Via Fall River and Newport.

THE SPLENDID

EMPIRE STATE,

Cabin, $4.   Capt. B. BRAYTON.   Deck, $2.50.

CARS leave the Station of the OLD COLONY & FALL RIVER R. ROAD,
Corner of South and Kneeland Sts.

THIS DAY
Thursday, April 21, 1859,
At 5.30 o'clock, P.M.

TICKETS for this Route, Steamer Berths and State Rooms, obtained at the following offices, and at the Old Colony & Fall River Railroad Station, corner of South and Kneeland Streets.
KINSLEY & CO., NO. 11 STATE STREET, AND AT 15, 24, 31, STATE, AND 70 WASHINGTON STREET.

THROUGH TICKETS FOR PHILADELPHIA, BALTIMORE, WASHINGTON,
And all points South, South-west and West, obtained at No.11 State Street.

FREIGHT TRAIN.....Leaves the Boston Freight Station at 1.30 P.M.
Arrives at Boston from New York at 11.50 A.M.
Freight taken at the lowest rates and forwarded without delay.

GEORGE SHIVERICK, Agent
Bay State Line, No. 11 State Street.

In 1847 the Bay State Steamboat Company started operations from New York to Fall River, with a stop at Newport. No passenger steamship service under the American flag, not excluding the North Atlantic liners, was more beloved by the traveling public or more greatly mourned when it was no more.

This 1924 photo of New York harbor shows the Fall River Line's terminal.

A naval architect once wrote of these ships that "the passenger steamers of the Fall River Line are absolutely the finest ships in the world for passenger service on inland waters...We may well be proud of the Fall River Line boats as creations distinctly American."

Even their first ship, the *Bay State*, was a pretentious vessel, measuring 352 feet overall, with an extreme beam of 82 feet. Each new ship incorporated improvements in speed and accommodations.

William Webb, famous builder of clipper ships, also built two of the most celebrated sound steamers, the *Bristol* and *Providence*, later acquired by the Fall River Line. They were 352 feet long, cost $1,250,000 each, and were renowned for their "magnificence and complete appointments." The owners could be excused for advertising them as "the mammoth floating palace steamers."

Typical of the elegance built into coastal vessels was the interior of the *City of Worcester* (1881) on the New London run. Known as the "Belle of the Sound," she had a saloon paneled in mahogany, and a wide mahogany stairway led from the spacious two-deck-high dining hall to a long promenadelike gallery lined with staterooms. She was the first sound steamer to have electric lights.

The *Puritan* of 1889 outdid anything else of the time in ornate decor and accommodations. She was 418 feet long and had 306 staterooms, plus 15 parlor bedrooms for honeymooners and others traveling in high style. Altogether, there were 964 berths on this liner. It took a crew of 224, mostly cooks, stewards, and waiters, to operate her.

The liners *Priscilla* and *Commonwealth* of the Fall River Line were the greatest of a long line of memorable Sound passenger ships.

It was claimed for these ships that they could carry as many passengers and as much freight as the *Lusitania* and *Mauretania* on about one-sixth the displacement, and that their accommodations were, on the average, superior to those on all but the most luxurious North Atlantic liners.

The steel-hulled *Commonwealth* measured 455 feet overall, with an extreme beam of 94 over the paddle guards, and was designed to be as safe as technology and the requirements of her service could make her. She had eight watertight compartments without doors, two fire bulkheads extending from the hull to the upper deck, a fire-sprinkler system with eighteen hundred outlets, and many other fire-resistant features in her construction. She was considered by many to be the safest ship on the Sound.

There was French decor in most of the public rooms. The library-social hall was furnished in cream and gold in the period of Louis XVI. The Grand Saloon was Venetian-Gothic, with decorative panels and lunettes. The Empire Saloon was furnished in Honduran mahogany with gold ornamentation. The cafe was done in Italian Renaissance. The main dining room, with windows providing spectacular vistas of sea and shore, sat 216 and was illuminated by indirect lighting set in three large domes in the ceiling.

The Fall River Line steamers were known as the "honeymoon boats," not only because they were popular with honeymooners but because many a romance budded and bloomed along the decks of the night boat as young couples fell under the spell of a summer sea, with the siren song of paddles and a sea moon painting seductive imagery over the waters.

Many a song and poem was written about the Fall River Line, but the best-known verse penned by some swain was this:

On the old Fall River Line,
The old Fall River Line.
I fell for Susie's line of talk
And Susie fell for mine.
Then we fell in with a preacher,
And he tied us tight as twine.
But I wish, oh Lord, I'd fallen overboard
On the old Fall River Line.

The line was suffering from changing times, especially auto and truck competition, in the 1930s, but its demise was speeded by a sitdown strike of seamen aboard the *Priscilla* and *Commonwealth* in 1937.

It was so greatly missed that a thousand residents of Fall River chartered a steamer in 1953 to retrace the route to New York and revive fond memories.

The steel-hulled Commonwealth *of the Fall River Line measured 455 feet overall, with an extreme beam of 94 over the paddle guards, and was designed to be as safe as technology and the requirements of her service could make her.*

William Webb, famous builder of clipper ships, also built one of the most celebrated sound steamers, the Bristol, *later acquired by the Fall River Line. It was 352 feet long, cost $1,250,000, and was renowned for its "magnificence and complete appointments."*

CHAPTER 12
TRAGEDIES & TRIUMPHS

Early issues of the *Maritime Register* often contained a long list of marine casualties; some minor, some tragic. There were strandings, collisions, dismastings in storms, and, more than just occasionally, this mournful notice of a failure to arrive: "Presumed lost and missing with all hands."

It was in the year 1872 that the New York brigantine *Mary Celeste* left port to become the most celebrated —and puzzling—of all mysteries of the sea.

Relics and memorabilia of the ship and her mysterious voyage are preserved in the "Mary Celeste Room" of the Atlantic Mutual Insurance Company at Wall and William Streets in New York. This company insured the vessel and its cargo and was involved in the lengthy investigation into what had happened to ship and crew.

A small vessel of 282 tons, *Mary Celeste* was towed out of pier 50, East River, on November 5, 1872, to an anchorage off Staten Island, where she awaited better weather before proceeding to sea. This she did on November 7, and the two or three ships that passed her as she headed out to sea probably were the last ever to see her people alive.

In command was a young but experienced shipmaster from Cape Cod, Capt. Benjamin S. Briggs. Accompanying him for a voyage to Genoa, Italy, were his wife, Sara, and their two-year-old daughter, Sophia. The crew included first and second mates, a cook, and four seamen.

Under hatches were seventeen hundred barrels of alcohol, the only cargo.

On December 4, the British brigantine *Dei Gratia*—captain, David R. Morehouse—bound from New York to Gibraltar with a cargo of oil in drums, sighted a small sailing ship off the port bow. Peering at her through his long glass, Captain Morehouse estimated the stranger to be about five miles distant, northwest by north. He was puzzled by her erratic behavior and by the fact that there was no one to be seen on her deck—no one at the wheel.

Judging the stranger to be in distress, Morehouse sailed as close as he could to the seemingly deserted vessel and hailed her: "Halloo aboard the brigantine...halloo...halloo." There was no response to repeated calls and, setting his sails aback to slow the ship, Morehouse launched a boat with First Mate Oliver Deveau and two seamen to investigate.

As the men boarded the mysterious craft all was deathly quiet, except for the swishing of loose lines, and the wash of the sea against the hull. Deveau looked into the forward house, the crew quarters—no one was there. The men peered down the cabin hatchway: "Halloo in the cabin!" No answer.

To a seaman's eye a great number of things about the ship were most puzzling. Only two sails were set, despite the fact that the wind was fair. The main staysail was hauled down and left lying, in a very unseamanlike fashion, over the forward deckhouse, as though it had been lowered in a great hurry to take way off the ship. There were three and a half feet of water in the hold, although the pumps were in good order. Some of the running rigging was in disarray and the wheel was spinning as the ship yawed about with no one at the helm. Ordinarily, a crew leaving the ship probably would have lashed the wheel to keep her on a course. The binnacle had been knocked loose and the compass was smashed. The ship's boat was missing, an indication that all hands had left the ship for some inexplicable reason.

Most puzzling of all were the crew's quarters. Clothes and personal effects were hanging on hooks and stowed in

In 1872 the New York brigantine Mary Celeste left port to become the most celebrated and puzzling of all mysteries of the sea.

the sailors' sea chests. Even their pipes were there, where they had put them down after the last smoke. And what sailor would leave a ship without his pipe and tobacco?

Ships like the *Mary Celeste* kept a log book in which all the pertinent facts of the voyage, such as courses, bearings, wind direction, state of the sea, and unusual events, were recorded daily. These bits of information were transcribed to the book from a slate on which information was recorded during each four-hour watch.

The ship's log book was missing, but on the table in the after-cabin was the log slate and its notations during the last watch kept aboard the *Mary-Celeste*. The last entries had been made on November 25. The ship evidently had been drifting about for nine days!

Captain Morehouse and his crew agreed they would take *Mary Celeste* into Gibraltar, the nearest port, and claim salvage rights. Shorthanded though he was, Morehouse decided that First Mate Deveau and two sailors should bring the deserted ship to safe harbor.

Both ships arrived safely in Gibraltar, albeit with their reduced crews in a state of near exhaustion, and *Mary Celeste* was turned over to the British Admiralty Court. Instead of a quick award of salvage money, however, the crew of *Dei Gratia* were questioned intensively by a suspicious court and the hearings dragged on for many weeks. After eighty-seven days the *Mary Celeste* was released, and the men who had saved her were awarded $8,300 in salvage money.

Many explanations have been advanced for the seemingly hasty abandonment of a well-found ship in mid-ocean but, barring the unlikely finding at this late date of additional evidence, the New York brigantine *Mary Celeste* will continue to be the most intriguing and most puzzling of all mysteries of the sea.

Many tragedies of the sea have occurred close to land.

On the 30th of July, 1871, the ferryboat *Westfield* had just loaded hundreds of passengers and was preparing to pull out of her slip at the foot of Whitehall Street for the run to Staten Island. As the lines were being cast off there was a crashing sound, followed by the hiss of escaping steam and in a second or two the forward decks were thrown into the air and "fell in all directions in a thousand pieces." The boiler had exploded. As the incident was further recounted, "passengers...were blown into the air to the height of thirty or forty feet, falling back into the wreck or into the water...scores of men, women, and children who escaped the full force of the explosion were immediately enveloped in a scalding cloud of steam." Some

A painting depicting the sighting of the abandoned Mary Celeste *by the astonished crew of the* Dei Gratia, *December 4, 1872.*

forty or fifty people were killed outright and many more were injured or maimed.

On June 15, 1904, the excursion steamer *General Slocum* was steaming up the East River to Locust Grove park grounds on Long Island. It was the annual outing of St. Mark's Lutheran Church and the boat was filled with a gay crowd of picnickers, mostly women and children. Counting the crew and bandsmen, who were playing sprightly marches, polkas, and waltzes on the lower deck, there were 1,358 people on board. Children ran and played about the decks. The mothers, most of whom lived in the tightly knit community of "Little Germany" between Houston and 14th Street, were relaxing on benches along the decks in dresses of voluminous crinoline and voile, gossiping and enjoying the harbor breeze on this sultry summer day as the paddles churned their way upriver.

The *General Slocum* was almost abreast of 125th Street when there was a muffled cry of "Fire! Fire!," and a boy hastily ran to the pilothouse to tell Capt. William Van Schaick.

168

On the 30th of July, 1871, the ferryboat West-field had just loaded hundreds of passengers and was preparing to pull out of her slip at the foot of Whitehall Street for the run to Staten Island. The captain was at his post, the engineer was on his way to the engine-room, men were standing ready to unhook the chains, when suddenly there came a terrible crash, and in an instant the steamer was a wreck. The huge boiler had exploded.

Within minutes the aft part of the crowded excursion vessel was enveloped in smoke, so quickly did the fire become a conflagration. Women screamed for their children. A passing tugboat, the *M. D. Wheeler*, swung its helm over and the crew yelled to the *Slocum's* pilothouse, "Run her ashore! Run her ashore!"

Perhaps the skipper was looking for a likely place to do just that, but the boat continued on as the thick, black smoke enveloped the entire aft half of the decks. Billy Noble, the tugboat captain, saw that a tragedy was in the making. He signaled for full speed and tried to keep up with the burning *Slocum*.

To those on nearby boats and to hundreds on shore, it seemed like an eternity before Captain Van Schaick ran his boat aground by the bow just above North Brother Island. By now the wooden vessel was all aflame.

Few people in those days knew how to swim. Even if they could, the women were encumbered by the bulky clothing of the time. They huddled together, trying to shield the children, until they were felled by smoke or swathed in flames. In panic, some threw their children overboard and then jumped into the swift-flowing tide after them. Many did nothing, paralyzed by fright or trapped by smoke and flame and calling desperately for children who had been romping about the ship.

Tugs and small craft rushed to the scene, but the fire spread with hurricane quickness. Although the bow was imbedded in the shore, few of those aboard had time to reach it and jump into shoal water.

The holocaust lasted only ten minutes but they were, as one newspaper story so well put it, "the most horrible ten minutes in the history of New York harbor." The armada of small craft pulled in some survivors but many more of the passengers were burned, drowned, or suffocated. Bodies were taken to the 26th Street pier and laid out there for identification because the city mortuary did not have sufficient space. When the final tragic count was made it was revealed that 1,031 had lost their lives in this holiday horror.

So many families were decimated by the tragedy that scores of relatives moved to other parts of the city, unable to bear the memory of happier times in the old neighborhood. Some of the bereaved became suicides.

Captain Van Schaick was sentenced to ten years in prison for negligence, although he had stayed at the wheel until his clothes were aflame and he was almost overcome by smoke. After two years, he was pardoned by President Taft, who reasoned that the owners of the vessel were much more to blame for failing to provide usable lifebelts, fire hoses, and a crew trained in emergency duties.

The survivors and relatives of those who died continued to hold yearly memorial services to mark this most terrible of harbor accidents.

Although the *Slocum* disaster was the harbor's worst, there have been many other fires, collisions, and explosions within sight of Manhattan's sky-raking shoreline.

Tugs and other small craft have been frequent victims, as when the famous *Mauretania*, outward-bound one night in 1927 with some one thousand passengers on board, rammed a steel car float near the Statue of Liberty. The ship could hardly have chosen a more humble target. Many passengers were awakened by the jar and ran on deck thinking the ship might be sinking. Others slept right through it. The stewards hurried about, reassuring people that all was well and that the liner had "only nipped a barge."

Mauretania stopped and lowered a lifeboat, but discovered that the car float's lone deckhand had jumped to safety on the tugboat *Mattawan*.

As one of the *Mauretania's* English crewmen later put it: "I'm glad nobody got hurt but they oughta be bloody proud to be sunk by a blue ribbon lady like the old 'Maury.'"

In the days when nighttime departures were popular for liners, in order to make the most use of the daylight hours at dock, the French S.S. *Paris*, outward-bound in the upper bay, rammed the Norwegian freighter *Bessengen* at 1:45 A.M. on an October morning in 1927, near the Statue of Liberty. A three-hundred-foot vessel, the *Bessengen* had just arrived from Havana the day before with a cargo of sugar and was riding at anchor when the accident happened. The freighter went down in a matter of minutes.

The Staten Island ferryboats *American Legion* and *Brooklyn*, passing by, immediately stopped to render assistance. Realizing what was happening, quick-witted passengers threw life preservers toward the area lit up by the ferryboats' searchlights. A lifeboat from the *American Legion* was lowered and hurried toward the men seen struggling in the night waters. The boat rescued thirteen crewmen, including the freighter's captain, exhausted and nearly drowned from the exertion of holding up a woman and a small boy. A lifeboat from the *Paris* saved several more.

A number of men, who probably could not swim, were seen clinging to the *Bessengen's* bow as the ship went down. Six of her crew were drowned. The freighter was underwater almost before the ferries could break their headway and launch boats. It later surfaced and was floating keel-up off Staten Island when salvage tugs took it in hand.

While crowded traffic lanes were the cause of many accidents, the presence of numerous ships and small craft just as often averted greater catastrophe.

Consider the ramming of the *Lexington* of the Colonial Line.

The ship's orchestra was playing "Whispering," a hit tune of the time, as the ship headed up the East River on her regular overnight run to Providence in January of 1935.

Some passengers were still on deck, bundled up against the cold, to watch the fairyland spectacle of a night-lit Manhattan. Others were dancing to the orchestra or having dinner in the dining room, or had retired to their cabins when the vessel was suddenly stopped. A freighter had run into her with a frightening crash of splintering wood and grinding steel.

This dramatic moment was vividly described on the dock a few hours later by passenger Blanche Grossman in an interview with a *Herald Tribune* reporter. Blanche was only six years old, but her account was worthy of a very observant and articulate adult.

"I was eating some food," she

Excursion steamer, General Slocum, sinks into the East River after a fire aboard the vessel killed 1,031 passengers, June 15, 1904.

said. "It was a tongue sandwich with mustard and a cheese sandwich which we had brought from a Jewish delicatessen in New York. Suddenly I got mustard all over my face and there was a crash like a boom.

"The noise was terrible and I ran to a window, and what do you think I saw? A big, wide ship sticking right into us. Mamma wouldn't let me look any longer, but pulled me away and we ran to the deck.

"I got a life belt. Mamma got a life belt, too, but Papa didn't get any. He said not to run because it wasn't anything bad, but we kept running. Papa ran, too, but he ran to help two

old ladies who fell down.

"Then we went down some steps and found a boat right along where the water was coming in, and they lifted us into a tugboat and then I looked up and saw a big boat toppled over just like a table. That's just what it looked like.

"Then I cried because I thought Daddy was drowned and Mamma cried, too. Then they put us ashore and we found out that Daddy wasn't drowned after all."

Another couple told how they were sitting in their stateroom when there was a tremendous crash, and

before they knew what was happening their stateroom was half full of water. They ran up to the main deck where an officer was directing passengers to a tugboat and shouting, "Tugs are standing by! Keep calm and everything will be okay!"

There was no panic, thanks to Capt. William Pendleton and his officers, and to the orchestra's leader, who had the presence of mind to keep on playing as though nothing had happened. "Whispering" seemed too slow a tempo, so orchestra leader Wilfred Downes told his men to

"switch to number seven."

"We were whooping it up with 'Somebody Stole My Gal'," he said, "when the mate came up and said 'Boys, she's going down. Pack up your fiddles and get out of here.'"

The *Lexington* had been cut in two by the freighter *Jane Christenson* of the Arrow Line. Seven of the *Lexington's* crew were lost; none of the passengers. The quick response of nearby towboats prevented a more costly tragedy.

The *Lexington* seemed to be a marked ship. In 1919 it had rammed

and sunk the tug *Jameson* in the East River and, before that, it had been rammed in Hell Gate by the submarine 0-7.

One of the most unusual harbor accidents occurred in 1926 in the Hudson River, not to a liner or a puffing towboat, but to one of America's largest luxury steam yachts, the *Delphine*. This 257-foot steamer had been built for automobile tycoon Horace Dodge in 1920, and in 1926 had just returned from Hawaii with Dodge's honeymooning widow, Mrs. Hugh (Dodge) Dillman.

While the Dillmans were attending the opera one night, fire broke out on board the *Delphine* and she sank at her anchorage, mostly from the weight of water that fireboats had pumped into her.

While her crew of fifty-four were battling the blaze, Mrs. Dillman's maid, Della Devers, braved a smoke-filled passageway and saved a gem box filled with jewels worth $250,000.

Delphine was raised several months later and refitted. During World War II she was the flagship of the entire United States fleet, her named changed to *Dauntless*. Today this ship is used as a floating classroom by the Harry Lundeberg School of Seamanship in Piney Point, Maryland.

One of the most spectacular harbor disasters occurred in August of 1941 when a fire destroyed pier 27 in Brooklyn, along with the freighter *Panuco* of the New York and Cuba Mail Line, which was loading alongside.

This fire broke out during the noontime lunch hour, and police estimated that fifty thousand office workers jammed South Street and the Battery to see the action.

No one knows for sure just how the fire started, although the blame was put on a carelessly tossed cigarette. A man who was looking out of a window across the street from pier 27 at 11:44 A.M. said he saw a longshoreman run out of the pier with his clothes on fire and, just moments later, the entire dock seemed to erupt like a volcano. Flames shot into the air like fireworks. By the time the first fire truck arrived—and it came quickly—it was too late to control the flames, which quickly spread to the ship.

172

173

Opposite, Left, The Colonial Liner Lexington was cut in two and sank immediately when it was rammed by the freighter Jane Christensen January 3, 1935. Four crew members were lost but 180 passengers survived.

Hastily abandoning a doomed freighter, members of the crew leap overboard into the waters of the North Atlantic. Waves splash across the deck, already covering part of the vessel as it sinks after a Nazi submarine attack.

More than a hundred longshoremen were working on the *Panuco* and the pier at the time. Some jumped from the ship into the water. Others were trapped on the pier or in the holds of the ship. A few raced across cargo-laden lighters, which surrounded the freighter, to the safety of an adjacent pier.

Within minutes the flames had become a five-alarm fire. The tugboats *Fred Dalzell* and *William Dalzell* were summoned to tow the ship away and beach her, but by the time they arrived they barely could see the vessel amid the swirling smoke.

Streams of water from the *Fire Fighter*, said to be the world's most powerful fireboat, helped the tugs nose up to the ship, and daring firemen threw lines from the *Panuco* to the towboat crews. Undaunted by the fiery peril, the tugs edged the vessel out of her slip and beached her on the Gowanus Flats, where she burned for several days.

This battle enlisted the efforts of twenty-eight engine companies, six hook-and-ladder companies, four fireboats, five police launches and rescue squads, and several Coast Guard cutters. Hundreds of fire fighters took part. Nineteen crewmen and longshoremen lost their lives.

On the pier, the ship, and nearbly lighters had been stored sisal, wax, and hundreds of drums of oil and chemicals, a perfect mix for a roaring conflagration.

Equally sudden and dramatic was the destruction, just outside the harbor entrance, of the World War II destroyer U.S.S. *Turner*.

The *Turner* had arrived as part of an escort for a convoy from North Africa and was anchored off Rockaway Point on the cold, blustery night of January 3, 1944. There was heavy rain and snow squalls.

Suddenly, in the early morning hours, there was a tremendous explosion, and a burst of fire shot hundreds of feet above the ship.

At Fort Hancock, on the tip of Sandy Hook, the watch realized that a major explosion had occurred; the post was put on instant alert.

At the Sandy Hook Coast Guard Station, Commander George Morin heard the blast and knew instinctively that there had been a shipboard explosion. He called a general alarm and ordered every available boat to the scene of the sky-raking flames. An eighty-three-foot cutter, a seventy-seven-foot patrol boat, and a number of smaller craft set out as soon as the crews could start engines and cast off the lines.

Guided by the flames, the rescue craft sped to the wrecked ship. The eighty-three-footer, which arrived about the same time as a pilot boat, nosed up to the blast-wracked vessel and rescued many men. The pilot

boat took thirty-nine sailors off the flaming ship.

Several muffled explosions occurred during rescue efforts and, following one of these blasts, the *Turner* seemed to break in two, quickly sinking amid blobs of burning oil. The waves and the rain soon extinguished these floating fires, and the sea was dark except for the beams of searchlights probing for survivors.

One sailor had jumped from the sinking ship to the deck of a Coast Guard boat with a small bundle in his arms. He had rescued "Turn To," a mongrel mascot picked up in Casablanca.

Surviving crewmen told how the initial blast had torn five-inch gun mounts from the deck and sent them hurtling into the air, catapulting over and over until they hit the water and sank. Many men were believed killed by exploding shells from ammunition racks at the anti-aircraft guns.

There was no panic. Sailors stood by their stations, even in the engineroom spaces, until word came to abandon ship.

The cause of this disaster was never

The Italian liner Andrea Doria *drifts lifelessly on her side after colliding with the Swedish liner* Stockholm *in patchy fog 45 miles south of Nantucket Island. The crippled ship sank less than 11 hours after all but 45 of the 1709 passengers were rescued July 25, 1956.*

175

The two tankers Panclio and Spring Hill collided in the early morning of February 5, 1945, and the resulting blaze killed seven with sixty injured and many missing.

determined, but it was thought that a careless sailor may have tossed a lighted cigarette too close to ammunition. When the final count was made, it was found that 163 were saved; more than 100 were killed.

Almost as disastrous as the explosion on the *Turner* was a collision on February 5, 1945, involving the tankers *Clio* and *Spring Hill*, which was fully loaded with a cargo nearly as lethal as TNT. In her tanks were 120,000 barrels of high-octane gasoline.

There was an immediate explosion and fire on the *Spring Hill*, and gasoline cascaded over the sides in flaming waves, engulfing the Norwegian tanker *Vivi*, anchored less than a hundred yards away. The *Vivi*, fully loaded with diesel oil, tried to hoist anchor and escape, but the flames spread too quickly.

According to an account in the *Herald Tribune*, "a series of explosions shook both ships, hurling men overboard. Others leaped into the burning oil and gasoline and swam desperately underwater."

176   A fleet of thirty city fireboats and

Coast Guard craft converged on the scene to pick up survivors and fight the fire. The fireboats used more than twenty thousand pounds of powdered foam, which was mixed with water and shot through hoses to choke the fire.

More than 120 men were picked up from the water, many of them badly burned. About twenty were killed or missing, some of them trapped aboard the fire-swept ships.

Many books could be written—and some have—about the myriad accidents that have occurred in the harbor and nearby waters, or to vessels, such as the famous *Vestris* and *Lusitania*, that had sailed from this port, or that, like *Morro Castle* or *Titanic*, came to grief while New York-bound.

Of all the calamities that have occurred to New York ships few were more dramatic or had more far-reaching consequences than the burning of the *Morro Castle* off Asbury Park, New Jersey.

This turbo-electric ship, flying the house flag of the Ward Line, was

The crew of the SS American Merchant lowers lifeboats from their ship in a thrilling mid-ocean rescue of twenty-two survivors of the British ship, SS Exeter City, which sprung her seams during a storm. Four men, including the captain, were lost in the rough seas which disabled the English ship.

Of all the calamities that have occurred to New York ships few were more dramatic than the burning of the Morro Castle off Asbury Park, New Jersey, September 8, 1934.

Below: *Friends and relatives anxiously await the arrival of Titanic survivors. The White Star Liner crashed into an iceberg in the North Atlantic seas near Newfoundland the night of April 14, 1912.*

returning to New York on a regular run from Havana when fire broke out on the morning of September 8, 1934. What followed is a sad story of confusion and ineptitude by the ship's crew which, together with dense smoke and spreading flames, resulted in the loss of 124 lives, mostly passengers. One lifeboat contained thirty-two crew members and no passengers.

This disaster, which occurred close to shore, resulted in a drastic revision of America's maritime safety laws, especially as they applied to ship construction, and stricter requirements for the certification of merchant seamen.

New Yorkers have thrilled to innumerable dramas of harbor waters—and to sagas of the sea involving the city's ships and seamen. Participants in ocean dramas have docked here to receive the front-page acclaim that sea-minded New York has always given to salty seadogs and heroes of the rolling ocean.

Few of them were more often honored than Capt. Giles C. Stedman, for it seemed that every time the North Atlantic ruffled her feathers Stedman was Johnny-on-the-spot to rescue crewmen from some sinking ship.

Stedman, who later was to command the New York-based liners *Washington* and *America*, first made headlines here in 1925 when, as first mate of the S.S. *President Harding* of United States Lines, he commanded a lifeboat crew that rescued twenty-eight men from the sinking Italian freighter *Ignazio Florio* in a North Atlantic storm.

In January of 1933 Stedman was master of the S.S. *American Merchant*, bound from London to New York, when he received an SOS from the British freighter *Exeter City* and a message saying it was helpless and taking water in a vicious midwinter gale.

Proceeding to the site with the aid of radio bearings, Stedman found the battered ship after an excellent feat of navigation. He hoped to stand by till the gale moderated so as not to endanger a lifeboat crew, but the British ship started to go down and there was no time to spare. The *American Merchant's* crew poured oil in the lee of

the *Exeter City*, and a boat's crew of volunteers made their way to the helpless hulk through the pounding waves, made less dangerous by the oil slicks. Huge seas had swept away the entire bridge section of the *Exeter City* and had taken the captain and several men with it. The rest of the crew were safely ferried to the *American Merchant* in a display of courageous small-boat handling.

Stedman and his crew received no ticker-tape parade up Broadway, but they did receive the city's "well done" in the form of front-page

accolades when their ship reached port.

No saga of the sea involving the city's ships and seamen ever thrilled New Yorkers more than Capt. Kurt Carlsen and his *Flying Enterprise*.

On a westbound crossing from Europe to New York in late December of 1951 the 6,700-ton freighter, owned by the Isbrandtsen Company of New York, was battered by a storm with huge seas and winds of hurricane force. Under this vicious battering, a crack developed across the deckhouse and along the hull. Although

Capt. Giles Stedman, heroic skipper of the SS American Merchant, *stands with members of the crew of the ill-fated British freighter* Exeter City, *after their arrival in New York on the rescue ship* American Merchant. *The captain, third officer, and two crewmen of the* Exeter City *were reported washed overboard, January 26, 1933.*

Carlsen tried to heave to, the crack opened wider, letting tons of water into the forward holds. Shifting cargo and the weight of flooding water sent the ship over on its port side in a dangerous list. Forty crewmen and nine passengers were taken off the helpless ship, but Carlsen refused to leave, saying, "I will stay with the ship until she reaches port or until she goes down."

For thirteen days Carlsen rode his storm-tossed freighter, mostly alone, while New Yorkers—and the rest of the world—followed his heroic efforts through headlines and radio news bulletins.

Salvage tugs finally got towlines aboard and headed for the English coast, three hundred miles away, but another storm came up and the *Flying Enterprise* could take no more. Carlsen was taken off just before his ship disappeared beneath the waves.

Kenneth R. Dancy, chief mate of the British salvage tug *Turmoil*, had joined Carlsen on the canting freighter several days before. He left the *Flying Enterprise* as it went down.

180 Few other heroes or famous visitors have received the acclaim accorded Carlsen during a civic welcome on January 18, 1952.

Ships in the harbor sounded their whistles in his honor. More than three hundred thousand New Yorkers waved and cheered as Carlsen was paraded from the Battery to City Hall. He rode in an open car preceded by an honorary guard of mounted police, an army band, and various military units, including the seven-hundred-man cadet corps from the U.S. Merchant Marine Academy at Kings Point.

The heroic captain received many awards, but they were all summed up in the inscription on a plaque presented to him by President Harry Truman on behalf of the Veterans of Foreign Wars. It read simply: "To Captain Kurt Carlsen, for adding to the highest traditions of the sea."

In a way, Carlsen's heroism epitomized the deeds of hundreds, perhaps even thousands, of seamen sailing out of the port of New York who have, in war and peace, upheld such traditions over the city's three hundred years of close association with the sea.

The dramas of the port have by no means all been centered around calamities and disasters.

The bustling activity in New York harbor was always a spectacle in itself, entrancing the daily ferryboat commuter as much as the tourist: the parade of stately liners, the stubby freighters—loaded down to their marks with cargoes of all kinds from ports all over the world, puffing tugs, tankers, and all the rag-tag-and-bobtail of the harbor, from squatty canalboats to grimy coal barges.

Pressing in tight crowds along downtown Broadway, thousands of clamoring New Yorkers cheer Capt. Kurt Carlsen as he is led by marching cadets of the Merchant Marine Academy. Ticker-tape and the greeting "Well done" fill the air around the 37-year-old skipper of the doomed Flying Enterprise.

Opposite, A most momentous occasion took place on October 28, 1886, when the monumental Statue of Liberty was unveiled on Bedloe's Island and presented to the people of the United States as a gift from the people of France.

No other harbor in the world offers a better vantage point than New York's Battery for viewing this daily harbor drama. From colonial times it has been a favorite promenade. For harbor excursionists there was always a pulsing, colorful nautical show, all free for the watching.

Most of the big excursion fleet is long gone now, but excursion trips around Manhattan by the Circle Line and trips to the Statue of Liberty and Ellis Island from the Battery, not to mention the famous ferry ride to Staten Island, are among the city's major tourist attractions.

New Yorkers have always loved a show and the harbor, in one way or another, has given them some of the greatest spectacles to be seen anywhere.

New York's maritime fraternity had an important part in one of the city's first spectaculars, a great parade held here in July of 1783 to celebrate the adoption of the Constitution. All the city's craftsmen were represented. In the maritime section were horse-drawn floats on which nautical crafts were demonstrated as the parade moved along. Sailmakers cut and sewed a foretopsail; blacksmiths forged an anchor and boat builders constructed a ship's boat. There were pumpmakers, ship joiners, block and tackle makers, and others.

Riggers carried a banner saying:
"Fit me well and rig me neat,
And join me to the Federal fleet."

There have been harbor fêtes and celebrations too numerous to list. The 4th of July was an annual occasion for boat races, regattas, and fireworks displays, as well as parades. One of the great harbor fêtes marked the opening of the Erie Canal.

A most momentous occasion took place on October 28, 1886, when the monumental Statue of Liberty was unveiled on Bedloe's Island and presented to the people of the United States as a gift from the people of France. It was a wet, foggy day and the shrouding mists prevented the multitude of onlookers crowding every available space at the Battery, in Brooklyn, Staten Island, and the New Jersey shore from seeing much of the ceremonies, including the dramatic moment when the sculptor, Frederic

A. Bartholdi, severed the ropes that held the vast drapery and Miss Liberty was revealed in all her grandeur.

But the guns of warships off Bedloe's Island signaled the unveiling and as ships all around the harbor sounded their whistles and bells, the throngs ashore joined in with resounding cheers.

President Grover Cleveland and French dignitaries were on hand and Chauncey M. DePew, noted lawyer and politician, delivered the oration, customary for all major occasions. "We dedicate this statue," he said, "to the friendship of nations and the peace of the world."

Millions of seaborne travelers have gazed at Miss Liberty as their ships steamed into the harbor and millions have visited her by way of excursion boats from the Battery.

Inscribed on a bronze plaque in the pedestal of the statue is the sonnet by Emma Lazarus, "The New Colossus," with the famous lines:

"Keep, ancient lands, your storied pomp!" cries she
　with silent lips. "Give me your tired, your poor,
Your huddled masses yearning to breathe free,
　The wretched refuse of your teeming shore.
Send these, the homeless, tempest-tossed, to me.
　I lift my lamp beside the golden door!"

There was a dramatic harbor event on April 27, 1893, when an international naval flotilla gathered here for a grand review. The U.S.S. *Dolphin*, with President Grover Cleveland on board, passed between columns of war vessels flying the flags of England, France, Germany, Holland, Italy, Russia, Spain, Argentina, Brazil, and other nations. Guns boomed out a thunderous applause to America's head of state as the *Dolphin* passed down the lines of anchored ships. The salvos reverberated from the Narrows to the Palisades.

New York had never before seen a show as elaborate as that which was staged in the harbor for Admiral George Dewey, who had led his fleet to a resounding victory over the Spanish at the Battle of Manila Bay, May 1, 1898. Dewey's dash and vigor at Manila, achieving his victory with-

out the loss of a single sailor, had made him the hero of the hour and New York was determined to outdo itself in a hero's welcome.

A naval parade on September 29, 1899, was the climax of the celebration. "There was someone standing on every available foot of viewing space," said the *Times*, "...from piers to rooftops." An estimated million or more turned out to see this harbor spectacular.

The admiral's flagship, the *Olympia*, with his four-starred blue pennant flying from the mast top, led a parade of three hundred warships, steam yachts, and other vessels across the bay and up the Hudson to Grant's Tomb, where the *Olympia* anchored and reviewed the gaily decorated fleet. "Everything that could float," reported the New York *Times*, "was filled with sightseers and merry sounds filled the air. The densely packed humanity at the Battery sent up cheer after cheer, yell after yell, as the *Olympia* steamed by."

A frenzy of cheering erupted as the *Olympia* passed the jampacked piers at 23rd

The victorious crew of the Olympia *parades down Broadway in a celebration honoring Admiral Dewey. September 26, 1899.*

Manning her yards in honor of Queen Kapiolani of the Hawaiian Islands, the USS Atlanta *docks at the Brooklyn Navy Yard, May, 1887.*

Street. There was a brief rain, the sun came out brightly, and a brilliant rainbow shone over the famous ship, as though the gods had crowned her with a special glory for her role in America's new awakening to the importance of naval power.

The great gala staged for Dewey was outdone by another harbor spectacular, this one honoring Henry Hudson and Robert Fulton. The celebration continued from September 25 to October 9, 1909, and included an elaborate parade with historical tableaux and floats, boat races, and

twelve torpedo boats, four submarines, plus other vessels. Warships were also in line from a dozen foreign nations.

Excursion boats were recruited from as far away as Boston and Norfolk to handle the demand for space afloat. "The S.S. *Hendrick Hudson* of the Albany Day Line," said the *Times*, "was so thickly packed that she looked like a giant beehive."

More than a million people packed every available foot of viewing space in Manhattan to see the harbor parade and the awesome display of

184

other events. But the *piece de' resistance* was the harbor show on September 29, with a grand parade of ships led by a replica of Fulton's *Clermont* as well as a replica of Hudson's *Half Moon*, a gift of the Dutch people and manned by a Dutch crew in seventeenth-century seamen's attire. There were sixteen miles of ships in line behind these historic replicas. More than eight hundred vessels of all kinds took part, from sleek steam yachts to battleships. The American naval contingent included sixteen battleships, six cruisers,

lights and fireworks that followed after nightfall.

"Such a crowd," said the *Times*, "has never been seen in New York before."

But this spectacular was to be outdone, too.

New York has never seen a harbor show more thrilling than Operation Sail, the parade of windjammers staged to celebrate the nation's bicentennial on July 4, 1976. More than two hundred sailing ships flying the flags of twenty-eight nations took part in this dra-

matic sail-in, before which many of them had raced from England to the Canary Islands, Bermuda, and Newport, Rhode Island. Millions of people watched the tall ships from any vantage point along the harbor and from a huge fleet of excursion boats and small craft. It has been estimated that as many as 100 million followed the nautical parade on television as the full-rigged ships, barks, barkentines, ketches and schooners stood majestically through the Narrows and spread out through the harbor in a mass extravaganza that

when tall-masted, white-winged ships course by. "Nothing," said one paper, "has ever fired so many dreams or woven such magic or aroused the best instincts of our people."

The *Seafarer's Log* of the Seafarer's International Union summed it up well in these words:

"Followed by 15 other tall ships and 200 smaller sailing vessels, the U.S. Coast Guard bark *Eagle* led the Operation Sail flotilla up the parade route as millions drawn by their magic were joined together in the joy and

186

has never been seen here before and probably never will be seen again. Anchored warships lined the Hudson as the tall ships glided by, a tribute from the age of steam and atoms to the yesteryear of "wooden ships and iron men," and to the nation's 200th birthday.

It was New York's grandest day. Although an estimated six million jammed Manhattan's waterside, the police reported less crime than on an average day. It was the magic of ships and sail and the aura of romance that holds almost anyone spellbound

excitement of a very special bicentennial celebration, a celebration of our heritage and our unique bonds with the sea."

It was a New York harbor triumph.

The U.S. Coast Guard bark Eagle *led the Operation Sail flotilla up the parade route during the American bicentennial celebration, July 4, 1976.*

Operation Sail, the magnificent massing of tall ships on July 3-4, 1976, stirred the hearts and imaginations of all who saw this great display.

The crew of the USS Nautilus stand quarters for muster as she enters New York harbor. One of many tugs displays her greeting to the submarine which, in August, 1958, made a transpolar voyage under the arctic ice.

CHAPTER 13
THE PORT GOES TO WAR

The port of New York has served the nation in many wars, embarking troops and supplies for the Mexican war in 1846, the Civil War, the Spanish-American War, the two world wars, the Korean War, and the war in Southeast Asia.

New York was the principal base of supplies for Union forces in the Civil War and was headquarters for the Department of the East. Here were acquired and outfitted a large part of the fleet of transports and blockade ships, and here was built a fleet of monitors and other vessels for war service. Huge amounts of supplies were shipped from New York.

Many thousands of soldiers left for Civil War battlefields from New York piers. The city probably never before or since has witnessed the feverish excitement of April 19th, 1861, when the city's beloved 7th Regiment, preceded by a band of colorful Zouaves, marched down Broadway to Cortlandt Street to take ferries for New Jersey and thence the trains for Washington.

They were preceded a few hours by the 8th Massachusetts.

"The piers, landings, and house tops of New York, Jersey City, Hoboken, and Brooklyn were filled with people," said one observer. "Thousands upon thousands sent up cheers of parting."

Business life in the city again came to a standstill on the 21st when the 6th, 12th, and 71st New York militia regiments marched to the waterfront amid wildly cheering crowds and embarked on the steamers *Baltic*, *R. R. Schyler*, and *Ariel*.

One New Yorker recalled how thrilling it was to see the blue-clad volunteers striding along toward the docks, flags flying, long muskets on their shoulders, regimental bands playing stirring airs of the time.

"We all went down to Broadway this morning," she wrote, "to see Roger's company take a ship for the South. After much waiting we heard a noise of fifes and drums and then their band playing very gaily as the regiment swung into Broadway from where they had been mustered on a side street. The men looked so tall and bright and confident. It seemed so much like one of their summer parades and not at all like they were marching off to battle and many of them never to return."

Among the most colorful of all troops to set off brightly and smartly for southern battlefields were Col. Elmer Ellsworth's Fire Brigade Zouaves, known throughout the war as the Fire Zouaves. Enlisted from the ranks of the city's volunteer fire departments, dressed in bright red and blue jackets and baggy pantaloons copied after the uniforms of French Zouaves, they were, in martial array, every bit as cocky and proud as when they raced each other to Manhattan fires with their shining helmets and brightly painted engines.

In 1861, Fort Columbus on Governor's Island was the main army recruiting center for the entire Eastern Seaboard; it was also an assembly point for units awaiting embarkation to the South. There were as many as seven regiments encamped there at one time. It is not generally known that the island also had a prison camp for captured Confederates.

During the Civil War the federal government bought ships of all kinds for use as transports and for blockade duty off the southern ports. Typical of these was the sidewheel steamer *DeSoto*, purchased soon after outbreak of war and outfitted by the Brooklyn Navy Yard. She served with the West Gulf Blockading Squadron, capturing twenty-three blockade-runners during her war career. The Navy Yard also build many ships during the war years.

These war-built and war-acquired vessels had myriad adventures. The

One of the largest factors in the ultimate victory of the North was its sea power. The sloop-of-war Brooklyn, *2,000 tons, carrying fourteen guns, was one of the best fighting ships available at the beginning of the war. It was with such vessels and their successors that the Federal navy ultimately established its blockade of Confederate ports.*

189

150-foot *Albatross*, for instance, was an almost-new ship when the federal government bought her at Brooklyn in 1861 and had her armed and outfitted for blockading duty. This former merchantman served well, taking part in the capture of Port Hudson, the passage of the batteries at Grand Gulf, Mississippi, and in a sea battle with the Confederate raider *Beaufort*. Her log shows numerous other actions, including the attack on Fort DeRussy, Louisiana, in 1863, when a rebel cannonball smashed through the wheelhouse and carried away the wheel. She captured four blockade-runners, including an Englishman. This gallant merchantman-turned-fighter served throughout the war.

In June of 1865 regular commerce was restored throughout the nation by order of the President, with the port of New York enjoying the effects of this almost immediately. The New York *Times* of June 28 heralded the return of normal business operations and reported the first "legitimate" shipment of cotton from New York to Europe in four years.

190   "Shipping has been engaged in this

Col. Elmer Ellsworth was officer in charge of the Fire Brigade Zouaves, one of the most colorful of the volunteer groups.

Right, *New York was headquarters for the Department of the East in the Civil War. Thousands of recruits were processed. This scene is of the U.S. Naval Recruiting Office in 1861.*

Below, *The Albatross recaptured the schooner* Enchantress *off Hatteras Inlet, July 20, 1861.* Enchantress *had originally been captured by the Confederate privateer* Jefferson Davis, *two weeks earlier.*

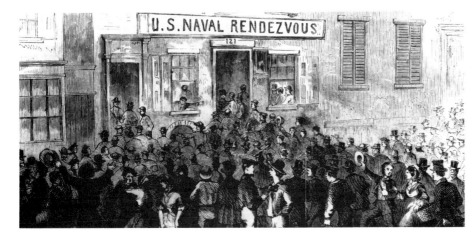

Below, *An 1861 view of Fort Lafayette in New York Harbor "where political prisoners are confined."*

Bottom, *New York's renowned Twelfth Regiment posed for photographer Matthew Brady. Some of the men are dressed as Algerian Zouaves.*

191

port alone, within a few days, for the transportation of 8,000 bales to Liverpool and vessels are also being laden at other Northern ports," it said.

The Brooklyn Navy Yard (which has been known under several names) built fourteen ships for the Union navy during the Civil War. More than six thousand men were employed there.

Three warships named *Brooklyn* had prominent roles in the nation's wars. The first *Brooklyn* was a screw sloop build by Jacob A. Westervelt and Son in 1859, with Capt. David

Farragut commanding. She served with the West Gulf Blockading Squadron during the Civil War, taking part in many actions. At the battle of Mobile Bay, *Brooklyn* was hit twenty times by Confederate shells, with eleven killed and forty-three wounded. The ship was decommissioned at the New York Navy Yard and sold out of the navy in 1891.

The second *Brooklyn* was launched in 1895 at the William Cramp and Sons yard in Philadelphia. It was part of the famous Flying Squadron during the war with Spain in 1898, flying the flag of Commodore W.S. Schley. She took a leading part in the battle of Santiago on July 3, 1898, when the Spanish fleet was destroyed. *Brooklyn* served with the fleet until 1921.

The third *Brooklyn* was launched in 1936 at the New York Navy Yard. In 1942 she rescued 1,173 troops from the transport *Wakefield* when that ship caught fire in the Atlantic. *Brooklyn* took part in the invasion of North Africa, the invasion of Sicily, and the landings at Anzio and southern France. She was given to the Chilean navy in 1951.

The activities of the port in the Civil War and the Spanish-American War were overshadowed by the huge job accomplished in World War I, when New York was the major embarkation port for troops and, by far, the principal shipping port for supplies for the American Expeditionary Force and our Allies.

Throughout that war the Allied Purchasing Mission preferred ordering their purchases "FOB New York," despite urgings to disperse their shipments among other ports. New York had the reputation for being able to deliver, and many of those associated with the Purchasing Mission had prior experience with the port.

Between 1914 and 1917 half of the world's entire stock of gold was centered in New York, much of it arriving from England and France in the strong rooms of the speedy Atlantic liners.

This money paid for the guns and other war supplies shipped to England and France, no small part of it in the holds of returning liners. From 1914 to 1916 the United States shipped $500 million worth of munitions and

Left, An engraving of a Matthew Brady photograph of Admiral David Farragut, the great American naval hero.

Commodore W.S. Schley, in his stateroom aboard the USS Baltimore, was later captain of the USS Brooklyn. Launched in 1895, Brooklyn was part of the famous Flying Squadron of the Spanish-American War.

The mighty USS Maine stands anchored in New York harbor. Her sinking was the central action precipitating the Spanish-American War.

193

In a show of naval strength the USS Brooklyn steams past Grant's Tomb in a review in 1939.

other war equipment, mostly from the port of New York.

There were occasional bottlenecks in cargo handling and ship fueling in World War I. In those days most steamers burned coal, and refueling ships became a major problem. At one time, with the harbor so blocked with ice that coal lighters could not get out to anchored ships, more than 150 vessels were waiting for coal. Some thirty thousand freight cars were, at one time, sitting on tracks waiting to unload into lighters or ships.

Edward N. Hurley, wartime chairman of the United States Shipping Board, was shocked by congestion in the port of New York. It was so bad early in 1918 that long lines of wagons waited for hours, even days, to get onto the piers. To avoid losing their place in line, teamsters would unhitch their horses and stable them for the night, leaving their wagons in the waiting line.

"It happened time and time again," Hurley says in his book *The Bridge to France*, "that at some New York terminals eleven or twelve hours were consumed in loading one truck.... The conditions at New York amounted almost to a blockade...coordination in loading and unloading of steamers was practically non-existent."

A Port and Harbors Facilities Commission was established, and, by late 1918, cargo was moving much more smoothly and quickly. The commission also provided more drydocks, ship-repair facilities, and bunkering docks.

World War I signaled an end, temporarily, to the transatlantic liner business in New York but brought on a boom in steamer movements to the nonbelligerent nations of Italy, Spain, Portugal, Holland, Sweden, and Norway. Interestingly, it also created a demand for sailing ships, and not only were many windjammers brought out of retirement in the demand for bottoms at any price, but shipyards in New England and the Northwest built many big schooners and barkentines for domestic and foreign buyers.

New York, a neutral port and free to trade with all nations, suddenly found itself even more of a hub of world trade. Many ship brokers and others having business with cargo shipping moved to New York from London and other ports in Europe.

The shipping district of lower Broadway, according to a news account of 1915, had become a "babel of tongues," with Britons, Dutch, French, Norwegians, Greeks, and yes, even Germans, vying for ship charters. In 1913 a total of 4,448 ships entered the port. In 1916 the total jumped to 5,189. There was a significant recovery in American-flag shipping, too.

Dock space was at a premium during these boom years. Pier rentals zoomed from about eighty dollars a day at prime piers to as much as three hundred dollars a day.

Shipyards expanded their facilities to handle the increased demand for repair work, especially the rejuvenation of old ships which came out of lay-up, and not a few right out of junkyards, to satisfy the demand for bottoms. "Bottoms at any price," became the cry among the ship brokers of Manhattan.

Outbound goods ran the gamut

Opposite, far left, *The George Washington takes on coal November 25, 1918. Note the latest in mechanical coalloaders used to transfer the fuel from barges alongside.*

Left, *During preparations for the Great War, a 12-inch gun was installed in the forward turret of the USS* Connecticut *at the Brooklyn Navy Yard, January, 1906.*

After the Spanish-American War there was a national welcome to the victorious navy. The fleet under the command of admirals Sampson and Schley, including the USS New York, Iowa, Indiana, Brooklyn, Oregon, Massachusetts, *and* Texas, *salutes Grants Tomb on August 20, 1898.*

from corned beef to cigarettes, lumber to lard, wheat to wool. Thousands of horses and mules were shipped out of New York. Hundreds of ships loaded up with coal and coke. Machinery of all kinds was exported. There were continual shipments of explosives, too.

The government set up the Emergency Fleet Corporation to build a bridge of ships to Europe, and it negotiated with private firms to construct a number of very large shipyards to turn out several types of standardized freighters on a mass-production system. One of these plants, at Newark Bay, New Jersey, was operated by the Submarine Boat Corporation for the government. This yard had twenty-eight shipways and built many five-thousand-ton freighters. The war ended before it could fulfill its contract to build 150 ships of 750,000 deadweight tons.

Another yard was operated by the Federal Shipbuilding Company at Kearny, New Jersey, where a 9,600-ton class of freighter was produced.

A number of German ships were seized in the port of New York when the United States entered the war against the Central Powers. The largest and best known of these was the great *Vaterland*, which was renamed *Leviathan* and became the queen of the American merchant marine.

The port contributed substantial transportation expertise toward the goal of moving eighty divisions to France by the end of 1918, the aim of General Pershing and the U.S. Shipping Board. The war ended before anywhere near this number of troops

196

INSPIRING CABLEGRAMS

CHAIRMAN EDWARD N. HURLEY *cables:* "* * * We want you and the boys in the trenches to know that the men in the yards are going the limit to provide in record-breaking time the ships that will carry more Men, Food and Munitions to the intrepid American Expeditionary Forces."

GENERAL PERSHING *replies:* "The launching of nearly 100 ships on the Fourth of July is the most inspiring news that has come to us. All ranks of the Army in France send their congratulations and heartfelt thanks to their patriotic brothers in the shipyards at home. No more defiant answer could be given to the enemy's challenge. With such backing we cannot fail to win. All hail, American Ship-Builders!"

Wartime propaganda in the form of inspirational cablegrams from port director Edward N. Hurley and General "Black Jack" Pershing.

The USS Texas, fully prepared for war, steams past the skyline of lower Manhattan in 1916.

197

The largest part of the two million troops sent to France during World War I were from the Port of New York. Here is but one of the huge troopships being boarded in 1918.

went overseas but, still, more than two million men were sent to France, the greater part of this army embarking from New York.

One of many regiments that sailed to the war from Manhattan aboard the British liner *Olympic* was the 59th Infantry. Its voyage turned out to be more than routine. Near the coast of Ireland the *Olympic* sighted a submarine, and before the U-boat could take evasive action the liner made a sharp turn, rammed, and sank it. In appreciation for the keen-eyed lookout who spotted the U-boat in the

camouflaging was set up under Henry Grover, and by war's end it had trained 150 men in this unique form of seagoing art.

Another novel project was undertaken by Hudson Maxim, the famous inventor and expert on explosives, and New York naval architect Morgan Barney, who collaborated on developing a torpedo-resistant ship. Their idea was to line the inside of the hull below the waterline with cylinders that would act as insulators from an exploding torpedo. The cylinders would be

198

dark of a moonless night, and for the alert bridge watch that ordered the instant maneuver, the troops of the 59th donated a plaque to the *Olympic*, which the famous ship carried to the end of its days.

New York had a leading role in one of the most unusual projects of the war. It was believed that ships would be safer if camouflaged by designs painted on the hull (angular stripes and varying shades of color) to confuse submarines about the vessel's size, speed, and course. A school for

filled with water or pulverized coal that could be piped into the boilers like oil. But hostilities ceased and an armistice was declared before the idea could be tried.

A wreck and a feat of salvage strikingly similar to that of the *Normandie* took place in World War I when the War Department requisitioned the liner *St. Paul* and had her towed to pier 60 on the North River for conversion into a troop transport.

While she was being warped into dock, she took a sudden and un-

The heroic British transport Olympic *in New York, 1918. She later rammed and sank a U-boat near the coast of Ireland. Note the use of camouflage to confuse U-boats.*

A royal welcome was given to Commander and Mrs. Albert C. Read just after a successful flight of the USS Zeppelin in June of 1919.

The camouflaged USS Robinson escorts a ship filled with troops out of New York in 1918.

explained list to port, causing water to pour through open portholes and hatches. Within a few minutes the big ship was sitting on the bottom, almost perpendicular, in a bed of mud.

Righting and raising the ship involved a challenging job of salvage for the Chapman Derrick and Wrecking Co., later to become one of the world's biggest salvage outfits under the name of Merritt, Chapman and Scott.

The *St. Paul* was armed with heavy guns at that time and, as guns were in short supply, the number one priority

an even more herculean service for the nation and its allies during World War II. Piers which berthed the world's greatest passenger liners were available for the embarkation of regiments and entire divisions. The port's piers were used to handle millions of tons of cargo. From the tanker docks at Bayonne was shipped a large part of the oil and gasoline that fueled the ships in foreign ports and ran the trucks, tanks, and planes of the invasion forces.

One of this nation's most dramatic contributions to the Allied cause in

was removal of her deck armament, all but buried in mud. This the divers accomplished in a seemingly impossible assignment, working at great risk amid a tangle of jagged steel and ships' fittings.

The liner sank on April 25 and on the 11th of September it rose up from the river bed on an even keel, ready for ballasting and cleaning. The entire job had been accomplished without a single casualty.

Tremendous as its contribution was to World War I, the port performed

World War II came in June of 1940, with the New York port area having an important role.

In the evacuation of British and French forces from Dunkirk in May-June of 1940, the British army had to leave all its equipment behind, including 2,300 pieces of artillery, 120,000 vehicles, 90,000 rifles, and 7,000 tons of ammunition. Britain then faced an anticipated German invasion almost denuded of the arms to repel it.

Prime Minister Winston Churchill

The USS George Washington *sails out of New York Bay, March 5, 1919, with president Wilson on his way to sign the Treaty of Versailles. This photograph was taken from the deck of an accompanying submarine chaser.*

200

A massive crash construction of submarine chasers in the New York Navy Yard, August, 1917.

201

Franklin D. Roosevelt, Mayor F. Hyland, and Admiral W.S. Benson review a victory parade after the Armistice in November 1918.

dispatched an urgent call for help to President Franklin D. Roosevelt and the American government responded generously and immediately.

Within a few days, American arsenals were virtually stripped and trainloads of arms and ammunition were rolling toward the New York port area in six hundred freight cars. A dozen British freighters were at dock to meet them and almost within hours ships started steaming with their vital defense cargoes toward embattled Britain. In their holds were half a million rifles, with ammunition, 900 field guns with a million rounds of ammunition, and 80,000 machine guns, plus much other equipment.

"We ferried these precious weapons safely across the Atlantic," said Churchill, "and they formed not only a material gain, but an important factor in all calculations made by friend or foe about invasion."

In 1942 and 1943 the port of New York handled twice as much cargo as it did during the 1917-18 war. And it did so with a minimum of confusion, thanks to much advance planning. In fact, the machinery of cargo handling moved so smoothly throughout the war that the port never reached a point of saturation. There was always an ability to handle additional cargo, despite what seemed to be an archaic system of cargo movement, with shipments having to be transferred from railroad terminals in New Jersey to piers or shipside in Brooklyn and Manhattan.

Such a system would seem to be an open invitation to disaster in wartime. That it functioned smoothly, efficiently, and with an always greater potential was due in large measure to the farsighted formation in 1940 of a committee to expedite shipments and eliminate bottlenecks.

This committee was formed by the Maritime Association of the Port of New York, the General Managers Association, and the Association of American Railroads. It consisted mainly of representatives of steamship lines and of railroad lighterage departments. E. J. Carr, vice president of Calmar Steamship Company, was chairman. The committee met twice a month to solve lighterage problems.

Fast and expeditious lighterage was the key to smooth freight handling in New York, which was unique in its system of railroad-to-dock and railroad-to-ship cargo transfer.

Shipments through New York increased greatly, of course, after the United States entered the war. In the first four months of 1942, for instance, 114,129 railroad cars were unloaded and their contents, for the most part, loaded aboard ship, compared to the 80,369 cars handled in the same period of 1940.

There was also a truck-pier coordinating committee to expedite handling of shipments to and from the piers, shoreside. The work of this committee, it was later claimed, "virtually eliminated delays to trucks at steamship piers."

The Maritime Association also organized a Joint Committee on New York Port Protection, which worked with the Coast Guard, the Navy, and other agencies to protect piers, ships, and cargoes from sabotage, careless fires, and explosions.

The June 1943 issue of the *Maritime Exchange Bulletin* explained how the

Wartime New York could handle fourteen hundred railroad cars everyday. This photo of the New York Central Port Yards was taken in 1943 at the height of port activity.

Wartime cargo taxed the ingenuity of port directors. Here an entire fighter is carefully loaded for the European theatre of operations.

202

port functioned so smoothly during the war years:

Clogging in the port is avoided by control of shipments to the docks by the Transportation Control Committee, made up of representatives of the Army and Navy, the Office of Defense Transportation, the United States War Shipping Administration, and the British Ministry of War Transport. The Committee meets every day and sets quotas for permits to move goods to all ports, depending on the number of ships available.

Storage facilities are kept clear by a system of shipment permits and open-ground storage and by organizing cargoes in depots some distance from the port, called 'storage banks.'

Thanks to its peacetime role as the busiest passenger and cargo terminal in the world, the port had a great pool of expertise in all phases of rail, marine, and truck transportation. Experience and know-how meant as much as facilities and hardware in enabling the port of New York to perform its job as the nation's number one port in the war effort.

204

This port, of course, was ideal for concentrated use in a war emergency, with protected anchorages in the lower harbor and the Hudson River available for a large number of ships. A huge convoy coming in from Europe or the Mediterranean could be dispersed to docks and anchorages without choking channels and blocking access to piers. On one day in 1943, the port handled 275 ships at dock without approaching capacity! Probably no other port in the world could have exceeded this capability, much less duplicated it under war conditions.

According to the Association of American Railroads, New York in 1943 had a capacity for handling fourteen hundred railroad cars every day. Only a very small percentage of war shipments arrived in the port by truck. Some traffic, including petroleum, was handled over the New York State Barge Canal.

Said an editorial in the *Maritime Exchange Bulletin* in 1943: "Experts who look upon the port's facilities as archaic, marvel that such efficiency and flexibility have been achieved." Half the piers in the port during the war years, it should be remembered,

had no railroad connections and were dependent on barges, lighters, and car floats.

This system of freight movement made New York the busiest port in the world as far as maritime traffic was concerned. In 1943, the port's vast armada of floating equipment moved the contents of 430,386 railroad cars!

At the peak of the war effort, in 1944, the port of New York employed 500 tugs, 55 self-propelled derrick lighters, 1,200 open lighters and scows, 900 covered barges and lighters, 135 covered scows, 323 car floats, and 75 grain boats. There were also some 300 canalboats moving into the harbor from the state barge canals.

In 1944, it was reported that New York was handling more ships than any other port in the history of the world.

While it is always hazardous to engage in superlatives, this was a statement hard to contest. Through the Narrows and out to sea toward England, the Mediterranean, South Africa, the Middle East, Russia, the Far East, and Latin America went sixty percent of all the nation's deep-sea

Opposite, right, In 1943 alone, the facilities of the Port of New York moved the contents of almost half a million railroad cars. Here, jeeps are loaded for shipment to Europe.

A portion of the fleet at anchor in New York Harbor in 1939. All photography of wartime activity was banned shortly thereafter.

The USS Missouri, destined for fame in the Pacific, is launched at the New York Navy Yard, January 29, 1944.

shipping.

Few people knew then that New York was the "brain center" for organizing, dispatching, and controlling convoys that left this port for Atlantic crossings.

Commodore Frederick J. Reinicke, the navy's port director in New York, headed a staff of eleven hundred men and women who supervised the flow of ships and goods of war from the world's busiest port. It was termed "the world's biggest marine traffic job."

The port director's people inspected every ship entering the port and interviewed every returning captain about his voyage and the capabilities of his ship. They decided which ships had to go in convoy and which, because of superior speed, priority of cargo, or the route to be traveled, could hazard the voyage unescorted. They dispatched the convoys and kept track of their progress en route. They also kept track of every vessel in the harbor, plotting its daily positions on a huge wall-chart for quick reference.

206 Other big charts in the port director's headquarters showed the daily position of the convoys and the best-known position of German U-boats on their course. Convoy routes and courses were changed from this office to avoid U-boat concentration.

In 1943, this "brain center" directed the ocean progress of ten thousand ships! Hundreds of troop-transport sailings from New York were directed from this office, too, and not one was torpedoed or prevented by the enemy from reaching its destination.

The port director's office made up all the convoys sailing out of New York, assigning ships to various convoys according to destination and readiness to sail. There were so-called fast ship convoys and slow ship convoys, a fast convoy being one that could consistently make ten to twelve knots or better. A slow convoy was generally a six-knot group, many of which made up in St. Johns, New Brunswick, or Halifax, Nova Scotia. They contained many an old ship that had long since seen its best days and now was an attractive target for submarine wolf packs waiting for such convoys to hobble along.

The world's biggest marine traffic job—directing a staff of eleven hundred during World War II—was ably handled by Commodore Frederick J. Reinicke, the navy's port director in New York.

Troops with full battle gear hastily depart the Port of New York for an unknown destination in 1944.

Convoys leaving New York later in the war sometimes comprised eighty or more merchant ships, plus naval escorts that joined them after the ships had left harbor.

Before a convoy sailed, a conference of all the captains was held in the port director's headquarters, with the convoy commodore, usually the most experienced of the merchant-ship captains, and one of the senior officers of the naval escort group.

In the conference room was a large blackboard on which the make-up of

According to a navy report in 1945, not a single convoy was delayed for lack of pilots. The Sandy Hook pilots handled as many as 243 ships in a single day. Considerable traffic was handled also by the Hell Gate pilots, who directed vessels transiting Long Island Sound to and from New York and the Cape Cod Canal, which many ships bound for convoy make-up points in Boston or Canada used to avoid the more exposed trip around Cape Cod.

The stevedoring companies certainly deserve special mention, too.

sugar, rubber, ores, and other cargoes needed by the civilian population and the war effort.

The stevedoring firms also contributed in another way: by training more than a thousand young Navy Seabee officers, and more than a thousand soldiers from the Army Transportation Corps, in cargo handling techniques necessary for the invasion staging ports of Great Britain for the great invasion of Europe; on the Normandy beaches, in North Africa, Italy, and the South and Western Pacific; from remote island storage

the convoy had been diagrammed, showing the position of each ship. On entering the room each shipmaster was given a sealed envelope marked "secret," containing a card showing the position of his ship in the convoy and directing when he was to move out and head for the Narrows and the harbor gate. Convoys were organized and dispatched with trainlike precision.

No little credit for the smooth functioning of the port during the war must go to the harbor police, too.

The longshoreman—the "man with the hook"—was the one who performed the manual labor of loading the crates and the barrels, the trucks and tanks and guns onto the outward-bound ships. Despite bitter cold or sweltering heat, the longshoremen turned out day and night to sling the cargoes on board and speed the convoys on their way. They also worked the incoming ships, which were as important to the war arsenal as were the outgoing ships to the fighting fronts, for they brought

depots to the shell-swept shores of Iwo Jima.

The extent of the port's contribution to the war effort in know-how and expertise was far-flung and complex. Only a detailed reporting of this vast effort—and none has been done —could give credit to all those who took part. The full story is yet to be written.

209

Opposite, left, *A huge dump truck is angled into the hold of a freighter to be unloaded only a week later on the French coast, 1944.*

Navy Waves in tight formation head a parade honoring the Fleet Admiral Chester Nimitz immediately after the war's end, October 9, 1945.

CHAPTER 14
A TIME
OF CHANGE

I f you had walked along the New York waterfront on a warm spring day in 1870 you would have been in a nautical paradise. Ships of all kinds, from just about every seafaring nation, lined the docks along the East River. This was still the age of sail. Windjammers outnumbered steamers by ten to one or more. There were clipper ships: slim, sharp-nosed survivors of the great age of the China tea trade. There were many more utilitarian square-riggers, full-rigged ships of heavier body than clippers, designed for cargo capacity rather than speed. More numerous were barks, three-masters, square-rigged on the first two masts and schooner-rigged on the third, a design that afforded almost as much speed as a full-rigged ship but could be handled by a smaller crew.

Even more numerous were brigs, little two-masted vessels carrying square sails on both masts; and brigantines, a compromise between a brig and a schooner, square-rigged on the foremast and schooner-rigged on the main.

Most numerous were the schooners, two- and three-masters mostly, for this was before the days of the great four-, five-, and six-masted coasting and offshore schooners, the queens of the fore and aft.

If you had stopped to talk with a suntanned, hard-fisted sailor from one of those little brigs or brigantines you might have discovered that he was just in from the Baltic or the Mediterranean or perhaps the Gold Coast of Africa. True, the coasting trades and the Caribbean were the primary domain of these small vessels in New York, but their adventurous owners, skippers, and crews knew no ocean bounds. Nested together at an East River pier, discharging everything from Russian cordage to Jamaica rum, you would see them in from Cuba, Mexico, Barbados, New Orleans, Texas, Halifax, the Azores, Le Havre, or Copenhagen.

The New York *Maritime Register*, published by the Merchants Exchange and News Association, is a rich source of marine intelligence for this, a golden age in New York shipping.

The issue of April 2, 1870, listed 424 ships in port. Seventy of these were full-rigged ships and 96 were barks. There were 89 brigs and brigantines, 105 schooners, and 64 steamers.

Ships in port were loading cargo for such far-flung destinations as Melbourne, London, San Francisco, Callao, Hong Kong, Cape Town, and Odessa. The riverside streets were filled with heavily laden drays pulled by weary horses, the teamsters vying for space along the cargo-filled piers. There was a continuous cacophony of sound: the clatter of hoofs and the shouts of stevedores, sailors, and cargo clerks tallying freight going in and out of the ships. Whistles of tugboats edging tall-masted outward-bounders out of dock into the stream. Sailors swaggering out of a Fulton Street saloon roaring the words of "The Shanghai Bumboatman."

And there were the waterfront smells and scents...of tea and molasses...tobacco and coffee...of lemons and oranges...wool and spices...of hemp and resin. And if you were around the Fulton Fish Market at Fulton and South streets there was always the smell of fish being forked out of the holds of boats in from the Banks.

And there were the cargoes. In the boxes and bales, the tins, the chests, and the hogsheads were the incoming products of the world beyond the horizon, plus a thousand items of all kinds bound from American farms and factories to buyers all over the world.

If you had walked the waterfront here on the second of April in 1870

The West Side Waterfront, 1809. This crowded view of the Hudson River docks, looking north on West Street from Rector Street, shows the busy life of the New York waterfront in the years just after the Civil War. The river is full of ships of all descriptions while along the piers are sidewheel steamers and sailing ships bound for destinations up and down the Atlantic coast.

you could have seen the bark *John Griffin*, just arrived from Havana with 516 hogsheads of sugar; or the brig *Selma*, also from Havana, unloading 175 hogsheads of molasses.

A few docks away was the British S.S. *Statira* from Messina, warping into her slip with a truly fragrant cargo under hatches— 578 boxes of lemons and 5,965 boxes of oranges, fancy fare for New York restaurants and the breakfast tables of families who could afford them.

From New Orleans on this second day of April was the S.S. *Lodona*, with a cargo of corn and cotton, and from Malaga there was the bark *Thomas*, bringing 3,142 boxes of raisins and 717 boxes of almonds, plus palm hats, orange peel, licorice, lead, and 200 casks of wine. Half unloaded after a voyage from Rio de Janeiro was the brig *Delphin*, with 3,700 bags of coffee.

If you had read the *Maritime Register* for that day you might have been interested to learn that some three hundred ships had cleared for the port of New York or were loading cargo for New York at foreign ports. New York-bound ships, according to the day's marine intelligence, were then loading in such places as Amoy, China; Palermo, Italy; Cadiz, Spain; and Montevideo, Uruguay. There were eleven ships then at Yokohama bound for New York; fifteen at the English ports of New Castle and Shields; eleven at Singapore and eleven at Marseilles. Liverpool still was one of the major trading partners for New York, with twenty-one New York-bound vessels in that port. The importance of New York's Mediterranean trade was evident in the presence of twenty-four New York-bound ships in the port of Messina alone. The Indian trade had become very important, too. There were twenty-seven vessels in Calcutta, loading cargo for New York or advertising availability for that port.

The New York-Liverpool trade contributed huge tonnages to the port, with as varied a list of merchandise as could be imagined. Much of it by 1870 was moving as premium cargo in the liners and the big steamships, but many sailing ships were still employed in this run.

The pages of the *Maritime Register*

for the second of April, 1870, carried a long list of New York-bound cargo waiting on the docks in Liverpool or already in transit, as reported by local agents for the cargoes. The list is indicative of the port's importance as a funnel for general cargoes that would be consumed in the New York area or shipped on to points all over the country. Due in from Liverpool were tin plate, hides, plate glass, cotton, cutlery, paint and books; also machinery, brushes, carpeting, and iron rails. In this list of incoming Liverpool cargo, which seemed to go

on ad infinitum, were hats, lace, figs, drugs, chandeliers, statuary, knives, sheeps' wool, cotton thread, furniture, wine, tea, and bottled beer. The list went on and on.

With the port's increasing commerce and traffic came the necessity to provide more services.

A very important addition to port services occurred on January 24, 1873, with formation of the Maritime Association of the Port of New York, with Thomas P. Ball as president. There were 140 members, who had paid twenty-five dollars each to join.

One of the vanished landmarks of the port, The Fulton Market, shown here in 1947, was destroyed for new facilities in 1952.

The New York Merchants' Exchange and News Association published the New York Maritime Register, *a rich source of marine intelligence for this, a golden age in New York shipping.*

Bowling Green and the new customs house in 1909. The scene is very much the same today with the magnificent building and its murals completely restored.

212

213

Headquarters were set up at 61 Pine Street.

The association was empowered by an act of the state legislature to "establish a Maritime Exchange for the collection and prompt dissemination of the news of the current hour, commercial, financial, and general, in advance of publication."

Reporting on vessel movements was its primary function, and the association established a telegraph station at Sandy Hook and at other strategic points in the harbor and along the nearby coast to record the

214

comings and goings of all ships doing business with the port of New York. This was not only of great help to the owners of ships and cargoes but to all those having business with ships—insurers, ship chandlers, towboatmen, customs officials, shipyards, and others. It was of great benefit to a shipowner, for instance, to know just when his vessel left the open sea and entered protected waters, for insurance purposes. And ship chandlers needed to know when a vessel was coming in and dispatch a man to the docks to ascertain her supply needs

and make a sale.

The association organized a system of marine intelligence to gather news on the movement of New York ships and cargoes all over the world. When shipmasters arrived in port they were given use of the Exchange, contributing information about the ports they had visited and vessel movements there.

In 1874 the association took over the Merchants Exchange and News Association. By 1875 it had 750 members, absorbed the Merchants Association, and enlarged its quarters sever-

Thomas P. Ball was president of the Maritime Association of the Port of New York from its founding in 1873 to 1874 and took the post as director from 1875 to 1877.

Left, This building served as the Maritime Association headquarters from 1904 to 1930 when it was replaced by the 35-story Maritime Exchange Building.

The riverside streets were filled with heavily laden drays pulled by weary horses, the teamsters vying for space along the cargo-filled piers.

al times within a decade. The association bought property at 78-80 Broad Street and moved into its own building there in 1904.

The tremendous growth of the port of New York just before and after the turn of the century was its greatest danger. To anyone who toured the harbor it was always a puzzle as to where another ship could be fitted at dock and how the maze of harbor traffic could go about its daily, round-the-clock business without wholesale tie-ups, rammings, and collisions. In fogs or snowstorms the harbor was a bedlam of whistles, from the shrill piping of little towboats to the deep-throated blasts from freighters and liners feeling their way in or out of the harbor.

Port congestion was causing concern as early as the 1890s, and in 1898 the governor of New York appointed a commission to look into the situation and make recommendations.

It appeared quite obvious, even by 1900, that the port was in danger of strangling itself.

From 1898 to 1913 the foreign commerce of the port increased by 131 percent—but wharfage space increased by less than 25 percent! There was such demand for all available pier space that in 1914 the Lehigh Valley Railroad was paying $65,000 a year (a very large figure in those days) for only partial use of pier 34 on the North River.

In 1914 the New York Merchants Association declared that the biggest problem facing the city was that of the harbor—how to relieve the daily congestion that resembled a bargain day at Macy's basement. The association put it this way:

> The citizens of New York have many problems, changing in form and degree with each generation, but the City...must ever deal with the one fundamental factor of its existence: New York is a seaport.
> New York's growth has been dependent upon its harbor. Could New York be conceived as losing its harbor, it would straightaway dwindle to a second or third rate city.

It seemed to many of the city's business and civic leaders, and especially to the maritime fraternity, that such a disaster would certainly occur unless the port was modernized to accommodate larger ships and handle cargo more speedily and efficiently.

By the early years of this century, New York seemed to be bound, as one report put it, "in a straitjacket of confined, limited, and outdated port facilities."

Almost all of the wharves in the harbor were finger piers, reaching from the shore out into the harbor, and most of the port's traffic was concentrated in just a few miles of Manhattan waterfront. Of the 578 miles of usable shoreside, only a relatively few were used for the handling of ships and cargoes.

"The commerce of the port," said the Merchant's Association, "has far outgrown its facilities."

The streets of lower Manhattan had become almost impassable because of trucks, drays, handcarts, and the thick melee of people doing business on the waterfront. It is a wonder that cargo was delivered at all but, amazingly, those having to do with cargo handling, from the ship's officers to the stevedores, the longshoremen, the Customs, steamship company

clerks, the draymen, lighterage crews, and all the others in that diverse and colorful army of waterfront workers managed to create purpose and direction in the midst of chaos. Crates of apples from New Hampshire, cans of olive oil from Italy, bales of cotton from Savannah, silks from Japan, African cocoa and China tea were unloaded, sorted, and loaded again on barges for Jersey and inland destinations, overseas, or consignees in Manhattan.

It seemed as if it could be accomplished only by magic—but somehow it was done.

It was a tribute to the commercial and financial strength of New York—to its powerful concentration of commercial interests—that other ports were unable to take advantage of this congestion and woo away much of the business. In Boston, Philadelphia, and Baltimore, there were little or no lighterage problems. Freight in Boston, as an example, could be unloaded from ships directly onto docks owned by railroads with transcontinental connections.

Almost all of the railroads serving the port of New York terminated in New Jersey, which meant that most of the seaborne freight, export or import, had to be barged from the New Jersey side to piers in Manhattan or Brooklyn.

"In no other harbor in the world," said one survey of the situation, "is there so much lightering done as in New York. Countless craft of every sort ply the waters of the North and East rivers. Each of the great railroads maintains its own floating equipment and there are many independent

Early in this century, almost all of the wharves in New York harbor were finger piers, reaching from the shore out into the harbor, and most of the port's traffic was concentrated in just a few miles of Manhattan waterfront.

By the early 1900s, the streets of lower Manhattan had become almost impassable because of trucks, drays, handcarts, and the thick melee of people doing business on the waterfront.

An 1880 view of South Street, as always, crowded with carts, wagons, and people scurrying about their duties on the waterfront.

companies engaged in this traffic."

It was estimated in 1914 that at least three thousand harbor craft—tugs, barges, scows, and floating derricks— did business in New York harbor, probably a conservative estimate.

Plying the harbor and bay on an average day were from fifteen hundred to two thousand railroad-car floats that carried cars from the New Jersey rail terminals to piers along a five-mile stretch of Manhattan and Brooklyn waterfronts.

It wasn't that nothing had been done to improve the port. Between 1870 and 1914 at least $115 million had been spent to build and repair piers in Manhattan, but the maintenance alone of facilities in a port as vast as New York could eat up a sum of money like this without any major effort toward modernization.

At the outbreak of World War I, cargo handling was still concentrated in Lower Manhattan, which contained less than ten percent of the port's usable waterfront. The New York Commissioner of Docks in 1918 stated publicly that between 30 and 40 applications for permanent vessel berths were in his department's files for which the city had nothing to furnish. This condition had existed continuously for at least 21 years and was symptomatic of the chronic neglect of the city's marine terminal needs.

Numerous plans were suggested for port expansion, however, including recommendations for large-scale pier construction in Queens and Staten Island and for development of a huge new port—an entire seaport in itself—in Jamaica Bay, with an entrance right onto the Atlantic.

An equally ambitious and perhaps more practical harbor development project, because of its excellent rail connections, was proposed in 1919. This proposal envisioned a huge ocean freight complex on eleven hundred acres of the so-called Jersey Flats, the Communipaw peninsula in Jersey City. It would have cost more than $200 million and, according to a preliminary design, would have provided berthing for more than a hundred ships; for fifty at the coal docks alone.

This project and the one in Queens

never materialized. As for Staten Island, a string of finger piers was built by the City of New York north of the Narrows during the 1920's. Port Newark, a remote marshland on the western shores of Newark Bay, was the site of marine terminal development during World War I and was the subject of much discussion during the twenties and thirties for additional building. In Bay Ridge, Brooklyn, the federal government started a large complex of piers and warehouses during May 1918. The project was completed quickly but not until after the Armistice in 1918. Called the Brooklyn Army Terminal, this facility thrived as one of the busiest marine terminals in the port for the next 40 years.

The Port Newark and Brooklyn Army Terminal projects were both attempts to cope with the strains put upon the port's facilities after the United States entered the conflict in Europe. The port not only suffered breakdowns during this period but railroad congestion. Rail, being a virtual transport monopoly at the time, was so great that there were severe shortages of coal, then the dominant fuel for power, industry and homes. The Port of New York, nevertheless, accomplished a fantastic job in logistics. Three-fourths of the troops and supplies that went to France cleared the Narrows, and more would have passed through New York had not the federal government diverted a considerable amount to other East Coast ports.

The tribulations of traffic congestion in the rail terminals, on the streets and piers, caused by a lack of any unified control, were forcefully brought home to the public and their legislators. Interests in New Jersey also were calling for rail rates lower than those for deliveries to the New York side of the harbor. A clamor that something be done led to the creation of a New York & New Jersey Harbor Development Commission. After four years of study, a comprehensive report and subsequent presentations before the New York and New Jersey state legislatures, identical laws were passed in both States. A compact between the two states was later ratified by Congress to

One of the many plans for additional port facilities was detailed in a magazine in 1910. Kennedy Airport now occupies the area on the extreme right.

218

SCIENTIFIC AMERICAN

[Entered at the Post Office of New York, N. Y., as Second Class Matter. Copyright, 1910, by Munn & Co., Inc.]

A POPULAR ILLUSTRATED WEEKLY OF THE WORLD'S PROGRESS

Vol. CIII.—No. 1.
Established 1845.

NEW YORK, JULY 2, 1910.

[10 CENTS A COPY.
$3.00 A YEAR.

create The Port of New York Authority in 1921.

As one of the founding fathers of the Port Authority put it, the 185 municipalities that comprised the Port District of New York, the 1,500-square-mile area in which the Port Authority mandate was to prevail, did not become an economic entity through the compact of 1921. Instead, he maintained, "The economic unity of the district is a reality. The interdependence of the (185) communities within the district is a reality."

What followed during the twenties under the Comprehensive Plan that guided Port Authority activities was the new bi-state agency's attempt to better coordinate the Port District's transportation system by planning a series of railroad belt lines. The objective of the proposed belt lines was to enable loaded freight cars of the dozen railroads then serving the port to be delivered intact to any point in the port, without breaking bulk or unloading the cars prior to reaching the final terminal. A tunnel connection between New Jersey and Long Island was among the intraport tunnels and bridges proposed to attain this objective. The plans for the belt lines died aborning, primarily because of the then dominant railroad's lack of enthusiasm, if not outright opposition.

Consequently, the Port Authority focused its attention and resources on interstate bridges and tunnels for motor vehicles that would link Staten Island with New Jersey as well as Manhattan with the Garden State. Most of these vehicular crossings, which were to have a dramatic impact on the port's commerce in future years, were completed, for the most part, between 1927 and 1931.

The world-wide depression of the thirties that followed prompted federal funding of mid-Manhattan's transatlantic piers, facilities which were to berth the greatest passenger liners of all times. Throughout the thirties, forties and fifties, celebrities and tourists, the rich and not so rich, made these piers the capital of international travel. Gradually, the glamour and efficacy of ocean travel were eroded by jet aircraft, a trend that was to wipe out the transatlantic luxury

hotels twenty years later.

The heyday of transatlantic liners during the post war years also saw the beginning of the period during which the most comprehensive building program of freight handling piers at the port took place. During 1948, the Port Authority leased Port Newark from the City of Newark and immediately began a program to rehabilitate that sector of the port. The waterfronts of Manhattan and Jersey City were also examined in depth by the Port Authority in 1949 and 1950 and the bi-state port agency sub-

mitted extensive plans to the two cities for the redevelopment of their waterfronts. Both plans were rejected. Hoboken, New Jersey and the federal government, on the other hand, turned to the Port Authority several years later for the modernization of Hoboken's major piers—a task the Port Authority rapidly completed.

By 1955, the Department of Marine and Aviation of the City of New York suddenly came to life by announcing a $200 million pier rebuilding program for Manhattan. The city then had juris-

When New York's Brooklyn Bridge was built in the last half of the 1800s, its architects did not have supertankers in mind. The Brooklyn, the largest U.S. flag commercial vessel ever built, is shown heading out to sea, November 11, 1973, passing under the Brooklyn Bridge with about four feet to spare.

220

221

*The marvelous George Washington Bridge
before the addition of the second deck.*

diction over some 80 piers in Manhattan and Brooklyn. During the same year, the Port Authority moved to acquire the antiquated piers of the New York Dock Company along the two miles of Brooklyn waterfront south of the Brooklyn Bridge. It was also during 1955 that the Port Authority took the first step to purchase 400 acres of unused marshland in Elizabeth, New Jersey as the site of a future marine terminal.

The city's ambitious plans for rehabilitating the East River and Hudson River waterfronts did not materialize front took place along the two miles of Brooklyn shoreline. In a $100-million building program spaced over six years the Port Authority demolished twenty-five old piers and built twelve new terminals in their place. Described as "the greatest marine terminal development ever undertaken on the New York side of the harbor," this renovation provided twenty-seven new berths at twelve new cargo terminal buildings.

Late in 1958, the Port Authority augmented its Brooklyn waterfront program when it acquired the old Erie

Cargo containerships have completely revolutionized the port facilities. These containers will be aboard trucks and trains with hours of this photograph.

222

terialize completely. The projects were percolating at the very same time that a revolution was on the verge of taking place in ocean transportation—the advent of containerships and intermodal transport technology requiring spacious marine terminals.

Crowded Manhattan was a poor site for the new type of shipping technology. This fact was emphasized by the influential Citizens Budget Committee which also pointed out that the city didn't have the kind of money it was talking about. Even as late as 1963, the Department of Marine and Aviation adamantly stood by its program of eight years earlier by announcing another ambitious plan for Manhattan nearly three and one-half times the cost of its initial program. The few products of this modernization scheme that came to fruition on the Hudson River cost in excess of $50 million for terminals briefly used, if at all.

While the planned redevelopment of Manhattan's piers was stalled, an actual rebirth of the East River water-

Basin Terminal, one of the port's oldest cargo facilities, and spent nearly thirteen million dollars in modernizing it. Unfortunately, like the piers in Manhattan, it was closed to shipping when the container era greatly reduced the need for break-bulk piers with little or no upland area to marshal containers.

The Port Authority meanwhile had an ambitious program to develop containership facilities in Port Newark and Elizabeth. This development began well ahead of the full impact of the container revolution of the mid-

A 1963 view during construction of the Erie Basin Bay Breakwater connecting bridge shows the newly poured concrete deck. Asphalt pavement will soon be applied over the bridge deck.

223

The Brooklyn Port in 1968 was laden with cargo as much of the Manhattan facilities closed.

sixties, so the port was well equipped to accommodate containers and containerships when this technique transformed the ocean freight business.

In retrospect, it is evident that it would have been an impossibility to accommodate container shipping in Manhattan, or even large-scale container movements in Brooklyn, with its shortage of upland or spacious areas adjacent to the vessels berths in which the 20- and 40-foot-long containers could be marshalled.

At the outset of the container changeover it was believed that each containership berth would require about 15 acres of land for parking containers and maneuvering them to shipside. Now, however, for the new generation of larger containerships, some port authorities are planning as much as fifty acres of open land for each container berth. The New York-based containership *Austral Entente*, for instance, is 813 feet long and carries seventeen hundred containers.

Containers are aluminum/steel "boxes" resembling truck trailers that are equipped with special corner fittings enabling them to be lifted and otherwise handled by all modes of transport. They come in three major lengths—20, 35 and 40 feet—and are generally eight feet wide and high. Containers hold any kind of cargo, from transistor radios to shoes, surgical instruments, toys, and hardware. Some are refrigerated or cooled for perishable products. By using containers, cargo can be shipped, for instance, directly from a factory in Tokyo to a department store warehouse in New York with handling only at origin and destination. The reduced manhandling of cargo saves time and money while pilferage and breakage are held to a minimal level.

"Containerization and container terminals saved this port from a big slide downhill," says one New York port official. "No other port in the world is better equipped than this for containerized cargo." About seventy-five per cent of all general cargo moving in and out of the port is now carried in containers.

Between 1946 and 1977, the city, the Port Authority, and private interests

spent nearly $700 million in pier modernization and new construction, more than any other port in the world. This money paid for 120 new berths in Port Newark, Elizabeth, Brooklyn, Staten Island, Hoboken, and Manhattan. Much of this investment was directed to container terminals, so that the Port of New York now has 5 modern container terminals with 37 berths. There are also 72 berths for conventional break-bulk cargo handling, plus berths for bulk and specialized cargoes. The five container terminals handled close to two million of these big cargo boxes (20-foot equivalent TEU's) during 1978.

Approximately two-thirds of this volume is handled by containerships that berth at the Elizabeth-Port Authority Marine Terminal, which qualifies it as the container capital of the world, not only because of the unmatched number of containers but by dint of its size, buildings and specialized equipment. Encompassing 1,165 acres of land and pier areas, Elizabeth's facilities include 18 container cranes which serve containership berths along 16,934 linear feet of wharf. Twelve huge cargo distribution buildings, with over a million square feet of space, eight cargo buildings, and 50 miscellaneous service structures are other indications of the construction that transformed Elizabeth from unused marshland less than 20 years ago to its present position of eminence in world shipping.

Nearby Port Newark has 23,387 feet of berthing space on Newark Channel and the north side of Elizabeth Channel where two major containership terminals are situated. Imported automobiles—a specialty for Port Newark's vast open paved areas—arrive regularly in quantities of up to 5,000 cars per vessel. A wharf also has been specially constructed to accommodate extraordinary heavy-lift cargo, enabling huge pieces of machinery to be delivered to the wharf and then transferred by ship's boom or floating derrick onto a freighter. Consolidation of so-called project cargo is also accomplished conveniently at Port Newark because of its abundant open area and availability of firms specializing in export packing.

Pittston Terminal is part of the Port Newark-Port Elizabeth complex, which provides docks and backup areas for lumber, automobile imports, and bulk cargoes.

An artificial dawn comes early to the Fulton Fish Market. The noise, clutter, and aroma begin to saturate the area at 2:30 a.m. as the harvest of the sea, the main entree on many a restaurant lunch menu, is delivered to the market's fishmongers.

This photo was taken during construction of the 39th Street Brooklyn pier for the Mitsui Steamship Co., Ltd. The terminal, built in 1960 and leased by the New York City Department of Marine and Aviation, was the first to be constructed in New York for a Japanese shipping line.

224

The Global Marine Terminal, a privately owned facility built at a cost of $20 million in Bayonne and Jersey City, is used by several container lines that provide services to Europe, the Far East, Australia and the Middle East. This terminal is one-and-one-quarter miles long and has eighty-four acres of backup storage area.

Port Seatrain in Weehawken, New Jersey, across the Hudson from New York's 42nd Street, is home port for the Container Division of Seatrain Lines, which inaugurated, during the 1930's, an early form of roll-on, roll-off freight handling using railroad cars. For many years, Edgewater, New Jersey, was the home port for Seatrain Lines. The line's current terminal, privately financed, can berth two containerships at a time and has 45-ton cranes.

The Northeast Marine Terminal at 39th Street, Brooklyn, is designed for LASH (lighter-aboard-ship), container, and break-bulk operations, and represents an investment by private capital of about $75 million.

At Howland Hook on Staten Island, the New York City Department of Ports and Terminals has built a container terminal equipped with five 40-ton-capacity gantry cranes. Howland Hook, the largest container terminal on the New York side of the port, has excellent rail service and easy access to the major highways linking Staten Island with Long Island and New Jersey.

Soon to join Howland Hook as a New York base of containership operations is the Red Hook Marine Terminal in Brooklyn that will be built by the Port Authority under a program funded by the State and City of New York. When completed in 1981, the Red Hook Terminal will have 1,000 feet of berth for containerships, 40 acres of upland area as well as accommodations for break-bulk and ro-ro ships.

Although the demise of the North Atlantic passenger liner, as well as containerization, put a crimp in the city's plans for the grand development of the Hudson River waterfront, a large passengership complex was provided by reconstructing several piers on the Hudson between 48th and 52nd Streets to boost the city's

share of the cruise-ship business, which was trending toward Florida bases. This $40-million terminal constructed by the Port Authority and financed by the city, was opened officially in November of 1974 when the cruise ship *Oceanic* of the Home Lines embarked 950 passengers for Nassau and the M/V *Sea Venture* prepared for a weekend "cruise to nowhere."

Described as the first integrated passenger-cargo terminal to be built on the New York waterfront, it came many years too late for the trans-

An Atlantic containership called a "ro-ro." These giants carry everything from loaded trucks to complete railway cars.

atlantic-passenger trade. It is hoped that it will encourage more cruise liners and more of the "fun ship" trade to patronize the Port of New York, which generates a large share of the cruise-liner business.

Tremendous changes have taken place in ocean shipping since World War II, changes which have affected New York as well as other ports. Thousands of tons of cargo a year were lost to the port when the coastwise cargo and passenger business died during and after World War II. More tonnage was lost when many of the once-prosperous intercoastal lines went out of business in the postwar years. In 1939, according to the 1940 annual report of the Port Authority, close to a hundred ships served the port in the coastwise trades. In that year they carried 4,400,000 tons of cargo between New York and South Atlantic and Gulf ports. Huge amounts of canned goods, candy, fruit, and other products also moved in the intercoastal ships, a business which largely has been taken over by trucks.

But thanks to its container-terminal

A modern passenger-ship complex, provided by reconstructing several piers on the Hudson between 48th and 52nd Streets, was officially opened in November of 1974.

developments, plus the continued strength of its commercial-industrial-transportation complex, New York has reversed a postwar shipping slow-down and once again can rightfully claim to be one of the world's busiest ports and the number one port in the nation.

In 1977 the port handled 121 million tons of cargo of all kinds, foreign and domestic, general and bulk. Foreign trade showed an increase during the year, but fell far short of 1973, biggest in port history.

Among the major exports are machinery, chemicals, steel products, vehicles, textiles, tallow, paper products, fruits and vegetables, drugs and cosmetics. Europe and the Far East are the port's major markets, but Central and South America, the Middle East, Africa, and Australasia are important also.

Principal imports are sugar, steel products, newsprint, lumber, liquor and wine, meat, vehicles, and chemicals. Bananas and coffee also are major imports, as they have been for many decades.

Exports and imports, of course, cover a wide range of raw materials and finished products. On the export side, besides the commodities mentioned, there are marble, salt, vegetable oils, alcohol, mineral tar, ink, drugs, glue, fertilizers, aluminum, tools, books, airplanes, thread, corn, and musical instruments, to name just a few items. Imports range from meat, sugar, and hides, to rubber, cotton, wool, paint, clothes, tires, copper, electric motors, asphalt, and automobiles. It seems incongruous that there are frequent duplications of imports and exports; autos, for example, are substantial imports and exports. But that is the fascinating nature of trade in a big port. Clothes are imported and exported; so are airplanes, fruit, and many other items.

* * *

The once-teeming waterfront of Manhattan is quiet and almost deserted now. Gone are the thousands of trucks, drays, and carts that once jammed the dockside streets. Gone, too, is the colorful variety of shipping that filled the Manhattan waterfront; the white-hulled coastal liners, the great western ocean sea queens with their towering hulls and their rakish stacks, and the myriad freighters with cargoes from Hamburg, Calcutta, Callao, and Shanghai.

Only a memory in picture books now are the towering masts of schooners and square riggers whose bowsprits stretched like a canopy over the dockside. The sailor haunts of South Street have been torn down to make way for look-alike skyscrapers. The huge fleet of tugs and other harbor craft is decimated, and the bay would seem almost empty to those who remember how it teemed with traffic half a century ago.

Changing times have changed the nature of the port. One ship now carries as much as four or five did a generation ago. Mechanization has replaced the iron hook that sweating longshoremen once used to man-handle the hogsheads, bales, boxes, and crates.

Romance gives way to bigness and automation and a port must change with the times. The ships are different now—huge, square-sterned cargo

droghers with containers stacked one upon another from bow to stern, looking very unlike the traditional ships of yesteryear.

But the ships still come and go, and if you watch the cargo being unloaded at Brooklyn or Staten Island, Weehawken, Jersey City or Port Newark, you'll see stenciled on many a box and crate the directive that long ago helped to create one of the busiest harbors in the world: "Ship Via Port of New York."

New York can rightfully claim to be one of the world's busiest ports and the number one port in the nation. Exports and imports cover a wide range of raw materials and finished products.

Lower Manhattan's skyline is dominated today by the giant twin towers of the World Trade Center. A great skyscraper, the Woolworth Building, is shown dwarfed in the background.

228

CHAPTER 15
THE SURVIVING
PAST

The face of the port has been changing constantly since its very beginning. Etchings, lithograph prints, slides, and postcards reflect the subtle yet substantial changes—of landscape, of the horizon and of the new technology.

The casual visitor will find, however, that a great deal of the colorful history of the port of New York has survived, much of it intact and much of it unchanged from whatever period it sprang.

Great efforts have been made to preserve and reconstruct sections of the port. Visitors to the Fulton and South Street areas are transported back into the nineteenth century. The cast iron fence around the Battery park has been maintained as originally constructed. The fireboat station stands today in Victorian splendor with the ultra modern World Trade Center as its backdrop.

Amid the architecture of the lower city, relics of the early life of the port exist almost unchanged. One can walk from the futuristic buildings of the Chase Manhattan Bank directly into the eighteenth century atmosphere of India House. Cast iron buildings, so typical of the flourishing commercial constructions of the early nineteenth century, stand next to the innovative modular structures of tomorrow's corporations.

Though the port has changed in a thousand ways it somehow continues to echo the cries of peddlers and merchants, the clatter of metal wheels on the cobblestone of South Street, and the shuffling of leather boots over the polished marble floors of the Custom House.

A bird's eye-view of the port of New York from the Battery looking south, by Currier & Ives, 1872.

An 1849 lithograph of Nathaniel Currier showing Manhattan as seen from Brooklyn Heights.

A unique architectural view of the Brooklyn Bridge in 1883 by R. Schwartz.

234

Immigrants landing at the Battery, 1855. The painter, Samuel B. Waugh, includes the Chinese junk Key

the background, the first such vessel seen in New York, although she actually visited two years earlier.

The clipper schooner Great Republic, built for speed in an era when speed meant survival.

The steamship James W. Baldwin *from an 1861 painting by James Bard.*

The skyline of lower Manhattan as it is today, dominated by the twin towers of the World Trade Center.

Bowsprit of the Eagle on Operation Sail.

In Winter, the port functions fully despite severe weather.

An outgoing freighter steams past the Manhattan skyline.

The Seamen's Church Institute.

Statue of John Ericsson, inventor of the torpedo, at the Battery.

The Fireboat Station stands ready at the Battery.

The basic skills of seamanship are still at the heart of port activity. The docking of a ship begins with a hand thrown line.

Tugboats are the powerful workhorses of the port.

Nautical scenes in stained glass at the Seamen's Church Institute.

War Memorial at the Battery commemorates those lost at sea.

Built in 1964, the Verrazzano-Narrows bridge has a suspension span of 4,260 feet, the longest in the world.

The bell of the Atlantic, lost at sea.

243

Brooklyn port facilities.

*A forest of tall ship masts sprang up for
Operation Sail, 1976.*

244

Cranes, like mighty pieces of sculpture, at rest.

*Figurehead of the sailing ship, Rosa Isabella.
Permission Museum of the City of New York,*

The bicentennial fireworks celebration over the Statue of Liberty, July 4, 1976.

CHAPTER 16
PARTNERS IN PROGRESS

From the moment Robert Fulton demonstrated the practicality of steamboat travel in 1807, to the introduction of the railroads during the 1830's, to the modern age of computerized containerization, New York's taste for private enterprise has fueled zealous economic ambition.

The port's heritage is the people and the wealth of the land. The histories of individual businesses are closely associated with and in many instances the very source of the historical meaning of the port itself. Risk, adventure, intrigue, knowledge, and imagination combined with the advantages of the land provide the formula for the success of many of the firms whose capsule histories follow. Behind them are the ghosts of mergers, obsolescences, and a community which has progressed from the lessons of history. Together they form the very foundation, the strength, and the sustenance of our harbor and haven—today and tomorrow.

247

What makes a great world port? A configuration of land and sea, people, enterprise, and the social and political environment in which free commerce and unbridled industry can flourish.

Almost from the very day the *Half Moon* lingered in the lower harbor under the flag of the East India Company, world-wide trade commenced. As the first ambitious thrusts were made into an unexplored world, seeds were planted which some two hundred and fifty years later would yield a thriving metropolis. The New World had become a haven to a flood of immigrants in search of the mythical touchstone of "a better life." As the country grew, the primal labor force established itself.

Industry and commerce boomed—shipping lines, banks, exchanges, terminals, insurance, communications, tugs and pilots, and professional associations. Raw materials, at first packed in casks, then on barges, on pallets, and finally in massive containers, flowed through the port. Slowly, the window of a new land opened to share its abundances with the rest of the world.

The intricate, far reaching roots of the port of New York sustained the drama and excitement of its role as an international city. The business and labor force provided the competitive setting in which countless entrepreneurs availed themselves of the natural resources of an emerging nation.

Wall Street, the financial center of the world. Much of the economic support of the Port of New York is generated here.

NEDLLOYD

The 21,500-ton multipurpose Nedlloyd Bahrain *joined the fleet in 1978.*

Poster recalls the early days of Rotterdam Lloyd service from Rotterdam to Java.

Nedlloyd was formed by combining the Nederland Line of Amsterdam and the Royal Rotterdam Lloyd of Rotterdam—two venerable shipping lines with more than a century of experience behind them.

Nederland Line and Royal Rotterdam Lloyd started their joint Java-New York and Java-Pacific Lines in the 1930s. Shortly after World War II, they established a joint liner service between the East Coast and Gulf ports of the United States and the Arabian/Persian Gulf, pursuing an old objective of both lines to "go where the oil is." The two lines had traditionally initiated services to serve major industries such as the oil, rubber, and coffee industries. The joint venture was operated under the name Nedlloyd.

The joint services concept culminated in 1970 in a formal merger, under the name Koniklijke Nedlloyd Groep, N.V. This group includes divisions engaged in liner operations on regular routes, bulk carriers, drill ships, and fleet management services. Other activities include stevedoring, shipping agencies, Rhine and inland shipping, road hauling, forwarding, real estate management, and tourism. In the United States, the group is represented by Nedlloyd, Inc., with offices in New York's World Trade Center.

From services originally designed to serve the Netherlands and the East Indies, Nedlloyd has become one of the world's largest and most diversified ocean carriers. The company operates twenty-nine liner services, both independently and jointly with other lines, and has a growing fleet of specialized cargo carriers. Much more than just a steamship company, Nedlloyd has developed a total transport service which, as it proudly states, can "move anything from a crate to a city."

Nedlloyd undertakes any transport assignment. One of its largest was the delivery, from factory to construction site, of 850,000 tons of cargo for building 32 high-rise apartments and support facilities at Dammam, Saudi Arabia.

At the end of 1977, the Nedlloyd fleet comprised 125 vessels, including general purpose cargo liners, container and roll-on/roll-off ships, conventional tankers, liquified gas tankers, chemical tankers, special product carriers, and drill ships.

The Nedlloyd fleet is being continually enlarged, modernized, and adapted to meet special trade requirements. Joining the fleet in 1977 was the *Nedlloyd Houtman*, a 49,000-ton ship carrying 2,450 containers. In 1978, Nedlloyd took delivery of two 21,500-ton multipurpose vessels, the *Nedlloyd Bahrain* and the *Nedlloyd Baltimore*. Before the end of 1979, seven more ships will be added to the fleet: two more multipurpose vessels, similar in size and design to the *Bahrain* and *Baltimore*; four ro-ro vessels, totaling 93,000 tons; and a container vessel of 48,000 tons. The latest in sophisticated ocean carriers, these vessels are designed to carry out Nedlloyd's motto: "shaping sea transport for tomorrow."

MCALLISTER BROTHERS, INC.

Family legend has it that on his way to the New World from County Antrim, Ireland, in 1864, James McAllister was shipwrecked off Labrador. Despite this inausupicious beginning, the 21-year-old James worked his way to New York, where he shipped out on a Ward Line steamer as a mate.

Within the year, James had saved enough money to buy a 40-ton sail lighter, which he sailed between ships at anchor and the piers of New York harbor. Soon, with his brothers Daniel, William, and Charles, James formed the Greenpoint Lighterage Company. With each partner sailing as skipper in his own lighter, the company, the progenitor of modern McAllister operations, opened its first offices on Manhattan's South Street only a few years after the end of the Civil War.

Forming a new partnership in 1888, James and his son James P. bought a shipyard on Newtown Creek, just south of the Greenpoint Avenue bridge in Brooklyn. Building tugboats, scows, and lighters in their yard, within a few years the McAllisters had a thriving tug and lighterage business, carrying products for the sugar and coffee king, John Arbuckle, among many others.

During the ensuing years, McAllisters' marine enterprises continued to branch out. By the turn of the century, McAllister Brothers owned part of the Yankee Salvage Company, one of the best known marine salvors along the Atlantic Coast. In 1905, they acquired another large shipyard at Mariner's Harbor, Staten Island. They also bought the Starin Line, a Staten Island company which every summer carried New Yorkers from the Battery to Glen Island on ten side-wheeler excursion vessels. In 1914, with the opening of the Interstate Park at Bear Mountain on the Hudson River, they acquired the famous side-wheeler *Bridgeport* (later known as the *Bear Mountain*), which carried picnickers from their city apartments to the rural park until 1939.

James died in 1916, and control of the company passed to his four sons—James P., John E., Charles D., and William H. Like their father, the four McAllister brothers continued the company's basic tug and lighter operations around the port, while expanding into other related businesses, including the deep-sea tanker service. They operated over forty 10,000-ton tankers for the U.S. Shipping Board for over ten years.

With the death of James P. McAllister in 1937, the partnership was dissolved, and the corporate entity McAllister Brothers Inc. was formed by the one surviving second-generation McAllister, William H., and James P.'s three sons—Anthony J., James P., and Gerard M. They were subsequently joined by Charles D.'s son, Roderick H. McAllister.

In 1974, control of the 114-year-old company passed to the next generation of McAllisters—the fourth. One of the most diversified organizations operating in the towing, lighterage, and marine transportation industry in North America, McAllister Brothers is now under the direction of Anthony J. McAllister, Jr., Bruce A. McAllister, Brian A. McAllister, James P. McAllister III, Neill A. McAllister, and William M. Kallop.

McAllister Brothers, although still regarding New York as its home port, now operates over 100 vessels along

McAllister vessels have been sailing past the Battery since 1864.

the Atlantic Coast, the Gulf of Mexico, Panama, Puerto Rico, the Netherlands Antilles, and further afield. It is only fitting, therefore, that the young mate aboard a tug in McAllister's newest venture—a towing company in Saudi Arabia—is named Jeffrey McAllister, one of the fifth generation.

ALEXANDER & ALEXANDER

The marine insurance division of Alexander & Alexander started with the placing of insurance on puffing tugboats and slow-paced harbor barges. Today, it deals with mammoth supertankers, huge containerships, integrated tug/barge units, deep-sea oil rigs, and LNG (liquified natural gas) carriers, the most sophisticated cargoes being transported.

Founded over eighty years ago in Clarksburg, West Virginia, the firm later moved to Baltimore where it became nationally known for its expertise in the many facets of railroad insurance.

A New York office was opened in 1918 to handle insurance on the great fleet of tugs, barges, and carfloats operated by many of the major railroads, such as the New York Central, the Central Railroad of New Jersey, and the Chesapeake system. This was a very important service for the firm as well as for shippers, for in those days millions of dollars worth of cargo moved by tug and barge over harbor waters.

World War I projected the company into the ocean marine field as well, and this growing activity resulted in the creation of a marine department. The marine business boomed in World War II and has been growing ever since, becoming highly complex and demanding with the vastly increased size of ships, new cargo-handling techniques, and exotic cargoes.

The marine division of Alexander & Alexander handles all types of vessel and cargo coverage. Included in their list of clients are Seatrain, Central Gulf Lines, United States Lines, Mobil, and Texaco. The company has become one of the world's principal marine insurance brokers and has arranged coverage for some of the largest and most costly ships afloat, including the 250,000-ton, New York-built tanker *Bay Ridge*, one of the largest vessels ever to fly the American flag.

Marine insurance is only part of the company's business.

Alexander & Alexander is a highly diversified insurance consulting, actuarial and employee benefits organization with over 6,000 employees serving clients of all kinds and sizes all over the world. It provides insurance and financial services for the special needs of such a diverse clientele as baseball teams, steel mills, hospitals, retail stores, refineries, museums, and family farms.

Since 1969, the company has merged with many insurance agency, brokerage, and consulting firms to make it one of the fastest growing financial service organizations in the country, dedicated to the "protection of people, property and profits."

Despite its preeminence in the industry and the large number of Fortune 500 firms among its clientele, Alexander & Alexander is equally proud of its service to hundreds of medium- and small-size businesses. It is proud, too, that its globe-girdling marine division grew out of small beginnings, from the little tugs and homely barges that moved the cargoes of the world in and out of the port of New York.

250

The marine division of Alexander & Alexander handles coverage for some of the largest and most modern vessels operating out of the port of New York.

The company has come a long way from insuring homely harbor tugs and barges to arranging insurance for such huge vessels as LNG (liquified natural gas) carriers, and their multimillion-dollar cargoes.

NAVIERAS DE PUERTO RICO

Puerto Rico has been an important trading partner with the port of New York for 300 years. From earliest colonial times, little sloops, brigs, and schooners braved storms, buccaneers, and other hazards of the fourteen-hundred-mile sea journey to carry flour, cattle, cheese, hardware, and other goods from New York to the Caribbean island and sailed home with molasses, sugar, and rum.

Under the impetus of Puerto Rico's successful industrialization program which has transformed the island into America's fifth-largest offshore customer in the world, trade between the port of New York and Puerto Rico has increased tremendously over the past quarter century. According to predictions, this trade will increase five fold by 1995.

Today, New York and Puerto Rico are served by Navieras de Puerto Rico, the largest single ocean cargo carrier in the United States/Puerto Rico trade. The Navieras house flag flies over a fleet of four swift 24-knot, 700-foot-long ro-ro (vehicle roll-on/roll-off) carriers and eight containerships.

In addition to ships, Navieras also owns some 18,000 trailers and containers and 10,000 chassis for complete door-to-door transportation. There are specialized containers and trailers for handling a wide range of cargo, such as reefers, insulated units for pharmaceuticals, open-top units for machinery, stainless steel tanks for oil, rum, and chemicals, car rack units for autos, and even "cattletainers" for humane and efficient movement of livestock.

More than $300 million has been invested by Navieras in ships, terminals, and mobile equipment in the ports of New York, Baltimore, Charleston, Jacksonville, Miami, New Orleans, and Houston.

The Navieras terminal at Port Elizabeth is a large cargo-staging area with room for some 2,800 trailers/containers and 700 vehicles of all kinds on any given day. Navieras is by far the gateway for a Puerto Rico trading area covering New York, New Jersey, all of New England, and Canada. From Port Elizabeth, Navieras also handles cargo from Europe and the Far East consigned to Puerto Rico and elsewhere in the Caribbean area, including the United States' Virgin Islands.

Navieras is committed to this prom-

Roberto Lugo D'Acosta is executive director of Puerto Rico Marine Management, Inc., which operates Navieras de Puerto Rico.

251

ise to both mainland and island shippers: "to move cargo reliably at reasonable rates while maintaining schedules that shippers can depend upon, and to offer total service, from shipper's origin to final delivery point, with the most modern, efficient, and professional system transportation technology has to offer."

JOHNSON & HIGGINS

Johnson & Higgins was founded in 1845 by Henry W. Johnson (left) and Andrew F. Higgins.

252

No company has deeper roots in the port of New York or a greater share in the city's maritime heritage than Johnson & Higgins—the oldest and one of the largest insurance brokers in the nation.

The firm's offices at 95 Wall Street are only a stone's throw from where it was founded in 1845. In those days, young Henry W. Johnson and Andrew F. Higgins could look out of their office windows and see many of the lofty sailing ships and the cargoes of their clients along the bustling docks of South Street. Shipmasters, merchants, longshoremen, and sailors from the seven seas were part of the colorful mix of people that continually thronged Wall Street and the nearby waterfront.

The partners early had acquired a reputation as experts in average ad-

justing—an aspect of insurance almost as old as seaborne trade. When part of a ship's cargo was jettisoned during a storm to save the ship, or was otherwise lost or damaged, the loss was shared or "averaged" with all those who had cargo aboard. Special knowledge was required to determine these losses and apportion them fairly.

In their first year as a firm, the young average adjusters earned themselves a name which encouraged shippers to call upon them for the purchase of marine insurance. Taking this step, Johnson & Higgins became insurance brokers as well. The principles of the function have changed little from that time. And the basic principle is that the broker

serves the buyer of insurance, not the seller.

By the time of the Civil War, Johnson & Higgins was so well known that the Secretary of the Navy, Gideon Welles, asked the firm to send an agent to New Orleans to survey the wreck of the battle-blasted Union gunboat *Varuna* and recommend what to do with her. The agent inspected the ship, recommended salvage, and then supervised her raising and refitting. She later rejoined the Union Navy's Gulf Blockading Squadron.

By the turn of the century, the company had opened seven branch offices, including one in San Francisco, where the discovery of gold and the resultant boom in shipping necessitated insurance services. Many a windjammer arrived in port sea-worn and battered from its rigorous voyage around Cape Horn. San Francisco was rapidly becoming one of the world's busiest ports, and Johnson & Higgins one of its busiest insurance firms. At the same time, the company was expanding into fire, casualty, and other types of insurance to keep pace with new business needs.

The reputation of Johnson & Higgins was greatly enhanced at the time of the disastrous San Francisco earthquake and fire of April 1906, when the San Francisco staff, aided by the senior fire adjuster from New York, settled all its clients' claims within six months.

When World War I again focused the country's attention on shipping, Johnson & Higgins was honored by having a senior executive of the firm named to the three-man advisory board of the Federal Bureau of War Risk Insurance. So capable was this board that of all claims submitted,

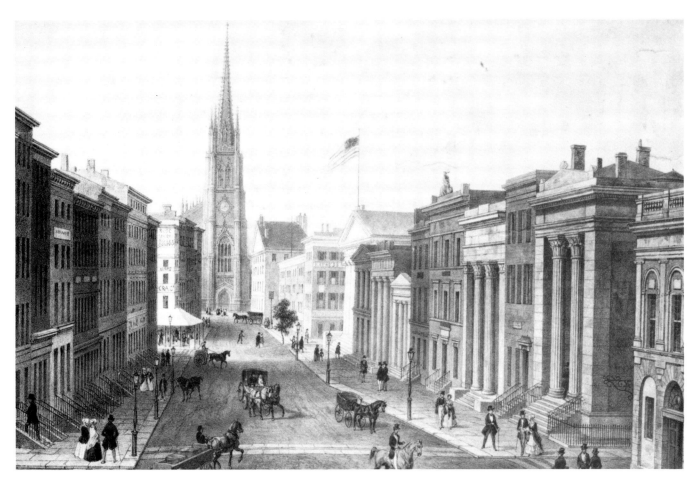

only one ended in litigation.

The company's most severe testing came during the long business depression of the 1930s, when insurance activity was almost strangled by business stagnation. Times were hard and business slim, but the company came through by stressing ingenuity in finding and providing insurance service. It was able, moreover, to keep its entire staff intact.

With World War II came a new era for the insurance business, with group insurance and pensions, hitherto a very small percentage of business payroll, developing into the elaborate employee benefit programs of today. The war also brought a boom in the marine insurance business.

When the federal government began to import strategic raw materials, leading marine brokers were appointed as an insurance committee to handle all the necessary insurance. Out of this group, Johnson & Higgins was selected to act as the serving broker.

During the 1950s era of business acquisitions, conglomerates, and multinationals, the company opened new offices and expanded its overall

This 1850 lithograph shows the view from the original office of Johnson & Higgins. Even in the mid-nineteenth century, Wall Street was already the banking and insurance center of the nation.

Today, the company is headed by Richard I. Purnell (seated), chairman and chief executive officer, and Robert V. Hatcher, Jr., president.

service base, creating a worldwide network of wholly-owned offices. Today, the company has more of its own people and more offices outside North America than any other broker. This network now includes thirty-four offices in the United States and Canada and thirty-four overseas offices in seventeen countries, serving all commercial centers of the free world. Despite its worldwide expansion, however, Johnson & Higgins remains a privately-held company, owned entirely by its directors.

The company has pioneered many "firsts" for the industry, which now includes benefit and actuarial consulting. It introduced the first nationwide dental insurance plan with local cost variations figured in—a concept that set the standard for all subsequent plans around the country.

It has been a long time since tall-masted clippers tied up within a "hail and a shout" of Johnson & Higgins headquarters in lower Manhattan. But the company remains proud of its long business tradition and, with the same spirit of creativity and enterprise that inspired those long-gone clippers, continues to serve the business needs of today—and tomorrow.

F.W. HARTMANN AND COMPANY

F W. Hartmann and Company, Inc., was founded by the late F. Wolfgang Hartmann in September 1944. Starting with rented desk space at 120 Wall Street, they soon leased their own offices in the same building, remaining there for more than twenty years before moving to 17 Battery Place.

When World War II ended, in cooperation with the United States government, Mr. Hartmann visited various European shipowners to advise on the rebuilding of their fleets. While there, he found a need for ship supplies and materiel. Back in the United States, he located a company demolishing war-built Liberty ships from whom he obtained ship generators, booms, tarpaulins, and even discarded seamen's uniforms, which he sold to the European shipowners.

By the early 1950s, the company controlled a substantial amount of American and European fertilizer chartering, which chartering had previously been transacted in the European markets. Contracts for coal from the United States to Europe were also arranged, as well as for scrap and wood pulp on the return voyage of the chartered coal carriers. The company was also involved in the sale of ships, the first being a tanker. Eventually, there were sales of three U.S. government surplus C1MAV1 vessels to a Swedish shipowner. Meanwhile, the chartering department diversified by introducing European-owned vessels into the American and Caribbean trade and eventually arranged for the employment of up to thirty-one vessels at a time in the Western Hemisphere.

By convincing shipowners to start regular berth service from the United States, the company was successful in being appointed general agents for German, Swedish, and Hong Kong shiplines.

After returning from Pacific duty with the U.S. Army, Mr. Joseph F. Daly joined the firm and soon became involved in all aspects of the business with Mr. Hartmann. It wasn't long before he was elected an officer and partner of the organization.

The founder's son, Peter W. Hartmann, after an apprenticeship in England and the Continent and service in the U.S. Army overseas, joined the New York Office in the mid-1950s. Four years later, his elder brother Rolf D. Hartmann, who also apprenticed abroad and who completed his military service with the U.S. Coast Guard, came into the company. Shortly before the senior Hartmann's death in 1968, both brothers became partners.

Today the company has expanded to nine offices in the United States and has approximately 200 employees. As general agents, they represent lines of various countries and specialize in the carriage and handling of equipment of unusual size and weight on vessels under American and European flags. In chartering, they are very active in the worldwide movement of bulk commodities, especially fertilizers.

Hartmann today also owns Containership Agency, Inc., located at One W.U.I. Plaza, New York. This company specializes in intermodal transportation and represents various container and roll-on/roll-off vessels and maintains sophisticated computer systems for the control of thousands of containers, trailers, and other equipment throughout the U.S.

All three partners of the organization are active in the company, and the firm is one of the few remaining agency and brokerage houses under private ownership.

254

F. Wolfgang Hartmann founded the successful company, which bears his name, in 1944.

R.B. JONES
OF NEW YORK

Benedict & Benedict, successor to Beecher & Benedict, maintained the company's original office in Brooklyn (shown here at left) and established a second office in Manhattan.

R.B. Jones of New York Inc., traces its origins to the partnership of Beecher & Benedict, founded in 1870. The office was located at the intersection of Court and Montague streets in the city of Brooklyn; the telephone number was 50.

Mr. Beecher was the son of Reverend Henry Ward Beecher. Seelye Benedict was a Yale graduate. In 1873, the firm obtained an agency with the Liverpool and London and Globe Insurance Company, now part of the Royal Globe Insurance Group. Mr. Beecher later withdrew from the firm, and Seelye Benedict took in his brothers, Andrew and Walter, as partners. In 1885, the firm became known as Benedict & Benedict.

Seelye and Andrew opened a new office at 45 Broadway in Manhattan, while Walter stayed in Brooklyn, where he became active in many philanthropic and civic affairs. To this day, the company still handles the insurance affairs of many schools, hospitals, churches, and banks in the borough of Brooklyn.

Over the years, the firm of Benedict & Benedict met the cargo insurance needs of a great many clients. In more recent times, it has handled insurance for fleets of tugboats, bridge builders, cargo loading operators, and other harbor-oriented accounts, especially since a merger with S.N. Eben Corporation, a marine insurance specialist, was accomplished in 1972.

By the late 1880s, the business handled by the firm began to change from meeting the insurance needs of prominent families in Brooklyn to a general insurance business of a commercial nature. By the early 1900s, automobile insurance began to be a major factor. Benedict & Benedict handled the insurance for the privately owned BMT subway system, prior to its acquisition by the city of New York.

Business continued to expand, including accounts from more than a hundred outside brokers in addition to those generated by the firm itself. By the early 1930s, the number of partners had increased from three to eight.

Among those particularly active in civic affairs was Benjamin W. Blakey. The senior partner of Benedict & Benedict at the time the Brooklyn Battery Tunnel was completed in 1950, Mr. Blakey contracted a severe case of the "bends" while on an inspection tour of the tunnel during the course of its construction.

By the 1950s, correspondent relationships had been established in various parts of the United States to accommodate the needs of national accounts. One of these correspondent relationships was with R.B. Jones Corporation, one of the leading agencies in the Midwest. In 1970, Benedict & Benedict merged with R.B. Jones, then in the midst of an expansion program and well on its way to becoming a prominent national brokerage operation.

The Brooklyn and New York offices of R.B. Jones of New York Inc., were combined in new modern quarters at 160 Water Street, New York, in 1970.

R.B. Jones, the ninth largest broker in the United States, merged with Alexander & Alexander Services, Inc., the second largest broker, on January 31, 1979. Both firms are renowned for their professionalism, which has enabled each to grow at a prodigious rate over the past decade.

MOORE McCORMACK LINES

W hen the freighter *Montara* steamed into Rio de Janeiro in July of 1913, it was the first time the inhabitants of that South American port had seen an American flag flying over a vessel in twenty-six years. Back in New York, Albert V. Moore and Emmet J. McCormack sat at desks facing each other in their single office, wondering what would become of the $5,000 they had invested to charter the small freighter and send it on its way with a full load of cargo that included dynamite.

256 That first successful voyage of the *Montara* signaled the start of a major steamship line; it also marked the beginning of an involvement with South American trade that to this day serves as a cornerstone of Moore McCormack Lines operations.

Known as Moore & McCormack Co. in its early years, the company soon became a major name in the trade, successful enough to earn the support of important financiers like J.P. Morgan and to raise a $100,000 loan in 1916 to expand its operations. By 1917, Moore & McCormack had fifteen sailings to South America. Soon Mooremack vessels were seen not only at Rio de Janeiro, but also at Pernambuco, Bahia, Santos, Montevideo, and in 1919, as far south as Buenos Aires.

Moore & McCormack continued branching out, inaugurating a Scandinavian service in 1918 that by the early 1920s made it the dominant U.S. carrier servicing Norway, Sweden, Denmark, and Finland. Soon Mooremack ships were calling regularly at ports in India, the Mediterranean, and the Middle East. They became the first American ships to call at Soviet ports, and played a major role in transforming the little fishing village of Gdynia into an important Baltic

Loaded with U.S. troops returning from Europe after V-E day, the Moore-McCormack passenger liner Brazil arrives in New York.

Model-Ts are being loaded aboard a Moore & McCormack vessel in 1926.

seaport. In the late 1920s, now a major American steamship operator, the company became known as Moore-McCormack Lines, Inc.

During World War II, Mooremack operated more than 150 merchant vessels for the War Shipping Administration. Guiding the vessels on 2,199 voyages during the course of the war, Moore-McCormack was responsible for moving approximately one million troops and over 20 million tons of cargo for the Allies.

At the end of the war, the company resumed its peacetime cargo and passenger services. In 1957, it took over the well-known Robin Line Service between the U.S. Atlantic Coast, South and East Africa, and Indian Ocean ports.

Albert Moore died while still president of the company in 1953, and Emmet McCormack retired as chairman of the board in 1959, but the company has carried on their innovative approach to the steamship business along with their names. Today, Mooremack carries a full range of cargo, from break-bulk to containers, between the U.S. Atlantic Coast and ports in South and East Africa, as well as Brazil, Uruguay, Argentina, and Paraguay. And although the ships bear little resemblance to the original *Montara*, it is with special pride that Moore-McCormack Lines carries its flag into the port of Rio de Janeiro, in its sixty-sixth year of continuous service.

SEALAND TERMINAL CORPORATION

Aaron Held, alive and alert at 96, was born in Austria. He immigrated to the United States at the age of ten. In 1915, married, with a three-year-old son named Irving, he bought a truck (probably horse-drawn) and founded a small business called the Held Haulage Corporation. A second son, Milton, was born five years later. About the time Irving joined his father, at the age of sixteen, Aaron acquired a second truck and engaged several employees. Subsequently Milton joined his father and brother, and all three worked in the driving, dispatching, and loading of trucks.

Today Aaron is retired; Irving is president and chief executive officer, and Milton is executive vice president and treasurer, of one of the best known stevedoring and terminal operating companies in the Port of New York and New Jersey.

The organization has developed over sixty-three years as the parent Sealand Terminal Corporation, with seven subsidiaries—United Terminals, Inc.; Held Warehouse & Transportation, Inc.; Genser Trucking Co., Inc.; Champion Truck Rental, Inc.; Ellison, Inc.; Great Eastern Maintenance & Service Corporation; and Anchor Stevedoring, Inc.

In the 1930s, Held Haulage operated a fleet of over one hundred trucks and a warehouse distribution center of more than 100,000 square feet. In the 1940s, they opened and operated the Jay Street terminal for the U.S. war effort, which involved one million square feet, in multistory buildings, for the storage and distribution of every item except firearms used by armed forces.

In 1945, they founded the Sealand Dock & Terminal Corporation, with four Brooklyn piers and four square

At Puerto Rico Marine Terminal in Elizabeth, New Jersey, ro-ro and container operations are handled by United Terminals, Inc., a subsidiary of Sealand Corporation.

Irving Held (seated), president of Sealand Terminal Corporation, confers with David Richman, secretary-counsel.

257

city blocks to serve six steamship lines. Today, on Manhattan's East River piers 36 and 42, Sealand performs terminal operations and stevedoring assignments for five steamship companies; the same services are performed in Gulfport, Mississippi, for four other companies.

United Terminals functions similarly in Weehawken and Elizabeth-Port Newark, New Jersey, for three large steamship lines and in Bayonne, New Jersey, for the U.S. Military Ocean Terminal. Anchor Stevedoring, Inc., services Seatrain Lines at Charleston, South Carolina, and the U.S. Army at

Cape Canaveral. Anchor, which is 80-percent owned by the Helds, was formed in 1974 as a joint venture with South Eastern Maritime Company of Savannah, Georgia. The Helds also operate 850,000 square feet of space as a public warehouse distribution center in Port Newark, Bayonne, and Brooklyn.

The corporation has a weekly payroll of some sixteen hundred persons, with an administrative staff of 110, under the direction of David Richman, vice president, secretary, and counsel.

AMERICAN BUREAU OF SHIPPING

In 1861 a number of New York marine insurance companies organized the American Shipmasters Association "to promote the security of life and property on the seas" and "to encourage a higher degree of efficiency and character amongst the masters and officers of vessels." Merchants, shipowners, and other members of the maritime industry became members. The Association awarded certificates of competency to officers who passed examinations in nautical science and seamanship and, by 1900, when this activity was taken over by the federal government, it had granted certificates to 6,817 masters and mates, an activity that contributed greatly to safety at sea and the improvement of the American merchant marine.

During these years the Association gradually became a classification society and began publishing its *Record of American and Foreign Shipping* in 1867, "a faithful and accurate classification and registry of mercantile shipping."

The first rule book for the survey of wooden vessels was published in 1869, for iron vessels in 1877, and for building and classing steel ships in 1890.

In 1898 the name was changed to American Bureau of Shipping, and since then the Bureau has grown steadily in usefulness and prestige until its activities now span the world. ABS is a not-for-profit, nongovernmental society dedicated to serving the marine industry.

Growth was speeded by the vast United States government shipbuilding program of World War I, when ABS was called upon to survey hundreds of emergency ships of various types; and again in the merchant marine rejuvenation sparked by the Merchant Marine Act of 1936.

The Bureau accomplished a herculean task in World War II when its personnel inspected 5,171 merchant vessels built for the greatest shipbuilding program the world has ever seen.

Activities were further expanded after the war, with the opening of a greater number of exclusive offices all over the world to handle the large number of American ships sold to foreign buyers. There was also a great postwar increase in the number of ships built in foreign shipyards classed by ABS; currently more than 15,000 vessels registered in ninety countries are in class with ABS. The Bureau has surveyors at all of the major seaports and shipbuilding centers worldwide, plus technical offices in Buenos Aires, Hamburg, Genoa, Tokyo, Rotterdam, Manila, Singapore, Madrid, and London overseas, and in Cleveland, New Orleans, San Francisco, and New York headquarters. There are now more than 750 field and technical ABS surveyors who serve the marine industry in eighty-eight countries.

The "rules" upon which classification is predicated are founded on established principles of naval ar-

An ABS surveyor is lowered from a helicopter onto the deck of a tanker as it rounds the Cape of Good Hope off South Africa.

chitecture, marine engineering and other engineering disciplines. The Bureau has many committees, of both technical and geographical (regional) makeup, the members of which are chosen because of their eminence in the marine field. They serve without compensation and assist ABS in developing the various rule books. As a result, the rules are impartial and authoritative and reflect the most current developments in technology and in scientific disciplines.

The annual ABS *Record* is invaluable to shipowners, shippers, underwriters, and shipbuilders for the essential data it contains on hull, machinery, the particular characteristics, and the ownership of 55,000 vessels and marine structures in the world. The *Surveyor* is a quarterly magazine distributed to the maritime industry, with articles on shipbuilding and other maritime subjects.

In furthering the objectives for which it was founded, the Bureau aids young college students in their study of naval architecture and marine

A crankshaft is inspected in Kobe, Japan—one of eighty-eight countries in which ABS maintains offices to provide classification services.

The whaling ship Charles M. Morgan, shown under sail during the last days of her career, is the oldest ABS-surveyed vessel in existence. She is now restored and open to the public at Mystic Seaport, Connecticut.

This certificate of competence was issued to a ship master in 1866 by the American Ship Masters Association.

engineering and awards a Valor Medal for especially noteworthy acts or deeds of valor at sea. It maintains a technical library, engages in extensive research, and maintains a complete file of ship registers published by other classification societies.

ABS pioneered in the classifying of welded vessels. Its 1936 "rules" were the first to state that welding would be acceptable for all parts of the hull. This pioneering effort, backed by much experimentation and research, helped make possible the vast welded ship program of World War II. The Bureau also helped to develop the use of aluminum as a structural material in shipbuilding, and was the first classification society to publish rules for the construction and survey of offshore mobile drilling units.

When a ship or other marine structure is "classed" by ABS, it means that every aspect of design and construction, from blueprints to sea trials, has been closely supervised by ABS surveyors for compliance with ABS rules and that the ship is maintained to standards of safety and efficiency for all of its useful life.

To accommodate its growing activities, the Bureau recently acquired a twenty-one-story headquarters at 65 Broadway in New York City, a building described as one of the most architecturally attractive in lower Manhattan. Here also are located other ABS functions, including the ABS Worldwide Technical Services, a certification and advisory service for land-based projects; EXAM Company, a pipeline inspection organization; and ABS Computers, a data-processing service for industry. The Bureau's computerized records contain data on some 55,000 ships.

Robert T. Young is chairman and chief executive officer of the American Bureau of Shipping.

259

THE SEAMEN'S BANK FOR SAVINGS

When The Seamen's Bank for Savings was chartered on May 11, 1829, the Port of New York was alive with the bustle of cargo being loaded onto the countless stately, square-rigged packet ships which dotted the waterfront.

Handbills had been circulated announcing the new bank's opening on the second floor at 149 Maiden Lane in Lower Manhattan for the purpose of "furnishing a safe and advantageous depository for the earnings of seamen and seafaring people, and those connected with the navy and merchant service."

The first depositor answering the advertisement was James Chappel, a stevedore.

Few banks have had more humble beginnings. The bank was open only one hour a day, Monday-Saturday, and there was one paid employee. There was no vault, so deposits were kept by the Fulton Bank.

But few banks in New York had more substantial sponsors. The trustees included such men as William Whitlock, Jr., who owned a line of ships running to Le Havre, France, and Captain Charles H. Marshall, principal owner of the famous Black Ball Line. All were concerned with the welfare of seamen.

In 1833, the bank extended its deposit service to people of all callings, and it experienced a modest but steady growth.

In its long history, the bank has survived fires, economic depressions, and financial panics. In the panic of 1857, it met all demands and emerged with a reputation as a bank that stood behind its obligations.

On May 23, 1871, the bank opened a new six-story headquarters at 74 Wall Street—the first Wall Street building with elevators. This came

just before more hard times and many bank failures, but Seamen's came through again with "all sail set" and steadily increasing deposits.

A new fifteen-story headquarters, at 72 Wall Street, was dedicated in 1926. However, continued growth necessitated even more space, and in 1955 the bank moved into the former U.S. Assay Office at 30 Wall Street, newly modernized behind a handsome stone facade. Next door is the historic Federal Hall National Memorial Building, the actual site of George Washington's inauguration as President on April 30, 1789.

Considering its historic surroundings and its 150-year association with sailors, ships, and shipping, it is only fitting that the Seamen's Bank decorates all its offices in a nautical decor, with authentic ship models, fine marine art, and memorabilia of

the sea. Its nautical calendars have long been collectors' items.

But this historical flavor has not hindered the bank's course toward the future. Today, The Seamen's Bank for Savings has twelve offices in Manhattan, Westchester, Nassau, and Suffolk with over 300,000 depositors, and assets of close to $2 billion. In keeping with its 150-year history, the bank continues to move ahead, following the sailors' tradition of "hold your course and steady as she goes."

Headquarters of the Seamen's Bank today is at 30 Wall Street, in the financial heart of America, right next to the historic Federal Hall National Memorial Building.

The Seamen's Bank opened in 1829 on the second floor of 149 Maiden Lane, close to the bustling East River waterfront and its ship-lined piers.

260

THE PORT AUTHORITY OF NEW YORK & NEW JERSEY

A century and a half ago, the states of New York and New Jersey squabbled like neighbors over a backyard fence. The principal bone of contention was jurisdiction over interstate commerce crossing the Hudson River and the exact location of the boundary line in the river. In 1834, the matter was settled by treaty.

Seventy-five years later, however, the old rivalry surfaced again with the tremendous volume of waterborne traffic generated by World War I. Then, as had been the practice since the port's origin, the bulk of the port's maritime commerce was handled at piers on the New York side, although most of the railroads had their terminals on the New Jersey side. It was during this period also that the initial impact of automobile and truck traffic was being felt. Congestion and delays were rampant. A bi-state investigative commission was formed, and its comprehensive report gave rise, in 1921, to The Port Authority of New York and New Jersey.

The Port Authority was established as a self-supporting public corporation. It was given full power to construct, lease, and/or operate a wide variety of transportation and terminal facilities then in use or contemplated, with the recommendation that interstate bridges and tunnels be constructed for the burgeoning vehicular traffic.

During the late 1920s and early 1930s, the Bayonne and Goethals bridges and the Outerbridge Crossing between Staten Island and New Jersey were constructed, as well as the Lincoln Tunnel and the George Washington Bridge between Manhattan and New Jersey. Another trans-Hudson crossing, the Holland Tunnel, was opened in 1927 and

The compact between the states of New York and New Jersey that established the Port Authority was signed on April 30, 1921, in the Great Hall of the New York Chamber of Commerce.

In the same hall, on August 24, 1978, Governors Brendan Byrne of New Jersey and Hugh Carey of New York signed the industrial park development legislation that will mean an expanded role for the Port Authority.

placed under Port Authority operation in 1930. Then followed a number of marine and other transport terminals: Port Newark and Elizabeth, New Jersey, which together comprise the world's largest containerport; Hoboken, New Jersey; the Brooklyn, Erie Basin, and Columbia Street marine terminals; the New York City Passenger Ship Terminal; and the New York and Newark Motor Truck Terminals.

Airports administered by the Port Authority are John F. Kennedy International, LaGuardia, Newark International, Teterboro, and the West 30th Street and Downtown heliports in Manhattan. Bus and mass transit facilities include the Port Authority Trans Hudson (PATH) System, the Journal Square Transportation Center, the Port Authority Bus Terminal, and the George Washington Bridge Bus Station.

Since its creation in 1921, the Port Authority has invested over $4 billion in terminals and facilities that in 1977 accommodated 83 million vehicles across its tunnels and bridges, nearly 11 million tons of general cargo at its marine terminals, some 45 million passengers at its airports, and 117 million passengers traveling through its bus and rail facilities. In addition, the World Trade Center serves as a nerve center for the port's international trade operations—banking, customs, freight forwarding, commodities trading, world trade information, and educational facilities, to name only a few.

Port Authority policy is established by a board of twelve commissioners—six appointed by the governor of each state—and is carried out by an executive director and a career staff of professional and administrative personnel. Its responsibilities have recently been broadened significantly to include participation in the development of industrial parks in Jersey City, Newark, and Brooklyn.

It would be difficult to imagine the New York-New Jersey metropolitan area today had not the farsighted planners of sixty years ago created the Port Authority—the first organization of its kind in the United States.

WATERMAN STEAMSHIP COMPANY

Among the most modern vessels in the Waterman fleet is the LASH barge and containership Sam Houston, shown here at dockside in Brooklyn, New York.

Although the Waterman Steamship Company was founded in Mobile, Alabama, it has long been closely associated with the port of New York and is now headquartered here.

In 1919, John B. Waterman, a young man with considerable experience in shipping, decided that the port of Mobile was important enough to be represented by a locally-owned, American-flag steamship line on world trade routes. Enlisting the support of other businessmen, he formed the Waterman Steamship Company with a capitalization of only $40,000—hardly enough to buy office furniture today.

At that time, the United States Shipping Board was using its huge war-built emergency fleet to put the American flag back on the seas, and Waterman, like other shipping entrepreneurs, was able to obtain a surplus ship at bargain rates and a subsidy for the run between the Eastern Gulf and the United Kingdom. From this shoe-string start grew an enterprising organization that was to become the largest operator in the American merchant marine.

Over the years, routes and services were expanded to include runs to Puerto Rico and intercoastal and coastwise services under the banner of the Pan Atlantic Line. The company continually updated its fleet with larger, faster, and more versatile ships. Stevedoring, ship repair, and shipbuilding subsidiaries were added over the years, along with a steamship agency that serviced the Anchor Line, which operated many famous liners into the port of New York.

By the outbreak of World War II, Waterman owned thirty-eight ships, with routes to Europe and the Far East in addition to domestic services. The Waterman house flag left American ports on twenty-five cargo ships every month.

During the war, the company operated thirty-seven ships of its own (some of which were sunk) plus about one hundred ships for the government. Much of this wartime activity was centered in the port of New York. After the war, the Waterman fleet helped to carry huge amounts of cargo for the rebuilding of wartorn Europe.

In 1955, the company was sold to Malcolm P. McLean, a trucking expert who introduced the idea of "trailer-ships"—the carrying of loaded truck trailers aboard ships. The idea was soon imitated by others. In 1965, McLean sold the company and its fifteen C-2 freighters to Cornelius Walsh, former head of States Marine Lines, and its headquarters were moved to New York.

Fleet modernization has continued in the 1970s, with the addition of several LASH (lighter-aboard-ship) vessels carrying barges and containers. These ships are used on the Waterman-Isthmian service from New York and Gulf ports to the Persian Gulf, Red Sea ports, India, and Pakistan. The Waterman Line also offers express cargo service from New York and Gulf ports to Korea, Manila, Taiwan, and Hong Kong and from Gulf ports to Belgium, Holland, Germany, Poland, and Russia.

With its big, modern fleet of express freighters and its far-flung cargo routes, Waterman is now, more than ever before, an important part of the worldwide shipping network serving the great port of New York.

CHEMICAL BANK

E choes of the American Revolution still sounded clear in the summer of 1824. At the invitation of President Monroe, Lafayette made an official visit to the United States, landing at New York harbor on August 16 amid a tumultuous welcome. Among those greeting him was Mayor William Paulding, whose uncle had helped to capture British war spy Major John Andre in 1780. Of the dozen banks then operating in New York, one had been founded by Alexander Hamilton and another by Aaron Burr.

With a population of 124,000, New York was already the commercial center of the United States. Its port handled $33 million in cargo in 1824. Within a year, the Erie Canal would give it a direct water route to the Great Lakes and the American heartland. A quarter century later, traffic in the port of New York would be worth $300 million.

On Monday, August 2, 1824—two weeks before Lafayette's arrival—Chemical Manufacturing Company opened its office of Discount and Deposit at 216 Broadway, across the street from St. Paul's Chapel. As the city's thirteenth bank, it was successful from the day its doors opened. Twenty years later, manufacturing operations were discontinued, and the name was changed to Chemical Bank.

The founder and first president of the bank was Balthasar P. Melick. The first cashier was William Stebbins. John B. Desdoity served as bookkeeper, at an annual salary of $1,200. Even five years later, when the business was well established, only two officers received more than $1,000. The cashier received an annual salary of $1,500, plus the upper room of the bank as his living quarters.

263

The bank's first half century of life was set against a background of considerable chaos in the nation's monetary system. There were financial panics in 1837, 1857, and again in 1873, complicated by the circulation of some seven thousand different acceptable currencies. Through these crises, the young bank earned a reputation for stability. During the panic of 1857, Chemical was the only bank in New York City that would redeem its notes in gold—a policy that earned it the nickname "Old Bullion."

Over the past fifty years, the bank has experienced rapid and steady growth as a result of acquisitions, international expansion, and diversification into banking-related business. Today, Chemical New York Corporation, with assets of $32.8 billion and deposits of $24.9 billion as of December 31, 1978, provides a

Chemical's first office opened in 1824 opposite St. Paul's Chapel, which was then considered "uptown."

wide range of financial services to individuals, businesses, and governments throughout the world.

Despite its far-flung interests, Chemical Bank retains a strong sense of civic pride and responsibility toward the city of New York. A number of its executives are on full-time loan to the city—among them, Deputy Police Commissioner Matt McPortland. The bank has sponsored or supported a number of civic programs, including the Met in the Park summer opera and the Museum Collaborative. It also runs a Metropolitan-area art competition for high school students; winners receive scholarships, and their works are displayed at branches of the bank.

INTERNATIONAL TERMINAL OPERATING COMPANY

T he year was 1921. New York piers were once again crowded with ships of all nations, as the world's maritime commerce recovered from the effects of the world war. Many of the famous North Atlantic liners had not yet returned to service, but there were a number of familiar names listed in the shipping news of the New York papers: the *Olympic* bound for Cherbourg, the *Albania* for Liverpool, the *Morro Castle* for Havana, and the *Saxonia* for Hamburg.

The Holland-America Line was back in regular service, but the famous German Lines were notably absent from the shipping news. They were rebuilding their fleets, however, and planning to restore their New York services.

That was the year that Captain Franz Jarka, a former officer in the German merchant marine, started the Jarka Corporation, later to become the International Terminal Operating Company. Just a few months later, North German Lloyd resumed its New York run. The S.S. *Seydlitz* arrived in port with 125 passengers and a mixed cargo, inaugurating the line's new semimonthly service. Within a year or so, Captain Jarka's new firm was handling both the freight and passenger business of Holland-America and North German Lloyd, which soon became again one of the most important lines linking New York and Europe.

During the 1920s, the company expanded its operations to Boston, Philadelphia, Baltimore, Newport News, Albany, and Portland and Searsport, Maine.

For many years, the company operated the big Erie Basin terminal in Brooklyn, one of the largest and busiest dock areas in the port until its

closing in 1965. This was the home port of the Robin Line and the globe-girdling fleet of the Isthmian Line.

Because of its expertise and versatility, the firm was chosen to operate the huge Brooklyn Army Base after World War I and the Newport News Port of Embarkation in World War II.

In 1953, the Jarka Corporation became International Terminal Operating Company, known throughout the industry as ITO, which in 1962 became a subsidiary of the Ogden Corporation, a diversified company. Today, ITO operates throughout the port of New York, handling LASH, containers, and break-bulk cargo in Brooklyn and Port Newark; almost exclusively containers in Port Elizabeth, where some of the newest roll-on/roll-off and pure containerships afloat call; baggage and ship stores at the passenger ship terminal in Manhattan, home of the cruiseship fleet.

At Port Elizabeth in New Jersey, ITO has a terminal capable of docking three 700-foot-long ships, with 95 acres of backup storage space for 8,000 containers. These berths are served by four huge cranes, each sixteen stories high and costing $1 million—an indication of the tremen-

This is a part of the fleet of twenty-one straddle carriers used by ITO at Port Elizabeth.

dous investment and equipment needed for modern stevedoring operations in New York, the nation's "container capital."

On an average day, International Terminal Operating Company employs about 20 percent of the longshoremen working in the port. It has a full-time staff of 275 office and supervisory personnel for its various port operations.

ITO played an important role in the port's container revolution of the 1960s when it leased a large section of the new Port Elizabeth terminal. The container revolution brought not only radical new developments in cargo-handling methods, but also a tremendous increase in the size of ships. Because containerships are so costly to build and operate, moreover, turnaround time must be minimized. ITO has handled 1,600 tons an hour at Port Elizabeth!

This versatile Russian break-bulk/container ship is being unloaded by ITO at Port Elizabeth.

Observing the ITO terminal area in operation has been described as "like looking at two dozen football fields in action simultaneously." All vehicles going to and from the wharves are directed from a control tower, which assigns slots in storage aisles for containers being unloaded from ships and directs vehicles to where outbound freight is to be picked up.

Every container carries an identifi-cation number on all sides. Thus, a typical message from the control tower might be: "Van carrier V. Box XYZU13254, slot M17 to interchange #21."

Thousands of the metal cargo boxes are piled in neat rows, stacked two high, over almost one hundred acres of backup area. Keeping track of these containers and directing them to and from the ships is a complex job involving coordination and elec-tronic record keeping that has in-jected an entirely new dimension into the business of stevedoring. While a container may cost as much as $10,000, the contents of toys, textiles, machinery, or expensive surgical equipment may cost in the millions. Locating and accounting for each container in the terminal and re-porting its destination necessitates a team of computer specialists to pro-gram and feed information into the computer. While they never physical-ly handle a pound of cargo, they are as important to modern stevedoring as any vehicle driver or longshore-man.

In the days of Captain Jarka, steve-doring firms were run by men who came up from the ships or from the

Shown here are three of the four enormous cranes used by ITO at its Port Elizabeth con-tainer terminal.

docks. In the intervening years, steve-doring has become so sophisticated and investment-intensive that the company has long been recruiting graduates of the merchant marine academies and other colleges to complement those with practical, dockside know-how. Starting with the firm in 1955 and having worked all parts of the harbor as pier superin-tendent, terminal manager, and sales-man, John J. Farrell, Jr., graduate of Holy Cross College, is now President of ITO and an industry spokesman.

Huge cranes have now replaced booms and tackle for most cargo handling in the port. Ships today carry five times as much cargo as the freighters of 1921. But while it must adapt to fast-changing conditions, the business of stevedoring, says President Farrell, will remain a vital function of the port, contributing the experienced manpower, imagina-tion, and expertise in cargo handling that enables New York to retain its position as one of the great centers of world commerce.

MANUFACTURERS HANOVER TRUST

W hen clipper ships docked at South Street, not only the voyages themselves but most trading activities were financed by credit. Credit was the means by which Manufacturers Hanover, through predecessor banks, kept business and trade moving through the Port of New York for more than a century and a half. As trade and commerce prospered, so the banking industry grew. Mutually successful, they contributed to the development of New York into America's foremost seaport and the world's financial center.

At the very beginning of the Bank's corporate history, The New York Manufacturing Company combined the production of cotton looms and textile equipment with banking operations. Its founding in 1812 was advantageously timed with the shift of financial power from New England to New York and the rise of King Cotton, which within a decade would be exported almost entirely from New York.

Today's Manufacturers Hanover is the product of a series of mergers of more than eighty banks that began when the Phenix Bank acquired the banking business of the manufacturing company in 1817. The bank brought prosperity and growth to the country by advancing capital to Western wheat growers and Southern cotton planters, to importers and exporters, and to the builders of transcontinental railroads.

Manufacturers Hanover Trust Company was founded in 1961 with the merger of Manufacturers Trust Company and The Hanover Bank. In 1968, Manufacturers Hanover Corporation, a bank holding company, was formed to achieve more organizational flexibility and broaden geo-

Officers of Manufacturers Hanover Trust Corporation are John F. McGillicuddy (left), chairman and chief executive officer; John R. Torell III (center) and Harry Taylor, vice chairmen.

graphic and product markets. Two hundred branches serve the New York metropolitan area, with another forty operated by three subsidiaries upstate. One of the world's leading banks, MHT maintains an overseas presence through a global network of more than one hundred branches, representative offices, subsidiaries, and affiliates in some forty countries; its worldwide correspondent network extends to more than 1,600 banks in 122 countries.

But the character and caliber of a bank or a city are not determined solely by the success of its monetary and trading operations. Reputations for leadership have been won throughout MHT's corporate life by officers and directors who have not limited their financial ability and genius to their own enterprises, but have given generously of their time and energy to municipal, national, and maritime affairs.

Among those playing significant roles in the early years were Albert Gallatin, who, prior to assuming the presidency of National Bank, a predecessor bank, in the early nineteenth century, served as Secretary of the Treasury under Presidents Jefferson and Madison and then as ambassador to France and Great Britain. Moses H. Grinnell, president of the Phenix Bank from 1838 to 1840, was a member of the shipping firm that owned the record-breaking *Flying Cloud* clipper ship, which sailed from New York to San Francisco in fewer than ninety days. A number of officers and directors were prominent in New York commercial circles, serving as presidents of the New York Chamber of Commerce. Today's Manufacturers Hanover, a $35 billion worldwide organization, continues this proud tradition of financial and community leadership.

266

COLUMBUS LINE

In the foreground of this historic painting is the Corrientes, built for Hamburg-Sud in 1881. At left is the Santos II, and at right is the Rio—one of the first three ships bought by Hamburg-Sud in 1871.

The Columbus Australia is shown passing under the Sydney Harbour Bridge

Established in 1957, Columbus Line is a relative newcomer among steamship lines. It traces its ancestry, however, to Hamburg-Sud, a veteran company that initiated regular first class liner service between Europe and the East Coast of South America in 1871. Beginning in 1912, Hamburg-Sud also operated a regular service between the United States and Brazil, but this service was soon interrupted by World War I.

The original New York staff of Columbus Line consisted of ten veterans of the disbanded International Freighting Corporation, working out of the offices of the line's agents at 44 Whitehall Street—cheek-by-jowl with such giants of the steamship business as the United States, Cunard, French, Italian, and Hapag-Lloyd lines. At that time, the entire Columbus fleet consisted of two break-bulk vessels, the *Santa Rita* and the *Burg Sparrenberg*, offering a modest service to the East Coast of South America.

So well did the new venture prosper that in less than a year it had moved to its own offices at 26 Broadway. Now there were five ships and a doubled staff of twenty—five of whom are still with the company.

The company proved so successful in the handling of perishable cargoes that, in 1961, it was approved by the New Zealand Meat Board to transport beef and lamb to the Pacific Coast of the United States. A new service was established with two vessels, and an office was opened in San Francisco to operate it. In 1963, service was inaugurated to Australasia from the East Coast, making Columbus the first in the North America/Australia/New Zealand trade to offer simultaneous service from the East and West Coasts of North America.

During the 1960's, it was decided to convert to the revolutionary containerization concept, necessitating the replacement of the existing fleet of nine break-bulk vessels with three fully containerized ships designed specifically for the Down Under trade. By this time, Columbus had withdrawn from the South American trade. In 1973, three new containerships were added to the West Coast fleet.

The spring of 1977, which coincided with its twentieth anniversary, brought Columbus to the Gulf Coast, with a new company office in New Orleans to cater to that and the Houston territory. Three more containerships, designed especially to meet the particular demands of the Gulf route, were ordered at a cost of $95 million for delivery in 1979. These will replace the chartered tonnage now employed. Each vessel in the new, modern fleet will have a computer system that allows different kinds of refrigerated cargoes to be carried at the differing temperatures required for the safe transportation of meat, fish, fruit, vegetables, and other perishable goods.

Today Columbus Line maintains its headquarters in the North Tower of the World Trade Center, in full view of its cargo-laden vessels as they pass through the Port of New York.

NORTON LILLY & COMPANY

Founded in 1841 when John Norton first chartered a ship to carry kerosene from New York to Buenos Aires and La Plata, Norton, Lilly & Company is considered to be the oldest operating shipping business in the United States.

John Norton had come to New York from Maine to open a trading business, and like many merchants in the early 1800s hired the vessels that carried his goods. Soon, however, John Norton & Company found itself supplying sailing packets for other city merchants, first under charter and later with its own sailing ships as the Norton Line.

The advent of steam-powered ships in the late nineteenth century changed the shipping industry radically, and Norton & Son, as the company was then called, expanded rapidly under the direction of Edward Norton. Unable to obtain U.S. government assistance to purchase steamships for Norton Line, Edward traveled to London, where he convinced three British shipowners to establish direct steamship service from America to India, to South America, and to Australia and New Zealand. Pioneering what would become a mainstay of the modern steamship cargo business, Norton & Son became the general agents for the British lines.

As general agents became an established part of the maritime industry, Norton & Son continued to grow, expanding beyond its original Wall Street berth to piers on the Brooklyn side of the harbor, and forcing the company to move from its original offices at the corner of Wall and South streets to larger quarters at the new Produce Exchange Annex in 1895.

The company changed its name for the third and last time in 1907, when J. T. Lilly, a member of the firm since the age of 16 and at that time its senior manager, became a full partner.

While continuing to act as agents for the British Lines, Norton, Lilly & Company also helped establish a worldwide network of agents at the close of World War I for the first successful American cargo line in the long distance trades to India, China, Japan, and the Straits Settlements—the Isthmian Line. In addition to finding overseas representatives for Isthmian, the company expanded its own operations, opening offices in major ports on the U.S. Atlantic, Gulf, and West coasts, as well as in Panama.

When World War II broke out in 1939, Norton, Lilly began operating vessels for the British Minister of War Transport, as well as for the Norwegian Government's wartime agency, Notraship. And when the U.S. entered the war, the company stepped forward to help manage the War Shipping Association's Liberty and Victory ships which supplied Allied

John Norton founded the company that still bears his name back in 1841—making it the oldest shipping business in the United States today.

Flying the flag of her New York agents, Norton, Lilly, the schooner Berta of Ibiza departs New York in 1978 with the first commercial cargo under sail in thirty-one years, a fitting tribute to the company's early beginnings.

troops throughout the world.

In the postwar years, the century-old company returned to its extensive agency operations. Under new ownership and management from 1971, the company further expanded its office network, shipowner representations, and affiliated marine business interests. Today, representing sixteen liner operators and several score nonliner companies, with some 550 employees in its North American network of twenty-six offices, Norton, Lilly is not only the oldest steamship agency in the United States—it is also the largest.

HELLENIC LINES

World War II had just ended when Pericles G. Callimanopulos entered New York harbor for the first time on October 8, 1945. At the outbreak of the war, when Greece had been cut off from Northern Europe, the Greek government had asked him to start a service with the United States with the nine vessels in his Hellenic Lines fleet. With the war over, only one of these ships was still afloat; the other eight had been sunk crossing the heavily patrolled Mediterranean and North Atlantic.

Mr. Callimanopulos began his mar-

The Hellenic Valor, with an overall length of 190.5 meters and a gross tonnage of 17,000 tons, is one of three new roll-on/roll-off container vessels delivered at the end of 1978.

itime career as a shipping clerk in Alexandria, Egypt, in 1911. He bought his first ship, a small coastal vessel named *Valkyrie*, in 1918, then moved on to the coal business and the agency of regular cargo services. Eventually he began investing in seagoing ships, forming the Fenton Steamship company, in London. Deutsch-Hellenische Schiffahrtsagentur G.m.b.H. was formed in Hamburg, Germany, in 1934. Operating out of Piraeus, it was offering a regular cargo service be-

tween the Black Sea, the Mediterranean, London, and Northern Europe when it switched to the perilous North Atlantic run in 1940.

At the end of the war, the U.S. government allocated 100 ships to reequip the Greek merchant marine, and Hellenic Lines applied for six. It got five, all brand new Liberty ships, and found itself in the business of carrying peacetime cargo between the United States and the Mediterranean.

With his five new ships and new service to the United States, Mr. Callimanopulos made the decision to

Pericles Callimanopulos, founder and president of Hellenic Lines, is the recipient of numerous honors and awards from many countries in the world—including Greece, Belgium, Italy, Jordan and the United States—for his long and impressive record of maritime accomplishments.

stay in New York, opening a new Hellenic headquarters in the Cunard Building at 25 Broadway.

The steamship company expanded rapidly in the postwar years, soon opening branch offices in New Orleans and Houston. By 1951, Hellenic had outgrown its first New York headquarters and moved one block uptown to 39 Broadway, where it has remained ever since.

In 1965, Hellenic entered the shoreside business of ocean cargo, purchasing a finger pier at the foot of 57th Street on the Brooklyn waterfront. Along with an adjacent wharf leased from the U.S. Navy, the pier—the only privately owned general cargo pier in New York harbor—is the center of Hellenic's New York terminal operations.

From its fleet of five new Liberty ships plus the sole survivor of its World War II operations, Hellenic Lines has grown to forty-one modern motorships, including twelve new cargo liners built in 1975 and three roll-on/roll-off ships delivered in 1978.

Still under the active direction of its original owner and president, the line has continued to expand its services, which now include regular sailings from the U.S. to the Red Sea, the Persian Gulf, Pakistan, India, Sri Lanka, and Bangladesh. Hellenic has revived its original service between the Black Sea and Eastern Mediterranean ports and Hamburg, Rotterdam, Antwerp, and London, and also runs a service between Mediterranean ports and South and East Africa.

As a man who came to New York in 1945 with only one ship left in his fleet, Pericles Callimanopulos can be proud indeed of the past and present of Hellenic Lines—and equally confident of its future.

NORTHEAST MARINE TERMINAL

In a small square structure known as The Tower, a genial middle-aged man walks to and fro over a thick orange carpet as he talks about a modern miracle. The serenity of his office stands in sharp contrast to the scene of frantic activity below. The walls are decorated with pictures of sailing ships, dominated by a large lithograph by Montague Dawson, the famous marine artist.

This office is the chairman's office, center of Northeast Marine Terminal, located between 28th and 39th Streets in Brooklyn, New York. The man is Paul Friedman, who laughs a lot and loves to go deep-sea fishing.

Outside, all is noise and turmoil. Huge trailer trucks, carrying forty-foot containers, swivel and thrust every which way. They are serving the vessels of the half dozen or so steamship lines which regularly call at Northeast.

Northeast Marine Terminal is the only multipurpose facility on the Brooklyn side of New York harbor. The terminal can handle any type of ship—roll-on/roll-off, break-bulk, container, or LASH (Lighter Aboard Ship). Eleven large, ocean-going vessels can be handled simultaneously at the facility.

Northeast was built by the City of New York in 1962 for Mitsui Line, originally as a break-bulk facility, but the container revolution a few years later spurred changes in the handling of cargo and the design of ships, terminals, and equipment. As a result, with current engineering projects completed, 70,000 containers and 2 million tons of break-bulk cargo are to be handled annually at Northeast.

In 1977, Francis X. McQuade, with his lifetime experience in stevedoring, saw the inherent possibilities of the terminal. The large tract of land and its proximity to the entrance to New York Harbor made it the perfect site for development of an efficient containerport.

Current tenants are Prudential Lines, Delta Line, Jugolinija, Royal Netherlands Steamship Company, Medafrica Lina, Hellenic Lines, and Pakistan Shipping Corporation.

The terminal is within twenty minutes' steaming time of the entrance to the harbor. It has convenient truck access to the interstate highway system, with direct connections to major United States routes, thruways, and turnpikes to the North, West, and South. It also has its own rail depot, serviced by the New York Dock Railway, which connects with Conrail. By mid-1979, another forty acres will be added to the existing eighty acres of prime Brooklyn waterfront.

There are six warehouses—one, the largest in the area—for the storage and distribution of general merchandise. In the terminal are stored vast quantities of copper, antimony, lead, structural steel, and cupronickel— stored, explains Friedman, "until about four thousand tons accumulate and it is shipped to the Far East."

On the longest side, the terminal at

Northeast Marine Terminal stands out as the only intermodal center in Brooklyn.

39th Street has a width of 700 feet and a length of more than 1,060 feet. A continuous thirty-foot-wide apron extends uninterruptedly around the terminal's offshore sides for more than 2,300 feet. The terminal's large central court was designed to reduce cargo-handling time. It is presently being modernized to feature covered and well-lit loading platforms. The court enables trucks to discharge and load cargo close to the four-vessel berths served by the pier.

At an adjacent pier at 35th Street in the Northeast terminal complex, the ocean carriers consolidate or strip container shipments. This pier has a length of 1,750 feet and can work three vessels simultaneously. Nearby, and plainly to be seen from the chairman's office, are two immense Star Iron & Steel Starporter gantry cranes. One is a diesel-powered monster with a 133-foot outreach and a 65-foot backreach, 90-foot gauge, with a 70-long-ton capacity at 100 feet out and a 50-long-ton capacity at 133 feet. The other is also diesel-powered, with the same out- and backreach, but with a 50-long-ton capacity. A P & H mobile

The flexibility of Northeast Marine Terminal facilitates the turnaround of Prudential's LASH Atlantico with a full complement of LASH barges and containers.

crane is used as a backup and complement to the gantry cranes.

For the movement of containers and chassis through the terminal's facilities, there are twenty-one hustlers, three roll-on/roll-off hustlers, eight top loaders for stacking twenty- and forty-foot containers three high, plus three top loaders with twenty-, thirty-, and forty-foot expandable spreaders, and two fifteen-ton side loaders for handling or stacking empty containers. Also, there are 177 forklifts and six forklift trucks ranging from ten to thirty-five tons.

The efficiency and adaptability of the facilities of Northeast Marine Terminal are demonstrated most dramatically by the three new Hellenic Line ships which, with a full cargo, can be turned around between 8:00 A.M. and 4:00 P.M. of the same day, using the roll berth and container cranes simultaneously.

Thus, with its efficient new spirit of cooperation and burning desire to succeed, the dynamic new management of Northeast is committed to

the reinstatement of the port of New York to its preeminent position as the focal point of the waterborne commerce of the United States.

At the 39th Street pier of Northeast Marine Terminal, break-bulk cargo consigned to South American ports is being loaded onto the Prudential Lines freighter Santa Isabel.

UNITED STATES LINES, INC.

The present United States Lines evolved from the American Line, which came into being in 1871 with the financial sponsorship of the Pennsylvania Railroad. Thus, the house flag displayed from the masts of the earliest American liners, *Pennsylvania, Ohio, Indiana,* and *Illinois,* carried the rail company's keystone symbol of the state of Pennsylvania.

When the ship line changed ownership in 1893, it adopted the famous "blue eagle" that has remained its proud symbol ever since. The new house flag flew over the *New York* and the *Philadelphia,* then the crack liners of the North Atlantic trade. As the premier Yankee steamship carrier of passengers, cargo, and mail, the U.S.-flag company proudly maintained our nation's presence on the sealanes of the world.

The turn of the century saw the American Line join the U.S.-flag Atlantic Transport Company to form the nucleus of the International Mercantile Marine Company, one of the most fascinating enterprises in business history. It was headquartered at Number One Broadway in New York.

This huge American shipping combine, organized by Wall Street's financial wizard, John Pierpont Morgan, then acquired the famed British fleets of White Star Line, Leyland Line, Dominion Line, Oceanic Steam Navigation, and Shaw, Savill & Albion Ltd. At its peak, the International Mercantile Marine Company controlled more than 120 major passenger and freight vessels of 1.3 million tons and virtually dominated Atlantic shipping.

In the early 1930s, International Mercantile Marine merged with Roosevelt Steamship Company, which had been organized by Kermit Roosevelt, son of the former presi-

dent. The two companies then purchased the postwar fleet of United States Lines from the U.S. government.

In 1943, after gradually disposing of its foreign-flag tonnage, the corporation discarded its international designation and assumed the name of its principal subsidiary to become today's United States Lines.

For more than a century, United States Lines has served our country in peace and war, contributing significantly to its prosperity and security. The roster of famous vessels in recent years includes the famed ocean queens *Leviathan, Manhattan, Washington,* and superliner *United States*

On Washington's birthday in 1893, President Benjamin Harrison officiated as the new United States Lines' pennant was unfurled aboard the S.S. New York. The famous "blue eagle" still identifies the firm's modern fleet.

Future Port USA: The company's 200-acre modern marine terminal is located at Howland Hook, Staten Island, where upwards of 100,000 containers are handled annually. Other marine facilities and offices are maintained in more than one hundred cities around the world.

—holder of the legendary Blue Ribbon speed trophy for her record maiden crossing to Europe in 1952 in three days, ten hours, and forty minutes.

Today, the corporation is headed by Malcom P. McLean, with William B. Bru as chairman of the board, president, and chief executive officer. McLean—often called "the father of containerization"—created the first total intermodal system transporting cargo in standardized boxes door-to-door anywhere in the world. This innovation, which began in the 1950s, has revolutionized physical distribution. United States Lines' containerships now serve Europe, Canada, all coasts of the United States, Panama, Costa Rica, Hawaii, Guam, the Far East, and Southeast Asia via the company's Tri Continent Service.

SEATRAIN LINES

The Seatrain Havana in 1932 was one of the first ships in the world to carry a mile-long train of loaded freight cars.

Seatrain's Seamobile Service, inaugurated in 1958, combined the flexibility of highway container service with the economy of water transport.

In 1979 Seatrain Lines marked its fiftieth anniversary as an innovative ocean carrier serving the port of New York.

Seatrain was started in 1929 by Graham H. Brush and Joseph Hodgson. Brush had made an intensive study of ocean transportation and had come up with the revolutionary idea of hauling loaded rail cars, instead of loose cargo, to save time and stevedoring costs.

The first voyage was made in January of 1929 from New Orleans to Havana by the S.S. *Seatrain*, carrying a mile-long train of loaded rail cars.

Two more ships were built in 1932 and another two in 1940, all especially designed "seatrains." Routes were expanded to include New York, Savannah, Havana, New Orleans, and Texas City, Texas.

During World War II most of the Seatrain fleet was taken over by the Department of Defense, the ships being ideal for hauling tanks, trucks, and other vehicles. The Seatrain Texas was instrumental in turning back the Germans in North Africa: it rushed 250 heavy tanks, 50 tank destroyers, and other weapons to the British army in Egypt in a 35-day, unescorted, top-speed solo dash from New York through submarine-infested seas. The ship's 8,000 tons of vital cargo arrived in time to boost British firepower for the battle of El Alamein.

In 1965 Seatrain Lines was purchased by Joseph Kahn and Howard Pack, who had ventured into shipping in 1950 with one Liberty-type "tramp" and who, fifteen years later, were operating thirty-six ships. Their fleet later included the 115,000-ton supertanker *Manhattan*, at one time the largest ship in the American merchant marine. In 1969 the *Manhattan* was the first deep-draft commercial vessel ever to transit the historic Northwest Passage, the tortuous polar sea route around the top of North America.

Seatrain operates a worldwide container service with cargo interchanges serving the United States, Europe, the Middle East, the Mediterranean, the Far East, and Latin America. More than 60,000 containers are in use at any one time. A daily log of their movements is kept at the company's computer center at Seatrain Terminal, Weehawken, New Jersey. There is also a communications center there for contacting every ship of the fleet by satellite.

Seatrain also is active in port management in the Middle East and in the national and international chartering of ships. Its Seatrain Shipbuilding Corporation in New York has turned out four supertankers and is now building huge seagoing barges.

Energy is also important to Seatrain's long-range planning, with its Pride Refining Company in Texas and new involvements in petrochemicals in Alaska and coal in West Virginia.

Joseph Kahn, chairman of the company, predicts that Seatrain will continue to grow by use of new cargo concepts and innovative managerial skills. Seatrain, he says, is entering its second half-century as a company "on the move."

UNITED STATES NAVIGATION,INC.

S.S. ROCK ISLAND

Although the first freighter in America's World War I emergency fleet wasn't launched until twenty-two days after the Armistice was signed on November 11, 1918, in the next year over two thousand "Hog Islanders" came down the ways. Many of the ships went directly to the scrap yard. But in an effort to foster what had been a stepchild industry before the war, Congress created the U.S. Shipping Board and directed it to lease the Hog Islanders to anyone willing to compete against the established European steamship lines. Edward C. Oelsner was one of the few who decided to try.

In early 1919, with $10,000, five employees, and years of experience in both the American and European shipping agency business, Mr. Oelsner opened the first office of United States Navigation, Inc., at 66 Broadway in New York. On November 22 of the same year, just one year after the Armistice, his first chartered Hog Islander—the *Rock Island*—left New York for Hamburg, and he was in the steamship operating business.

U.S. Navigation rapidly developed into a major ocean carrier, operating up to ninety vessels either as owner or under general management contracts, and expanding from its original North Atlantic service to other U.S. trades. When the United States entered World War II, the company was appointed general operating agent for the U.S. government as well as for the Norwegian Shipping and Trade Mission. After the war, U.S. Navigation began diversifying, purchasing and operating tankers and dry bulk carriers, and serving as representative for the passenger ships of the North German Lloyd and Hamburg-American Lines, in addition to reestablishing its prewar general cargo services.

Although he retained an active interest in the business until his death in 1973, Edward Oelsner withdrew as president of U.S. Navigation before the war. His son, Edward C. Oelsner, Jr., joined the firm in July of 1937.

Under the leadership of Edward C. Oelsner, Jr., U.S. Navigation began concentrating on the steamship agency business in the early 1950s. Drawing on years of experience operating its own vessels, the company was soon acting as the U.S. representative for German, Indian, Norwegian, and other steamship lines, managing scheduled cargo lines for some of the world's major shipowners.

One of the first vessels in U.S. Navigation's fleet was a 4,300-dwt Hog Islander, the S.S. Rock Island. *Its first sailing, from New York to Hamburg on November 22, 1919, inaugurated the company's operations to Germany.*

The agency operations grew to become U.S. Navigation's major activity, and the company continued to develop its administrative and operational services, adding an extensive computerized container control system in the early 1970s. Gradually, the company established representation in all major U.S. and Canadian ports through agreements with other agencies, and opened its own branch offices in Chicago, Cleveland, and Milwaukee.

Today, with over four hundred employees, U.S. Navigation has come to manage one of the most diversified cargo liner operations in the world, including Hapag-Lloyd containership services from Canada and the U.S. to Europe and Japan, Indian-flag Scindia Line service to India and the Far East, Nicaraguan-flag Mamenic Line operations to Central America, Norwegian-flag Ivaran Line service to South America, and Turkish-flag Koctug Line service to Turkey.

FARRELL LINES

Farrell Lines Incorporated is proud of a seafaring tradition that dates back before the Civil War. Captain John Guy Farrell, an Irish immigrant, came to Connecticut in 1848, and became a merchant, sea captain, and ship-owner. He was lost at sea with his ship in 1878 when his son, James, was 15 years old.

James A. Farrell became a laborer in a wire mill and went on to become president of United States Steel Corporation. He inherited his father's love for the sea and for some years operated the full-rigged sailing ship

275

The SS City of New York, with accommodations for 68 passengers, was the first new ship built by the American South African Line (Farrell Lines) for its own use. Launched in 1929, the ship was lost to a torpedo in 1942.

James A. Farrell, Jr. (far left), James A. Farrell, Sr., and John J. Farrell are shown with a portrait of Captain John Guy Farrell.

Tusitala out of New York.

James' sons, John J. Farrell and James A. Farrell, Jr., acquired the American South African Line in 1925, after the United States Shipping Board accepted their bid to purchase the line along with five ships from the U.S. War Shipping Board. The first vessel built specifically for the Farrell fleet was the *City of New York*, launched in October 1929; it was lost to a torpedo in the spring of 1942 off the coast of Cape Hatteras. In 1947 the name of the line was officially changed to Farrell Lines Incorporated.

In 1965 Farrell Lines purchased the East and Gulf Coast Australia-New Zealand Trade Route along with six vessels from United States Lines. In 1975 they purchased Trade Route 27 from the West Coast of the United States to Australia and New Zealand from Pacific Far East Lines. In 1978 Farrell acquired the 59-year-old American Export Lines along with twenty-four vessels and five essential trade routes. All during this time Farrell Lines continued to build new ships for its various services.

John J. Farrell died in 1966, but his brother, James A. Farrell, Jr., lived to see the company, which had begun serving only South Africa and Mozambique, grow to be the largest privately-owned American-flag steamship company in the world. At the time of his death, September 15, 1978, Farrell Lines operated a fleet of forty-one modern vessels serving five continents.

The red, white, and blue Farrell Lines house flag is a familiar sight in its home port of New York. It will soon be flying over four new vessels presently under construction, as Farrell Lines continues to build and replace its ships with the fastest, most efficient vessels available. In addition to providing the world shipping community with the best service possible, Farrell Lines is constantly striving to make America's merchant marine the finest afloat.

INSURANCE COMPANY OF NORTH AMERICA

Insurance Company of North America, the predecessor company of INA Corporation, was founded in 1792 in Independence Hall, Philadelphia. In the same year, a group of traders meeting under an old buttonwood tree on Wall Street founded the New York Stock Exchange. INA opened for business in Philadelphia on December 15th in two rooms of a three-story building at 119 South Front Street. At the helm of the new business were two prominent Philadelphia merchants—John M. Nesbit, president, and Ebenezer Hazard, secretary.

The Irish-born Nesbit had been one of the organizers of the Bank of North America, and had rendered valuable service to the Army of the Revolution in the areas of finance and troop supply. Hazard, son of a wealthy merchant and well-traveled, was also a scholar. In the same year that he opened the subscription book for Insurance Company of North America stock at his residence, the first two volumes of his *Historical Collections* were published.

Founded by merchants, financiers, and scholars, the oldest of the marine insurance companies and the oldest stock fire insurance company soon earned the name of "aristocrat of insurance."

On December 18th, three days after Insurance Company of North America opened for business, President Nesbit signed policy number 10, insuring a shipment of cash from Charleston to New York. Since then, the company has regularly insured hulls and cargo in and out of the port of New York. In 1846, James Wright convinced the board of directors that it would be good for the company to appoint him its New York agent. He submitted requests for both fire and

The first office of Insurance Company of North America, in use from 1792 to 1794, occupied two rooms on the ground floor of this building at 119 South Street, Philadelphia.

marine insurance to the Philadelphia office. The following year, William W. Dibblee, a marine insurance specialist, joined him at 60 Wall Street.

New York City thereafter became INA's single most important American marine insurance service office. Prior to 1932, Insurance Company of North America's offices were variously located within the city. Fire insurance was handled on William Street; the Indemnity Company (INA's Casualty Company) was on John Street; and Alliance, for Marine, was on Maiden Lane. On January 1st, marine and fire were consolidated under the general management of Henry H. Reed, formerly New York Marine Manager. They moved into their permanent quarters, a newly built skyscraper at 99 John Street, in 1933. This building was sold in 1955, and INA moved to 79 John Street. A recent relocation has put INA's New York headquarters at 127 John Street.

John R. Walbridge, president of INAMAR, Ltd. and senior vice president of Insurance Company of North America, is the officer in charge of INA's marine insurance operation. He has been with the company for over thirty years and is active in the marine insurance community. Mr. Walbridge is a director and treasurer of the Security Bureau, director of the Maritime Association of the Port of New York, deputy chairman of the American Institute of Marine Underwriters, first vice president of the Board of Underwriters of New York, a director of the Foreign Credit Insurance Association, and past chairman of the National Cargo Bureau.

Insurance Company of North America gave rise to its parent company in 1968. Today the parent company is one of the nation's largest diversified financial institutions, consisting of some 300 companies with major interests in insurance, insurance related services, health care management, and investment banking.

Founded on the eve of the country's birth, INA has grown with the United States. On December 15, 1792, Mr. Nesbit insured the Ship *America* on a voyage from Philadelphia to Londonderry, North Ireland, a risk of

The present world headquarters of INA at 1600 Arch Street, Philadelphia, was built in 1925.

This edifice at 232 Walnut Street, Philadelphia, built in 1880, served as the company's head office until 1925.

In the archives of INA are numerous memorabilia of the great clipper ships whose hulls and cargo were insured by Insurance Company of North America. One of the last of these was the Governor Robie, built in Bath, Maine, in 1883. Until the mid-1890s, she sailed regularly out of the port of New York around Cape Horn to San Francisco and the Far East. A reproduction of the 1894 oil painting In the Days of the Cape Horn Trade, by Charles Robert Patterson, shows her in New York's East River after being towed under the Brooklyn Bridge. The fully rigged model was crafted of pine in 1929 by Captain Frederick Williamson of Staten Island.

$5,333.33. The premium was 2¼%, or $120, plus 50¢ for the policy. Within two weeks, the infant company's books showed a balance of $2,543.86 in cash from premiums. In 1977, according to the company's annual report, revenues from all activities totaled $3.7 billion. The marine and aviation underwriting profit was $8.4 million. INA currently insures some 350 of the 500 largest corporations in the United States, and is rapidly expanding its already considerable international operations.

HAGEDORN AND COMPANY INSURANCE SINCE 1869

The American Civil War was only four years into history when Henry Bohlen Hagedorn, an insurance broker, and John Miles Gillespie, a retired shipmaster, formed the insurance brokerage partnership of Hagedorn & Gillespie. The nation, healing its war wounds, was about to plunge into a great new era of trade growth and industrial expansion—an era of opportunity for those with the vision to serve the needs of a growing economy.

Hagedorn & Gillespie specialized in marine coverage, especially of cotton, insuring the crop from the time it was picked and processed through its loading onto windjammers on the docks of Mobile and New Orleans, until it arrived at the mills and warehouses of New England and Great Britain.

The partnership was dissolved in 1874 and the business was carried on by Mr. Hagedorn, who retained the original firm name. Young Daniel Schnakenberg, who immigrated from Germany in 1869 at the age of 17, entered the firm in 1874 and was soon the major voice in the business.

When Mr. Hagedorn died in 1882, the firm of Hagedorn & Company was formed, with Mr. Schnakenberg as principal owner. The company was incorporated in 1906, with Mr. Schnakenberg as president.

In the years that followed, under the leadership of Mr. Schnakenberg, his nephew Siegfried Gabel (president, 1932-1954), and Frederick D. Gabel (president, 1954-1978), the company expanded into property, casualty, and employee benefits. At the same time, however, it maintained its worldwide reputation for expertise in marine insurance, and until the 1930s, it handled most of the cotton exported from the United States as well as imports of Egyptian cotton.

Over the years, Hagedorn & Company has become prominent in all kinds of commodity insurance. For years, it has been a member of cotton exchanges all over the world. Today, it insures much of the tea, coffee, and cocoa coming into the United States.

Until World War II, most of the German steamship lines, including the big North German Lloyd and Hamburg-America Lines, placed their insurance with Hagedorn & Company, and its offices served as a kind of home-away-from-home for German shipmasters and agents. During the war, the company was selected as the government agency for insurance on all commodities shipped to and from the Western Hemisphere—a tribute to the firm's long association with the complex problems of commodity insurance.

Diversification has continued in recent years into such areas as insurance for trade associations, hospitals, colleges, and labor unions, and many other types of specialized coverage. The company was the first to introduce the advertisers liability policy, an insurance against suits for alleged misrepresentation in advertising, and for some years it was the only firm to offer this type of coverage. Staff members include experts in law, accounting, engineering, maritime operations, and other professional areas.

Officers of Hagedorn & Company are Frederick D. Gabel, chairman; F. Daniel Gabel, Jr., president; Richard Cobden, vice president; and E. Alexander Gabel, vice president. The company headquarters are at 225 Broadway, with over fifty affiliated offices in the United States through American Insurance Marketing Corporation and Associated Risk Managers of New York, as well as correspondent offices abroad.

Current officers of Hagedorn & Company—Frederick D. Gabel, chairman (left), and F. Daniel Gabel, Jr., president—are shown with portraits of their predecessors (left to right), Siegfried Gabel, Henry Hagedorn, and Daniel Schnakenberg.

278

UNIVERSAL MARITIME SERVICE CORPORATION

A freighter is nudged into her Brooklyn dock by puffing tugs. Hawsers are made fast to bollards on the pier. From the bridge the captain rings "finished with engines" on the engine-room telegraph, and the voyage is ended. The ship is now ready for the stevedore and his longshoremen.

The accommodation ladder is lowered, and a hundred longshoremen come trooping aboard, each man with a steel hook stuck in his belt, the time-honored symbol of the longshoreman's trade. Canvas covers come off the hatches, hatch boards

longer have booms or tackle. The longshoreman's hook is almost a museum piece, and the keeping of cargo records has progressed from manual bookkeeping to highly sophisticated data processing.

Since 1928, Universal Maritime Service has grown and changed with the times, adapting its equipment and its expertise to ever-bigger ships and to cargo-handling equipment that was not even dreamed of half a century ago.

At Port Newark in the vast New York harbor complex, Universal operates an 80-acre terminal designed

Versa Computer Service Corporation, a subsidiary of Universal, keeps a record of every export container arriving at the terminal according to steamship line, vessel, and port of discharge. For import containers, the system records the information from the ship's manifest and maintains it in inventory until it is picked up by the consignee's truckers. It also maintains a record of empty containers, keeping a history of each container's movement over a period of twelve months. This information is passed on daily to Universal's steamship-company clients.

are lifted off and stowed on deck. Tackle is rigged, booms are swung in place, steam is put on the winches, and the ship begins disgorging her cargo in boxes, crates, barrels, and bales.

That's how it was when Captain John N. Matthews founded Universal Maritime Service in 1928. Cargo was handled pretty much the same as it had been for a hundred years or more—by booms and tackle and the longshoremen's steel hook.

Fifty years later, the picture is very different. Today most general cargo moves in containers. Many ships no

Universal's Brooklyn terminals, a center for break-bulk operations, are directly opposite downtown Manhattan and easily accessible to all parts of the tri-state metropolitan area.

to handle simultaneously containerized freight, roll-on/roll-off vehicle carriers, heavy lift vessels, and traditional break-bulk cargo ships—a truly versatile cargo center. Universal also operates extensive marine facilities, serving twenty steamship lines, on the Brooklyn side of New York harbor. These are primarily break-bulk operations, although some containers are also handled.

Giant Paceco cranes, with up to 70-ton capacity, on-and-off load containers with speed and precision.

In scope, efficiency, and technical complexity, today's system of handling cargo is far removed indeed from old-time stevedoring. It is all part of the service by which Universal Maritime offers speed and economy to clients using the great port of New York.

GRIFFITH MARINE NAVIGATION

Griffith Marine designs, installs, and services navigation and communications systems for such large ocean vessels as these.

W hen Verrazano arrived in New York bay in 1524, he had navigated across the Atlantic by the use of currents and stars, and had taken his soundings by the use of a lead line to avoid the danger of dragging ashore in the narrows. Today, the human element is still present in navigation, but the navigator is now assisted by Loran C, Omega, Satellite Navigation, and radar. The electronic depth sounder has taken the place of the lead line and radio communication has replaced the voice trumpet of olden times. These latter-day aides to navigation and communications are the

An electronic-packed bridge aboard the 390,000-ton Atlantic *is typical of today's supertankers and huge freighters.*

concern of Griffith Marine Navigation. Griffith Marine designs, sells, installs, and services navigation and communications systems for all types of seagoing vessels.

As it exists today, Griffith Marine Navigation is the culmination of the dreams of the late Noel Griffith. A former shipboard radio operator who saw the need for fast, efficient shipboard electronic service at a reasonable cost, Griffith founded his company in 1963. His original concept included the idea that reliable elec-

tronic navigation and communications equipment had to be available to the ships' owners. He soon expanded these goals into a national distributorship for radar and other navigational aides. Today, Griffith Marine concentrates primarily upon the Middle Atlantic seaboard but will travel virtually anywhere, as evidenced by recent service in Halifax, Buenos Aires, Naples, Hamburg, and Singapore.

One aim of Griffith Marine is to give the best possible service in the least amount of time and at the fairest cost. To accomplish this, the company employs a staff of twenty-three persons, the majority of which are qualified technicians and engineers. Another aim is to sell and, where required, design the best navigation and communications equipment available. This particular combination of purpose gives Griffith Marine customers the ultimate in value.

The port of New York has grown remarkably in the last 450 years, and will continue to grow in the future. Griffith Marine Navigation intends to grow with it by maintaining its unexcelled reputation. This belief is reflected in the following statement by the company's president, Jim Chapman: "There was a time when riggers, sailmakers, and caulkers were a vital element of the marine industry within the port. Times change. The electronic age has come to the sea and harbor. The electronic specialist is as important now as the sailmaker was in the days of Verrazano, the China Clipper, or the Liverpool packet. We are proud to play a vital role in this new age of electronics in ships and shipping."

MARITIME ASSOCIATION OF THE PORT OF NEW YORK

In the mid-1800s, members of the city's maritime community traditionally gathered on the sidewalks of the "Five Points," where Beaver, William, and South William streets ran together, to exchange shipping information, make trades, and find cargo for vessels. But on the cold and blustery afternoon of February 5, 1873, representatives of some 140 firms moved to more comfortable quarters at 61 Beaver Street, as the new Maritime Association of the Port of New York opened its doors for the first time.

Led by Thomas Ball, the Association's founder and first president, the merchants, shipowners, and other members were interested in more than just a warm meeting place. New York was the country's busiest and most important port, yet it lacked a central source of accurate and timely shipping news. Within its first year of existence, the new Association moved to fill that void, and by 1874 it had acquired the Merchants' Exchange and News Association, as well as the Sandy Hook, Quarantine & City Island Telegraph, and had established a network of correspondents throughout the world.

The news service attracted a diverse membership, drawing not only shipping concerns, but also bankers, exporters, importers, foreign counsuls, and newsmen. Only two years old, the Association boasted 750 members by 1875, and when it purchased the Merchant Association that year, an average of 3,000 persons consulted the bulletin boards and open news ledgers on its Exchange floor each day.

In 1879, the Maritime Exchange, as it was commonly called, augmented its own extensive news-gathering system by becoming the U.S. representative for the world's most respected disseminator of ship intelligence, Lloyd's of London, an associ-

The Maritime Association has had its headquarters in the Maritime Exchange Building, 80 Broad Street, since 1931.

ation it still enjoys today.

Bursting at the seams with over 1,000 members by 1883, the Association moved its offices and Exchange to the new Produce Exchange Building at the foot of Broadway. In 1891, with their ranks almost doubled at 1,800, the Association's members voted to purchase and renovate the old Popham Building at 80 Broad Street for $350,000.

By the time the organization moved into the Popham Building in 1904, it had grown far beyond its original news-gathering activities and was deeply involved in promoting marine interests at both the local and federal level, joining in support for projects that ranged from driftwood removal in New York harbor to the widening of the Erie Canal. With most U.S. shipowners headquartered in New York, the influence of New York's Maritime Association extended to all major American ports, as well as overseas.

The stature of the Association continued to grow along with shipping activity in the new age of the steamship, and by 1927 the Association was again looking for larger quarters. Rather than move to a new site, the members voted to construct a 35-story Maritime Exchange Building at 80 Broad Street. On June 3, 1931, in a ceremony presided over by Mayor Jimmy Walker, the new Association headquarters was opened.

Today, the bulletin board and the open ledger are gone, replaced by highly sophisticated communication systems. But if the methods have changed, the results have not. The Maritime Association, more than a century later, still fulfills the same basic need for accurate and centralized information that attracted its original 140 members.

NEW YORK COFFEE & SUGAR EXCHANGE

The New York Coffee Exchange Market Report.

TUESDAY, June 6th., 3 P. M., 1882

FUTURE DELIVERIES.

On basis of Exchange Standard No. 7, with additions or deductions for other grades according to the rates of the Exchange existing on the afternoon of the 5th day previous to the date of the Warehouse Order. Delivery between the first and last days of the month, at seller's option, in lots of not less than 250 bags, upon 5 days' notice to buyers. Coffee to be of any grade between Prime and Common inclusive.

MONTHS.	First Call.		Second Call.	
	BID.	ASKED.	BID.	ASKED.
January	7.75	7.95	7.75	7.95
February	7.75	7.95	7.75	7.95
March	7.75	7.95	7.75	7.95
April	7.75	7.95	7.75	7.95
May	7.75	7.95	7.75	7.95
June	7.30	7.45	7.30	7.45
July	7.40	7.45	7.35	7.45
August	7.50	7.55	7.50	7.55
September	7.55	7.60	7.55	7.60
October	7.60	7.70	7.55	7.70
November	7.65	7.75	7.60	7.75
December	7.80	7.85	7.65	7.85

SALES.

FIRST CALL.

No sales.

Between First and Second Calls.

August—250 7.55. Total, 250 bags.

SECOND CALL.

No sales.

Between Second Call and Close.

No sales.

Total sales to-day, 250 bags.

MARKET—Quiet but steady.

Prices for Rings and Margins.

11:30 A. M.—June, 7.30; July, 7.40; August, 7.55; Sept., 7.55.

1:30 P. M.—June, 7.30; July, 7.35; August, 7.50; Sept., 7.55.

Transferable Notices will be issued at 7.65

Warehouse Deliveries.

DAYS.	Weeks Ending			
	June 3	June 10	June 17	June 24
Monday	7489	4884	....	....
Tuesday	....	....	....	....
Wednesday	6785	....	....	....
Thursday	5808	....	....	....
Friday	9643	....	....	....
Saturday	7872	....	....	....
Totals	37597	....	....	....

SPOT QUOTATIONS.

Exchange Standards of Rio. Settlements of Future Contracts on basis of No. 7, are made by the price of each grade quoted on the day on which notice of delivery is given.

GRADES.	PRICES.
No. 1 Prime	10.30
" 2 Good	9.80
" 3 Fair	9.30
" 4 Low Fair	8.80
" 5 Good Ordinary	8.35
" 6 Ordinary	8.10
" 7 Low Ordinary	7.60
" 8 Strict Good Common	7.10
" 9 Good Common	6.60
" 10 Common	6.10

MARKET—Weak.

Special Call of No. 3 Fair.

Deliveries to be within ¼c. per lb, either way of the grade stipulated, and settlement to to be made in all respects accordiug to the rules governing the sales of Futures.

MONTHS.	First Call.		Second Call.	
	BID.	ASKED.	BID.	ASKED
June	9.00	9.20	9.00	9.20
July	9.15	9.25	9.10	9.25
August	9.20	9.35	9.30	9.30
September	9.30	9.40	9.30	9.40
October	9.40	9.50	9.35	9.50
November	...	....	....	....
December	....	....	....	....
January	....	....	....	....
February	....	....	....	....
March	....	....	....	....

SALES.

FIRST CALL.

No sales.

Between First and Second Calls.

No sales.

SECOND CALL.

No sales.

Between Second Call and Close.

No sales.

MARKET—Quiet but steady.

Receipts at Rio for the Week Ending June 10th.

Monday	6,700
Tueday	....
Wednesday	....
Thursday	....
Friday	....
Saturday	....
Totals	....

VISIBLE SUPPLY,

First Hand Stock yesterday			98,586
Arrivals			
			98,586
Sales			
Withdrawals		18,909	
			18,909
Total First Hand Stock to-day			79,677
Second Hand Stock Yesterday	85,831		
Warehouse Deliveries Yesterday	4,884		
		80,947	
Taken from First Hand Stock		18,909	
Total Second Hand Stock to-day			99,856
Total Stock in New York			179,533
" " other Ports			100,938
Total Stock in United States			280,471
Afloat and Loading to May 15th		117,502	
Purchases since May 15 to June 5,	103,000		
" advised to-day	4,500		
		107,500	
			225,002
Total Visible Supply for United States			505,473

Daily Cablegrams to the Exchange.

(Quoted by the ASSOCIACAO COMMERCIAL.)

RIO DE JANEIRO, June 5, 1882.

Good First	9¼
Regular First	9
Ordinary First	8¼
Good Second	7⅛
Exchange	21⅛
Receipts	6,700
Market	Quiet
Stock	119,000
Sales to United States	4,500
Clearances by Sail	Nil
" Steam	"

(Quoted by Messrs. HAYN, ROMAN & Co.)

LONDON, June 6, 1882

Good Channel	40s.
Fair Channel	36s.
Market,	Unchanged.

☞ The above prices are per cwt.

(Quoted by Messrs. HAASE & Co.)

HAVRE, June 6, 1882.

Spot (Good average Santos)	fr.....
July	" 51
August	" ....
September	" 52
Market	Quiet
Stock in Havre	....

☞ The above prices are per 50 kilos.

Arrivals at New York for week ending June 10th.

JUNE 4.—S.s. Bessel	26,022
Totals	26,022

This market report was issued only three months after the opening of the New York Coffee Exchange in 1882.

In its edition of March 8, 1882, the *New York Herald* reported the first transaction on the New York Coffee Exchange—the sale of 250 bags of "Rio strict ordinary." The Exchange had opened the previous day, with 112 dealers and importers on the floor, amid "much enthusiasm."

No commodity was more important to the port of New York—either in tonnage or in value—than coffee. Strolling along the South Street piers almost any day of the week, one would have seen ships unloading bags of coffee, mostly from Brazil. The heady aroma of roasting beans was a pervading and pungent odor along the waterfront.

In 1880, major holders of East Indian coffee attempted to gain control over the supply of Brazilian coffee. The speculative effort backfired, however, creating huge surpluses of coffee, depressing the market, and ruining several of the largest coffee houses. In six months, dealers lost more than $6 million in the disastrous market collapse.

Out of this financial chaos was created the Coffee Exchange of the City of New York. Convinced that the

First president of the New York Coffee Exchange, from 1882 to 1885, was Benjamin Greene Arnold.

The trading floor of the ultramodern Commodities Exchange Center, located in the World Trade Center.

trade needed a more orderly process for buying and selling, plus some measure of self-regulation, a group of young merchants decided to adopt the same techniques already in use by the grain and cotton traders—an organized system for trading in futures and the end of uncontrolled speculation.

By creating the Exchange, they were able to set standards for different grades of coffee, establish a court of arbitration for disputes among traders, and provide a market in which growers, merchants, roasters, and wholesalers could protect themselves by hedging against losses caused by price fluctuations. There was another advantage, too: every transaction made on the Exchange was recorded, and these data were made available to all members.

The first President of the Exchange was Benjamin Greene Arnold, a legendary dealer who ruled the American market for many years. Known as "the Napoleon of the coffee trade," he, too, recognized the need for a

more stable industry.

In 1914, the outbreak of war in Europe forced the closing of the sugar exchanges in Hamburg and London, then the world centers for trading in sugar. In that year, the Coffee Exchange of the City of New York expanded its operations to include trading in sugar futures, and in 1916 the name was changed to the New York Coffee and Sugar Exchange, Inc.

Both coffee and sugar are among the oldest and most important cargoes in the port of New York. Coffee first came here from the port of Mocha on the Red Sea, and then from Java, Sumatra, the Caribbean Islands, and Brazil. And from colonial days on, the little sloops, brigs, and schooners that regularly plied the waters between New York, the Gulf of Mexico, and the West Indies almost invariably listed sugar among their cargo.

An old ship's manifest now on display at the Exchange attests to the arrival of the sloop *Betsy* from the West Indies in 1796 with a cargo of cotton, thirty-nine hogsheads of sug-

ar, and sixteen bags of coffee. By contrast, it is not unusual today for a huge freighter such as the S.S. *Delta America* to arrive in New York with a cargo of Colombian coffee worth $12 million or more, or for a freighter to carry 15,000 tons of sugar into the port.

The Exchange was located originally at 113 Pearl Street. In 1894, it moved to 26 Beaver Street, which remained its headquarters for 63 years. In 1957, it moved again, this time to 79 Pine Street.

In 1977, the Exchange joined the new Commodities Exchange Center in New York's towering World Trade complex. Described as the world's most technically advanced trading facility for commodities futures, the Commodities Exchange Center has a trading floor that accommodates 1300 members and employees from the four cooperating exchanges: the Commodity Exchange, the New York Cotton Exchange, the New York Mercantile Exchange, and the New York Coffee and Sugar Exchange.

Although this ultramodern facility is equipped with the latest electronic aids, providing instant data on prices and sales, trading is still done by the old "open outcry" system, with buyers raising their hands and shouting out their bids. A gallery overlooking the trading floor enables visitors to see how commodity trading operates and to share in the often feverish excitement of this fast-paced buying and selling.

The New York Coffee and Sugar Exchange is the world's leading market for futures trading in both of these commodities and is the fourth largest commodity exchange in the United States. There are 350 seats on the Exchange, each valued at $30,000 or more. In the 1890s, a seat was priced at $1,000.

In nearly a century of organized trading, contracts representing more than 900 million bags of coffee and 700 million tons of sugar have been traded on the Exchange. The dollar value of trades now exceeds $20 billion annually.

What may appear, to the casual spectator, as a hectic clamor of bids and shouting is, in reality, a colorful and effective way of organizing a vast market in these essential commodities.

283

ROYAL NETHERLANDS STEAMSHIP COMPANY

Steam power was just beginning to challenge sail on the ocean trade routes when the Royal Netherlands Steamship Company (K.N.S.M.) was founded at Amsterdam in 1856 and became an enthusiastic proponent of the steamship. During its first twenty years, the company commissioned thirty-three steamers. This ability to innovate and change with the times while adhering to sound and time-proven business principles has characterized the company ever since.

Initial services were to St. Petersburg, Gothenburg, Konigsberg, Memel, Danzig, Le Havre, and Bordeaux.

A major expansion took place in 1883 with the organization of the Royal Netherlands West India Mail service and the first sailing of the S.S. *Oranje Nassau* in 1884 to the Dutch colonies in the West Indies. This western venture was further enlarged in 1888 when the S.S. *Prins Maurits* opened a service from the West Indies to New York via Haiti, a service that is now a major part of the company's far-flung operations.

By 1900 K.N.S.M. was also operating an extensive shipping network to North Africa, Italy, the Near East, and as far away as Odessa on the Black Sea.

During World War II the company lost four passenger ships, thirty-seven freighters, and 180 of its seagoing personnel. After the war millions of dollars were spent in rebuilding the fleet and modernizing cargo facilities to meet new developments in transportation and cargo handling.

Following the war the company also expanded its South American routes and now provides a 5,000-mile network of cargo services from Paramaribo on the Atlantic to the port of Corral in southern Chile, with thirty-six ports of call in between.

The North American service now includes connections with Houston, New Orleans, Miami, Baltimore, Philadelphia, and New York. A number of versatile new ships have been added to this run to provide the utmost in fast and efficient service, with a capa-

These first K.N.S.M. vessels, built in 1857, were equipped with small steam engines; they also carried sails as auxiliary power.

bility for specialized cargoes.

The New York office is located in the huge World Trade Center and includes a staff of seventy. This office also represents a sister firm, Mammoet Shipping Company, specialists in heavy-lift operations.

The American operations of K.N.S.M. are headed by Maarten L. de Ruiter, general manager. Haye Van Noord, J.C. Kruiten, and John J. Lynch are assistant general managers.

Royal Netherlands Steamship Company can look back over its wake to a long, long line of ships, some of them pioneers in regularly scheduled steam cargo operations, and to a span of continuous service with few equals in the history of ocean navigation. It looks forward to continued success in meeting the challenges of an ever-changing industry and the needs of cargo shippers.

NATIONAL MARITIME UNION OF AMERICA AFL-CIO

Since its inception, the National Maritime Union has been dedicated to ending discrimination and promoting equal opportunity for all.

In 1937, the new union takes its organizing drive to the ships.

The National Maritime Union was formally brought into being at a mass rally of seamen in New York City on May 3, 1937. But the movement to create a truly democratic union of seamen had been building for over three years.

Although the International Seamen's Union had led the way in unionizing the American merchant marine, by the early 1930s there was a growing resentment among members who felt that they had lost control of their own union. Led by able-bodied seaman Joe Curran and others, these men put out a call for all interested in founding a new, democratic union to come to New York and help lay the groundwork.

At that founding rally, the new union's first constitutional convention was set for July 19, and a committee was elected to draft proposals for governing rules. Procedures were also set for election of convention delegates by all ships' crews, as well as by union members in the various East and Gulf Coast ports.

The convention opened two months later at the Manhattan Opera House with 135 delegates from 118 ships and 68 from 14 ports. The first action of the convention was to elect Joe Curran chairman; the second, to open the galleries to the press and "anybody else who is interested."

When the final version of the constitution emerged two weeks later, the new union was dedicated to organizing all seamen on all waters "without regard to race, creed and color," and to leveling the barriers that divided seamen by region and craft. The new constitution also established democratic procedures for electing officers, required membership approval of all constitutional provisions, and provided for rank-and-file control of shipping rules.

The constitution was ratified by the membership, and the new union became affiliated with an emerging labor federation—the Congress of Industrial Organizations. Joe Curran, the man who had led the battle for a new type of seamen's union, was elected the NMU's first president. Union headquarters were opened in a fourth-floor walk-up on New York's West Side, and within the first year 50,000 had joined the new union.

A prime objective of the NMU from its creation was to wipe out shipboard discrimination—to put an end to "white ships" and "black ships," and to eliminate the color line that restricted black seamen to the galley crew on ships that also carried white seamen. In 1944, for the first time in maritime history, a clause reading "no discrimination on grounds of race, creed, color or national origin" was written into the NMU contracts.

Under the leadership of Joe Curran until his retirement in 1973, and now with Shannon J. Wall as its elected head, the NMU has made great progress since 1937—not only in wages, but in the quality of life, including working conditions, union pensions, medical benefits, employment insurance, training programs, and scholarships for members' children. At the same time, NMU members can take a special pride in their union's history of social and political leadership in the American labor movement.

IRVING TRUST COMPANY

New York's piers were crowded with tall-masted, sharp-nosed windjammers when the Irving Bank opened its doors at 279 Greenwich Street on March 31, 1851. The city was still agog with gold fever, and New York yards were filled with clipper ships being rushed to completion for the California trade. A spirit of adventure, expectancy, and unbounded confidence was in the air. It was a propitious time for a new financial enterprise.

Washington Irving lent his name to the new bank and his portrait to its first bank notes.

Washington Irving, diplomat, lawyer, and America's first great man of letters, agreed to let the bank use his name. It was a name that conferred prestige—the feeling of substance, trust, and permanence that the founders hoped would be a hallmark of the new institution.

A picture of Irving graced the bank's first notes, for this was before the days of a national currency, when every bank was proud of its own beautifully engraved notes.

Number One Wall Street has been the Irving headquarters since 1931.

The new bank was launched with a modest capital of $250,000. There were another thirty-seven commercial banks at the time, most of them in the Wall Street area; nine of these would eventually merge with the Irving.

The new bank flourished. It survived the great financial panic of 1857 and the numerous other panics and depressions that followed. By the late 1800s, it was an important part of the business scene in this country, help-ing in many ways to finance the opening of the West and the transformation of the country into an industrial society.

In 1907, in the first of many mergers, the Irving and the New York National Exchange Bank joined to form the Irving National Exchange Bank. During the 1920s, there were five more mergers and name changes, but the name "Irving" was always retained. By 1926, on its seventy-fifth birthday, the bank had total resources of $741 million.

In 1913, the Irving moved into the new Woolworth Building, a skyscraper that was the marvel of New York and a pacesetter for the city's dramatic rise skyward. The bank moved to its present fifty-story headquarters at 1 Wall Street in 1931. This site, appropriately enough, once housed the law offices of Washington Irving.

Although the Irving had been active in international banking since the early 1900s, its global interests were greatly expanded in the 1950s. In 1958 it opened the first of a number of overseas representative offices, and in 1965 it began opening branch offices in the principal money centers of Europe and Asia. Today, Irving also has one of the strongest worldwide correspondent banking networks. Irving is banker to almost 1,800 governments, central banks, and foreign commercial banks, and is the fifteenth largest bank in the United States based on assets.

"Our record of growth and service," notes a recent report to stockholders, "reflects a long tradition marked by an unending quest for excellence. We affirm our commitment to that tradition and pledge our best efforts to pass it, enhanced and strengthened, to our successors."

UNITOR SHIPS SERVICE

T he modest environment of Unitor Ships Service belies the worldwide activities in which the organization is engaged. Housed in a low, modern building at Port Jersey, it faces the Brooklyn waterfront across Upper New York Bay.

The business of the ten-person staff of salesmen, drivers, warehousemen, and a secretary depends on the thousands of ships of all types that sail in and out of New York-New Jersey's great harbor. From the largest ship to the smallest, company representatives call upon captains, first officers, chief and first engineers, not only to sell the company's products, but also to render vital technical assistance on such problems as engine repairs and the proper maintenance of fire prevention equipment.

The forty-three offices of Unitor supply some 14,000 ships throughout the world with oxygen, acetylene, and inert gases in standard cylinders whose contents, when properly mixed, are used in welding. In addition, they supply all kinds of welding equipment. The company provides facilities at its Port Jersey plant where engine department officers can come for demonstrations and instruction in the newer methods of welding, so that repairs can be performed at sea.

Unitor supplies many other products that help to ensure the smooth and safe functioning of cruise liners, containerships, dry cargo vessels, and oil tankers. Among these are pneumatic and hand tools of various sorts, refrigerants and other chemicals, firefighting and safety equipment, and the special survival suits that wildcatters wear when helicoptering out to oil rigs at sea. All of this material is stored in efficient warehouse facilities that are part of the Port Jersey compound. Orders come not only from

The headquarters and central facilities of Unitor Ships Service are located in this modern plant at Port Jersey.

ships in port, but also by radio from ships at sea.

Unitor was established in 1936; its first New York office was opened in Queens in 1967. In 1968, the office was moved to Brooklyn, and then to Linden, New Jersey. This location proved too far removed from its sphere of operations, and Unitor moved to its present plant in Port Jersey in 1977.

The company maintains nine other offices in this country—in Philadelphia, Baltimore, Norfolk, Miami, New Orleans, Beaumont, Houston, Los Angeles, and San Francisco. In addition, one person is stationed in Rhode Island to service the offshore rigs of the various companies drilling for oil in the Baltimore Canyon.

HAPAG·
·LLOYD

288

In May of 1847 a group of German businessmen formed a company to operate a line of packet ships between Hamburg and New York. The name of this venture was Hamburg-Americanische Packetfahrt-Actien Gesellschaft, but to shippers and seamen alike it quickly became known as the Hamburg-Amerika or Hamburg-American Line —a name that has been famous in world shipping ever since. Even that name was shortened to Hapag.

The company's first vessel was the full-rigged ship *Deutschland*, which opened the trade to New York in 1848 with twenty cabin passengers and two hundred steerage immigrants. These were the first of millions of immigrants that Hamburg-American Line and its equally famous rival, North German Lloyd, brought to the United States through the port of New York.

Ever alert to progress, Hamburg-American Line soon gave up sail in favor of steam, and its first steamer, the *Borussia*, crossed from Hamburg to New York in 1856.

Just ten years after the formation of Hamburg-American, a number of small German steamship companies combined to form Norddeutscher (North German) Lloyd, which also became a very important name in the port of New York, and in world shipping in general. This company's New York service was opened by the S.S. *Bremen* in 1858. (Another *Bremen* was destined to become the world's fastest liner and holder of the "blue ribbon" of the North Atlantic in the 1930s.) By 1881 the company's S.S. *Elbe* trimmed the Hamburg-New York schedule to eight days, twelve hours, and fifty minutes. This popular ship set an envious record for other ships to shoot for, earning 25 percent of her cost in just five round trips, a

The Hamburg-American Line opened its trans-Atlantic passenger service in 1848 with this vessel, the full-rigged sailing ship Deutschland.

happy omen for the line's future success on the North Atlantic.

For more than half a century these two lines played important roles in New York's position as the American terminus of the "North Atlantic ferry," the route of the world's largest and speediest ships. A number of their great vessels captured the coveted "blue ribbon" for fastest time across the Atlantic. Renowned for size and luxury as well as for speed were Hamburg-American's *Furst Bismarck*, *Deutschland*, *Imperator*, and *Vaterland* and North German Lloyd's *Kaiser Wilhelm der Grosse*, *Kaiser Wilhelm II*, *Bremen*, and *Europa*. All were famous names in the port of New York.

While these majestic ships captured the headlines, the two companies were also building up extensive cargo services between Europe and North America and other parts of

the world. The motto emblazoned on the Hamburg-American Line's house flag was "My field is the world."

Two world wars played havoc with both fleets, but after each war the companies rebuilt, modernized, and expanded their services. During the 1960s they began operating joint services under the name Hapag-Lloyd, including a four-ship container express service between New York and Northern Europe. These four ships, with their 24,000-ton capacity and 21-knot speed, could carry an amount of cargo that would require twenty-one conventional break-bulk ships.

In 1970 the two lines merged to form Hapag-Lloyd AG, the foremost German shipping line and one of the largest in the world.

Hapag-Lloyd's versatile modern fleet includes huge containerships, such as the Koln Express, as well as break-bulk vessels and supertankers.

supertankers, bulk carriers, supply vessels, tugs, and the 21,000-ton passenger cruise liner *Europa*.

The container segment of the fleet includes twenty-two "super freighters" capable of carrying up to 48,000 tons deadweight. Each of these vessels is highly automated, and is equipped with an on-board computer system for cargo stowage and control. So fast are these ships that a North Atlantic turnaround, which includes ten ports, can be accomplished in twenty-eight days—about the time it took Hamburg-American's first ship to make the voyage from Hamburg to New York.

Hapag-Lloyd now services fourteen major trading areas of the world, calling at 231 ports, from New York to Nampo, Pusan to Penang, Tenerife to Timaru. No cargo is too large, too small, or too unusual. Some years ago the *Alster Express* carried four baby elephants from Rotterdam to New York, each pachyderm transported in its own specially built container.

Routes and services are supported by more than four hundred freight agencies around the world. United States Navigation, Inc. is the Hapag-Lloyd agent for the United States, with offices at 17 Battery Place, New York City. The offices of Hapag-Lloyd (America) Inc. are also located there.

"The blue ribbon was once a symbol of supremacy among the great ships of the North Atlantic," says Hans-Dieter Druegg, president of Hapag-Lloyd (America) Inc. "The huge racing liners are a thing of the past, but the spirit of competition is still as keen as ever. We try to fly a 'blue ribbon' for speed and service reliability on our trade routes all over the world."

This merger coincided with the advent of containerization, a dramatic increase in the size, speed, and automation of vessels, and the development of huge and highly sophisticated cargo terminals. To keep abreast of this shipping revolution, Hapag-Lloyd has become a total transportation system, with sea lift on some of the world's largest and fastest containerships and fast shoreside transfer in vast container terminals. All containerized cargo, from a box to a bulldozer, is monitored by electronic tracking and information systems—all part of the revolution in ocean shipping.

Hapag-Lloyd offers its customers an uninterrupted, door-to-door transportation chain for cargo. To do this, the line owns some 40,000 standard, tank, open-top, and refrigerated containers and some 5,000 chassis for carrying them over the road. At any one time, Hapag-Lloyd has about 10,000 containers in use in the United States.

As important as ship operation is the company's land-based equipment control, keeping track of the location, types, sizes, condition, and demand for this vast array of cargo equipment on ships, in terminals, or in transit on several continents. Container interchange agreements with railroads and trucking companies, container leasing arrangements, and container pools all help to complicate this intricate electronic record keeping.

A large and versatile fleet flies the Hapag-Lloyd house flag. Although containerization has taken over on many of the major trade routes, this fleet also includes more traditional types of ships for trade requiring a combination of container and break-bulk services. The fleet also includes

THE BANK OF NEW YORK

S oon after the last British warships and the last Redcoats sailed out of New York harbor, The Bank of New York opened its doors at 67 St. George's Square, now Pearl Street.

The little city of New York was still struggling to recover from a devastating war when a group of prominent businessmen, led by Alexander Hamilton, formed the bank as a means of bolstering its economy and promoting foreign trade.

The nation's capital was then located in the New York City Hall on Wall Street, and the city was also the state capital. Thus, the bank was closely associated with the beginnings of both national and state governments. It was also closely associated with shipping and commerce, for many of its principals were merchants and shipowners. Its first president, Gen. Alexander McDougall, was a merchant, a soldier of the Revolution, and a wartime privateer.

Founded before the days of a national currency, the bank at first conducted its business with Portuguese moidores, Spanish doubloons, British guineas, and other foreign coins. An important function in its early days was the weighing of coins to be sure they contained the right amount of silver or gold.

Outgrowing its original quarters, it soon moved to 11 Hanover Square, then to Wall and William streets, where its main office has been ever since. The present thirty-five-story headquarters was opened in 1928.

The Bank of New York played an important role in the nation's industrial expansion, helping to finance shipbuilding, foreign trade, and the construction of factories, railroads, and canals. In 1861, it joined with other New York banks in lending the

290

These private bank notes, issued by The Bank of New York, circulated in the mid-nineteenth century.

The constitution of The Bank of New York was written by Alexander Hamilton, shown here reading it to his fellow directors in 1784.

government $150 million to finance the Civil War—a prodigious financial commitment in a time of trial and uncertainty.

It has steered a safe course through many financial panics and severe economic depressions. In the panic of 1873, it was a financial bulwark, helping a number of other banks to survive. During the panic of 1907, one rich New Yorker had so much faith in the bank's soundness that he deposited $1 million while other banks were closing their doors.

In 1922, the bank strengthened its position even further by merging with the New York Life Insurance and Trust Company, a venerable institution known as the "Gibraltar of American trust companies." In 1948, The Fifth Avenue Bank joined The Bank of New York.

New York's oldest bank now has nine offices in Manhattan and 140 others throughout the state. It has overseas branches in London, Singapore, and the Cayman Islands, and a close working relationship with correspondent banks throughout the world.

Today, The Bank of New York retains the best aspects of a tradition almost as old as the nation itself, while adapting to the ever-changing demands of the present and the future.

SANDY HOOK PILOTS

In the long and dramatic history of the port of New York, no name shines more brightly than that of the Sandy Hook Pilots.

There have been harbor pilots from the earliest days of the port. These first harbor guides were probably fishermen or boatmen who knew every rock, shoal, and channel.

The first official provision for pilots was made by the Provincial Council in 1694. In 1784, the New York state legislature enacted laws on pilotage for the harbor. New Jersey also passed legislation for pilotage.

For many years, piloting was a highly competitive and dangerous business, with a fleet of pilot schooners ranging far out to sea in all kinds of weather to put their men aboard incoming ships. By 1860, there were twenty-one pilot boats in service, manned by licensed pilots from New York and New Jersey.

A disastrous storm in 1888 forced the pilots to pool their resources to build a larger vessel able to withstand all weathers. The first pilot steamer, the *New York*, was built in 1895 and served until 1951.

The pilots are especially proud of the tremendous job they did in World War II, when no vessel ever missed a convoy for want of a pilot. In one 24-hour period, the pilots guided 243 ships in and out of the harbor.

During Operation Sail, the great naval review and sailing ship extravaganza honoring the nation's bicentennial, the Sandy Hook Pilots guided more than 200 vessels safely through a harbor crowded with thousands of ships and boats. The visiting windjammers were piloted free of charge.

The Sandy Hook Pilotage Service includes the Sandy Hook Pilots Association of New York and the Sandy Hook Pilots Association of New Jer-

A pilot boards an early steamship to guide her into port. Sailing ship in the background is the pilot vessel.

sey, with a roster of highly skilled men. They share headquarters and facilities at the former Coast Guard Base on Staten Island.

The Pilots operate a fleet of eight vessels, including the 200-footers *New York* and *New Jersey*, which take turns maintaining station off Ambrose Lightship at the approaches to New York harbor. Pilots are transferred to and from ships by 45-foot tenders which accompany their "mother" ships in fog, storm, or hurricane, always ready to service ships needing a harbor guide. The Sandy Hook Pilots absorbed the Hell Gate Pilots in 1970 and now maintain a boat at City Island to service vessels using the treacherous channel known as Hell Gate.

A Sandy Hook Pilot is the product of a 15-year apprenticeship, during which he learns seamanship, boat handling, and the navigational intricacies of every foot of ship channel in the vast New York harbor complex. An apprentice school is maintained at pilot headquarters. Here, too, is a sophisticated communications system for supplying pilots to incoming and outbound ships.

In the pilot offices is a roll of honor recalling the names of many ships and men lost at sea maintaining the rich traditions of the pilot service. It was the skill of the Sandy Hook Pilots and their devotion to duty which impelled Sir Ivan Thompson, Commodore of the Cunard Line, to call these men "the world's most skillful pilots."

FIRST JERSEY NATIONAL BANK

The first impression of a visitor to the executive offices of the First Jersey National Bank in Jersey City is a breathtaking view of the twin towers of the World Trade Center. In fact, the World Trade Center in lower Manhattan is only four minutes away by the swift, spotless trains of the Port Authority Trans-Hudson (PATH) Railroad. Exchange Place is the first stop on the New Jersey side, and it is here that First Jersey National Bank has been headquartered since its founding in 1864.

The area was known as Paulus Hook in the days of the Dutch settlers who began arriving in Jersey City in 1623. In 1661, the first ferry between New York City and Jersey City was established, and many notable New Yorkers settled on the west bank of the Hudson. In fact, three mayors of New York—Richard Varick, Jacob Radcliff, and Cadwallader D. Colden—serving from 1789 to 1820, were founders and early residents of Jersey City.

But the Federalists who looked to the west side of the Hudson in hopes of building a new city that would rival New York met with many political and legal obstacles. In fact, when Jersey City's founders advertised "an easy and free navigation" to be enjoyed by purchasers of lots here, the city of New York announced ownership of the Hudson River up to the low-water mark on the Jersey side. To make public its posture, New York City advertised in newspapers on June 4, 1804, that anyone who "made improvements, constructed wharves, etc. between high and low water mark on the west side of the Hudson without getting their (New York's) official consent did so at his own peril." A treaty in 1833 finally settled the boundary dispute between the states of New York and New Jersey.

Exchange Place was created by landfill and offered the best potential for growth and development, situated directly opposite Manhattan. All trains from the west terminated at the Pennsylvania Railroad main depot, and nearly all trolley lines originated and finished their trips at Exchange Place. It was on Montgomery Street that all principal banks and professional offices were situated.

At One Exchange Place, on April 18, 1864, the First National Bank of Jersey City opened its doors in a rented room. In that year, when economic chaos was rampant, the value of paper currency fluctuated wildly from one state to another, and the nation was in the midst of a bloody Civil War, Abraham Lincoln marshalled congressional forces to pass the new National Banking Act of 1864, and First National was granted Charter No. 374. By the following year, the bank's assets were over $1 million, and the founding fathers purchased the five-story Exchange Place building.

By 1919, the bank had grown so rapidly that the board of directors decided to erect an elegant ten-story

Shown at the opening of the new bank building in 1920 are the General Ledger Department (seated along the windows) and part of the Proof and Transit Department.

building to house its expanded operations. Two massive black marble columns, the largest pieces of this type to have been brought to the U.S. at that time, flanked the bank's interior entrance. Groups of students visited the bank to see the columns, as well as the massive vault which had been built virtually as an impenetrable fortress. Forty feet below the water level of the Hudson River, the great steel vault was nested in bedrock, and its circular door, weighing forty-five tons, was one of the heaviest ever constructed. Minutes away from New York City, First National became known as the "Bank of Two Cities."

Edward I. Edwards was president of the bank when he was elected governor of New Jersey in 1919. Following this term of office, he was elected to the United States Senate. Born just months prior to the bank's opening in 1864, he was a protege of president E.F.C. Young who, during his forty years with the bank, also ran (unsuccessfully) for governor. Young was

to personalize checks. When a customer opened an account or needed more checks, a teller had to set the person's name in type, put it on the machine, and run off the checks.

In 1927, First National became the first national bank in the country to receive permission to operate branches and promptly opened two new offices. Today, as a result of subsequent mergers and acquisitions, twenty-seven banking offices serve customers in Hudson, Bergen, Essex, Union, Monmouth, and Ocean Counties. In 1968, the bank's name was changed to First Jersey National Bank to reflect its expanded activities and market area. One year later, a four-story administrative headquarters was completed at 2 Montgomery Street, across the street from the bank's original site.

As the bank's retail operations continued to grow, First Jersey recognized that its location at Exchange Place, minutes away from Wall Street, proved uniquely attractive to large corporations. The transfer of stock in New Jersey offered tax advantages over New York, and proximity to the world's financial center guaranteed prompt deliveries. As early as 1928, First National established a Trust Custody Division. As the mutual fund industry burgeoned in the 1950s and 60s, First Jersey earned an enviable reputation in the realm of automated financial servicing by installing the largest and most advanced electronic data-processing center of any bank in New Jersey. On July 19, 1971, First Jersey became the first bank in the country outside New York City authorized to act as a primary transfer agent for securities traded on the Big Board. Today, First Jersey handles more than a million shareholder accounts each day.

293

probably the richest, most powerful individual in Jersey City; during his reign, it was said that "all roads led to the First National." Today the bank is in the able executive hands of Thomas J. Stanton, Jr., chairman and chief executive officer, and Herman H. Suenholz, president and chief administrative officer.

Good penmanship was an impor-

First Jersey National Bank administrative headquarters at 2 Montgomery Street was built in 1969.

tant skill for a teller in the early days of banking when passbook entries were all done by hand. In the late 1940s, when checking accounts were introduced, tellers were supplied with a small printing press which they used

EAST RIVER SAVINGS BANK

Gold had been discovered in California, but news of this momentous event had not yet reached New York when the East River Savings Institution opened for business at 145 Cherry Street on May 22, 1848. Perhaps it is significant that this fledgling bank, which had close associations with shipping and foreign trade, should have started business on what is now National Maritime Day, the nation's annual tribute to the merchant marine.

John Leveridge, a prominent lawyer, had enlisted other well-known citizens in starting a savings institution as a safe place for working people to set aside money regularly from their meager earnings. Average pay for laborers then was about fifty cents a day; skilled mechanics earned about one dollar.

Leveridge suggested the name East River Savings Institution because the river was to New York what the Thames was to London—a pulsing channel of commerce, the very core of New York's growth and vitality. On its swift flowing waters moved ships and goods from all over the world, and on its restless tides merchants launched the bold ventures that made New York one of the great ports of the world.

Peter Hicks, a prominent Quaker merchant, was instrumental in obtaining a state charter for the new venture. Elias Guion Drake, one of the city's leading businessmen, was the first president.

The bank's opening coincided with

East River's first office from 1848 to 1850 was the home of the bank's founder, John Leveridge, at 145 Cherry Street.

a new state law giving women the right to have bank accounts in their own name, and twenty-five working women opened accounts during the first year.

By 1850, deposits had increased to $25,979, and offices were moved to a busier location at James and Chatham streets. Until that time, business had been handled by one paid employee, who received $41.66 a month. In 1853, the bank built a new home at 3 Chambers Street.

In 1911, a 19-story headquarters was built at 291 Broadway for the East River Savings Bank, as it was now called. During the depression years of the 1930s, the bank expanded by taking over two venerable institutions; the Italian Savings Bank and the Maiden Lane Savings Bank.

In recent years, East River has grown considerably, with a total of thirteen offices in New York and Long Island. In 1978, it merged with the 94-year-old Erie Federal Savings and Loan Association, with assets of $63 million, thus acquiring four offices in Buffalo and Erie County to provide the basis for a statewide operation. The bank now has assets in excess of $1.6 billion.

The East River Savings Bank moves into the future with a long tradition of service to the business community and the working people of New York. East River still adheres to the principles of conservative money management for its depositors that are as sound in the days of skyscrapers and supertankers as they were in the days of the great clipper ships.

BIBLIOGRAPHY

Albion, Robert. *Square Riggers on Schedule.* New York: Archon, 1965.

Albion, Robert. *The Rise of New York Port.* New York: Charles Scribner's Sons, 1970.

Allen, Gardner W. *A Naval History of the American Revolution.* Williamstown, Mass.: Corner House, 1913. Reprint, 1970.

Angus, W. Mack. *Rivalry On The Atlantic.* New York: Lee Furman, Inc., 1939.

Armstrong, Warren. *Atlantic Highway.* New York: John Day Company, 1962.

Bard, E. W. *The Port of New York Authority.* New York: Columbia University Press, 1942.

Barret, Walter (Scoville). *Old Merchants of New York City.* New York: Carleton, 1862.

Bierne, Francis F. *The War of 1812.* New York: Anchor Books, 1965.

Bonner, Willard H. *Pirate Laureate.* New Brunswick, N.J.: Rutgers University Press, 1947.

Bonner, William T. *New York, the World's Metropolis.* New York: R. L. Polk and Company, 1924.

Bowen, Frank C. *America Sails the Seas.* New York: Robert M. McBride and Company, 1938.

Brinnen, John Malcolm. *The Sway of the Grand Salon.* London: Macmillan, 1972.

Bryant, Samuel W. *The Sea and the States.* New York: Thomas Y. Crowell Company, 1967.

Cartwright, Charles E. *The Tale of Our Merchant Ships.* New York: E. P. Dutton and Company, 1924.

Clark, Arthur H. *The Clipper Ship Era.* New York: G. P. Putnam's Sons, 1910.

Clarkson, Thomas S. *A Biographical History of Clermont or the Livingston Manor.* Privately printed, 1869.

Coldman, Terry. *Going to America.* Garden City, N.Y.: Anchor Books, 1973.

Colman, Addie Cushing. *Captain Moses Rich Colman, Master Mariner.* Portland, Maine: The Anthoensen Press, 1949.

Cutler, C. C. *Greyhounds of the Sea.* Annapolis, Md.: U. S. Naval Institute, 1930. Reprint, 1961.

Cutler, C. C. *Queens of the Western Ocean.* Annapolis, Md.: U. S. Naval Institute, 1961.

Dalton, Sir Cornelius N. *The Real Captain Kidd.* New York: Duffield and Company, 1911.

Dayton, Fred E. *Steamboat Days.* New York: Tudor Publishing Company, 1939.

Dillon, Richard H. *Shanghaing Days.* New York: Coward-McCann, 1961.

Dugan, James. *The Great Iron Ship.* New York: Harper Brothers, 1953.

Emmons, Frederick. *The Atlantic Liners.* New York: Bonanza Books, 1972.

Encyclopedia Americana. International Edition. New York: Americana Corporation, 1976.

Encyclopedia Britannica. 15th Edition. Chicago: William Benton Company, 1974.

Fiske, John. *The Dutch and Quaker Colonies in America.* New York: Houghton, Mifflin and Company, 1899.

Flick, Alex C., ed. *History of the State of New York.* New York State Historical Society. New York: Columbia University Press, 1933.

Furnas, J. C. *The Americans, A Social History of the United States.* New York: G. P. Putnam's Sons, 1969.

Greenhie, Sydney and Marjorie. *Gold of Ophir.* Garden City, N.Y.: Doubleday, Page and Company, 1925.

Hill, Ralph N. *Sidewheeler Saga.* New York: Rinehart and Company, 1953.

Hughes, Tom. *The Blue Riband of the Atlantic.* New York: Charles Scribner's Sons, 1973.

Hurley, Edward N. *The Bridge to France.* Philadelphia: Lippincott Company, 1927.

Knox, Thomas W. *The Life of Robert Fulton and a History of Steam Navigation.* New York: G. P. Putnam's Sons, 1887.

Krafft, Herman, and Norris, Walter. *Sea Power in American History.* New York: The Century Company, 1923.

Lubbock, Basil. *Romance of the Clipper Ship.* London: H. Locke, 1958.

Lubbock, Basil. *The Down Easters.* Boston: C. E. Lauriat Company, 1929.

Lubbock, Basil. *The Western Ocean Packets.* Glasgow: J. Brown and Son, 1925.

Morrison, John H. *History of American Steam Navigation.* New York: Stephen Daye Press, 1958.

Morrison, John H. *History of New York Shipyards.* New York: William F. Gametz and Company, 1909.

McAdam, Roger Williams. *Commonwealth, Giantess of the Sound.* New York: Stephen Daye Press, 1959.

Paine, Ralph D. *The Fight for a Free Sea.* New Haven, Conn.: Yale University Press, 1920.

Paine, Ralph D. *The Old Merchant Marine.* New Haven, Conn.: Yale University Press, 1919.

Pendlebury, Jonas, and Stevens, Martin. *Sea Lanes.* New York: Milton, Balch and Company, 1935.

Perkins, Bradford, ed. *Causes of the War of 1812.* New York: Holt, Rinehart and Winston, 1962.

Porter, Kenneth Wiggins. *John Jacob Astor.* Cambridge, Mass.: Harvard University Press, 1931.

Powys, Llewelyn. *Henry Hudson.* New York: Harper and Brothers, 1928.

Roberts, W. Adolphe. *The Caribbean.* New York: The Bobbs-Merrill Company, 1940.

Rowland, K. T. *Steam at Sea.* New York: Praeger, 1970.

Rydell, Raymond A. *Cape Horn to the Pacific.* Berkeley: University of California Press, 1952.

Sears, Louis M. *Jefferson and the Embargo.* New York: Octagon Books, 1966.

Smith, Alexander R. *Port of New York Annual.* New York: The Smith Port Publishing Company, 1920.

Smith, Arthur D. H. *Commodore Vanderbilt.* London: Philip Allan and Company, 1928.

Smith, Eugene W. *Trans-Atlantic Passenger Ships, Past and Present.* Boston: George H. Dean Company, 1947.

Spratt, H. Philip. *Transatlantic Paddle Steamers.* Glasgow: Brown, Son and Ferguson, 1951.

Stiles, Henry R. *A History of the City of Brook-*

lyn. Brooklyn, N.Y.: Private printing, 1869.

Stokes, I. N. Phelps. *Iconography of Manhattan Island.* New York: Robert H. Dodd, 1926.

Turnbull, Archibald D. *John Stevens, An American Record.* New York: The Century Company, 1928.

Villiers, Alan. *Wild Ocean.* New York: McGraw-Hill, 1957.

Williamson, W. M. *Henry Hudson.* New York: Museum of the City of New York, 1959.

W. P. A. Writers Project. *A Maritime History of New York.* Garden City, N.Y.: Doubleday, Doran and Company, 1941.

ILLUSTRATION
CREDITS

American Museum of Immigration, Statue of Liberty National Monument; National Park Service, U.S. Department of the Interior: 90, 91, 92 right, 95, 97 top, 100, 102 middle, 102 bottom.

Atlantic Companies: 166, 168.

Author's Collection: Cover, 48, 51 top, 56 left, 72, 99 middle.

Blinn, Jeff, Moran Towing Corp.: 238, 239, 240 241, 243

Cunard Line: 132, 133.

D.T. Valentine's Manual: 12 left.

Department of Marine and Aviation, City of New York: 225 bottom.

Frank Leslie's Illustrated Newspaper: 40, 41.

Fuschetto, Robert: 243

Gleason's Pictorial Drawing-Room Companion: 33 bottom.

Harper's Weekly: 55 top, 73 top, 144, 151 top, 152, 154, 156.

King's Booklets: Frontispiece, 7, 9 top.

Library of Congress: 2 left, 2 right, 5 top, 6, 10, 11 top, 11 bottom, 13 bottom, 16, 17, 21 top, 31 top, 43 top, 51 bottom, 64 top right, 65 top, 65 bottom, 66 bottom, 92, 93 top, 96 top, 96 bottom, 99 bottom, 101 top, 102 top, 117 bottom, 119 top, 119 bottom, 126, 128, 131 top, 131 bottom, 133 top, 141 top, 147 bottom, 151 bottom, 159 top, 159 bottom, 162, 174, 176, 177 bottom, 193 top, 202, 203, 205 top, 213 bottom, 215, 217.

Liverpool University: 114.

Museum of the City of New York: 3 top, 4 right, 29, 32, 35 top, 35 middle (J. Clarence Davies Collection), 35 bottom, 50 top, 60 bottom, 71 bottom, 93 bottom (Byron Collection), 94 top, 94 bottom, 97 bottom, 101 bottom, 140 (Byron Collection), 146, 161 (Harry T. Peters Collection), 185 top (Byron Collection), 181 (Painting by Edward Moran).

National Archives: 23 bottom, 25 bottom, 46, 47, 61 bottom, 63 top, 80, 81, 121, 135 middle, 191 bottom, 197 bottom, 206, 207, 208.

Naval Historical Center: 13 top, 15 top, 15 bottom, 18, 24 left, 24 right, 25 top, 45, 50 bottom (*Iconographic Encyclopedia*), 52, 55 bottom, 62, 63 bottom, 64 top left, 64 bottom, 66 top, 67 bottom, 71 top, 75, 76, 77, 78, 79 top, 79 bottom, 85 bottom, 88, 122, 182, 183, 184, 185 bottom, 187 bottom, 190 top, 190 bottom, 191 top, 191 middle, 192 left, 192 right, 193 bottom, 194, 195 top, 195 bottom, 196, 197 top, 198, 199 top, 199 bottom, 200, 201 top, 201 bottom, 204, 205 bottom, 209.

New York Historical Society: 20, 21 bottom, 59 bottom, 60 top, 61 top, 155, 171.

New York Public Library, Picture Collection: 3 bottom, 4 left, 5 bottom, 9 bottom, 14, 38, 39, 43 bottom, 53, 59 top, 82, 85 top, 86, 87 bottom, 89 top, 89 bottom, 117 top, 120, 147 top, 165 bottom, 169, 210.

New York State Library: 23 top, 27, 31 bottom, 68, 70.

Redding, James: 240, 242, 243

Oregon Historical Society: 26.

Port Authority of New York and New Jersey: 150 right, 222 top, 222 bottom, 225 top, 226, 227, 228.

Queens Borough Public Library: 138, 141 bottom (*Herald Tribune*).

Operation Sail: 239, 244

Sandy Hook Pilots' Association: 153 top.

San Francisco Maritime Museum: 135 bottom.

Seafarer's Log: 67 top.

Seamen's Church Institute of New York: 33 top (Conrad Library), 118 (Conrad Library), 139 bottom (Conrad Library), 148 (Conrad Library), 149 top, 149 bottom, 163 (Conrad Library), 165 top (Conrad Library), 173 (Conrad Library), 178 (Conrad Library), 216, 217 bottom (Conrad Library), 221 (Conrad Library).

Smithsonian Institution: 36, 73 bottom, 125 top, 125 bottom.

South Street Seaport Museum: 57, 213 top, 224.

Transportation Institute: 54.

United Press International: 134 right, 135 top, 136 top, 137 top, 137 bottom, 153 bottom, 172, 175, 177 top, 179, 180.

United States Coast Guard: 186.

United States Lines: 139 top.

University of Baltimore Library, Steamship Historical Society Collection: 134 left, 158.

Wide World Photos: 220, 223.

296

INDEX

297

298

302